D0352083

THE ART OF
RESILIENCE

THE ART OF RESILIENCE

STRATEGIES FOR AN UNBREAKABLE MIND AND BODY

ROSS EDGLEY

HarperCollins*Publishers*

HarperCollins*Publishers*
1 London Bridge Street
London SE1 9GF

www.harpercollins.co.uk

HarperCollins*Publishers*
1st Floor, Watermarque Building,
Ringsend Road,
Dublin 4, Ireland

First published by HarperCollins*Publishers* 2020
This edition published 2021

1 3 5 7 9 10 8 6 4 2

Text © Ross Edgley 2020
Illustrations by Liane Payne © HarperCollins*Publishers* 2020

Ross Edgley asserts the moral right to be
identified as the author of this work

A catalogue record of this book is
available from the British Library

ISBN 978-0-00-835695-8

Printed and bound in Great Britain by
CPI Group (UK) Ltd, Croydon

All rights reserved. No part of this publication may be reproduced,
stored in a retrieval system, or transmitted, in any form or by any means,
electronic, mechanical, photocopying, recording or otherwise,
without the prior written permission of the publishers.

MIX
Paper from
responsible sources
FSC™ C007454

This book is produced from independently certified FSC™ paper to ensure
responsible forest management.

For more information visit: www.harpercollins.co.uk/green

Thank you to my dad, the most stoically strong man I know.

CONTENTS

FOREWORD

By Ant Middleton

You only have to look at the numbers: 1,780 miles, 157 days at sea, half a million calories burned, over two million swim strokes completed. Staggering. And do you know what's even more mind-blowing? Zero sick days.

Here was I thinking it would be hard enough to sail around Great Britain: who whould be crazy enough to *swim* all the way around it?

That's why I wanted to be one of the first to congratulate Ross when, after five months out at sea, he got himself back to Margate beach at the end of his mammoth Great British Swim. One of the things I remember most about that day was that he was exhausted, he was hungry, he looked like an alien from another world ... and yet he had this huge smile beaming across his face.

One of the key mindset principles that has got me through life is *positivity*. And for those who know him, you don't need me to tell you that Ross has that in bucketloads. It means you have more mental energy. You're smart. Your positive mindset can get you out of those dark places (and when you've read this book, you'll see that Ross has been to a few of those).

What gives you the motivation that drives you through the pain barrier and the resilience to cope with any obstacles that nature throws your way? What is it about the mind that is so powerful it can lead you to achieve incredible things? How did Ross find the unbelievable strength to go against the grain of human nature and tackle something which has never been done before?

When I think of the answers to these questions, I reflect back on my time in the Special Forces and how training taught me how to play the odds. So in a combat situation I would be thinking about what would happen when I went through that door with an armed enemy on the other side. Is he going to get me before I get him? What are the risks of me getting a bullet through the head that kills me instantly? In most situations I'd calculate the chances were slim, so I'd say to myself, 'Fuck that, the odds are with me, I'm going in.'

Ross overcame all the odds. The jellyfish in the Corryvreckan, the tankers crossing his path, the treacherous currents and tides, the winds and the waves, the storms. It's a wonder the odd Atlantic shark didn't decide to join the welcoming party!

With his physical and mental capabilities, backed up by his professional sports science qualifications and understanding of nutrition, if anyone was going to make the Great British Swim a success, it was Ross. You could be the best swimmer in the world but you wouldn't make it past the first week without mental fortitude, resilience and flicking yourself into survival mode.

The transformative lessons you can learn from this daring endeavour are countless. Don't let other people define you. Overcome that fear of the unknown. Purge your mind of everything apart from you against the water. Crack on, get in the zone, and get the job done.

Ross is one of the most humble and inspiring individuals you could ever wish to meet. From reading this book, the message that comes shining through is this: *you can achieve anything.*

Who dares swims. Good luck, mate – I couldn't be prouder to call you a friend. You are one of a kind, a true British hero and I can't wait to see what's in store for your next big (and hopefully dry) adventure.

PROLOGUE

It's 10.00 a.m. on 31 January 2018 at the Royal Marines Commando Training Centre in Lympstone, Devon. I had just completed a 48-hour training swim (covering 185 km in the centre's training pool) in preparation for my quest to set the record for the world's longest current-neutral swim in an ocean, sea or bay. I was planning to take on this challenge around Bermuda where the waters were warm, the food was great, and I knew lots of people with boats so plenty of support would be at hand.

Entering the officer's mess (an area where military personnel socialise and eat) I sat down with my good friend Ollie Mason, a Royal Marine Captain, head rugby coach and my temporary training instructor, to reflect on the last few days. Perched on a couple of grand leather sofas, we drank tea and spent the first few moments in silence.

Looking around it always felt like such a privilege for me just to be here. Hundreds of officers would have passed through these doors over the years. Yet this place still possessed a kind of timeless, old-fashioned opulence and came complete with solid-oak bookcases, polished brass door frames, a grand piano in the corner and a huge painting depicting a group of commandos receiving their green berets and becoming fully-fledged Royal Marines.

The silence was broken as we were joined by one of the older officers.

'You boy,' he said pointing at my shrivelled feet and hands. 'I heard about your 48-hour training swim. What is it that you are training for?'

He was tall with massive hands that made the teacup he was drinking from look comically puny. He also had an equally impressive moustache. You couldn't have designed a better Royal Marine Officer if you'd tried.

'I'm possibly training for the world's longest current-neutral swim,' I said.

He paused and sipped his tea, looking pensively into the bottom of the cup as if searching for clues before giving his verdict.

'Can I be honest with you, young man?' he asked.

'Yes, please do,' I replied, intrigued as to what he could possibly say.

'That just sounds a bit shit.'

Needless to say, I wasn't expecting this response. Nor did I actually ask for a response. In fact, I was still yet to introduce myself and learn his name. But it seemed the usual pleasantries had been forgotten and we'd gone straight into an impromptu brainstorming session.

Ollie then intervened. 'I'm going to be honest, mate. I think you should just man up and swim around Great Britain.'

'Why would I do that?' I asked stunned at the scale of his proposed swim.

'Well, I can think of at least three reasons,' he said. 'It's about 1,800 miles so would be the longest staged sea swim in human history. You'd be bringing that record back home to British waters. And it doesn't sound as shit as a current-neutral swim in Bermuda.'

I paused to consider his logic.

At first, I dismissed the idea. Sipping my cup of tea in a semi-conscious and heavily-chlorinated state, I laughed, shook my head and shuddered at the thought of spending my summer ploughing through some of the most treacherous currents in the world up and down the coast of Britain.

But as the night wore on, and the tea supply ran low, I have to admit it no longer seemed like the worst proposition in the world.

Maybe I wasn't thinking straight due to sleep deprivation, but as I sat there comatose in my giant leather chair the thought of swimming around this big rock we call Great Britain continued to play on repeat in my head. I began to think about the Great British adventurers of old, from Captain James Cook to Ernest Shackleton; it seems adventure and exploration are engrained in our British DNA, and the idea of following in their footsteps (in my own smaller way) had now lit a fire under my belly that even an energy-sapping 48-hour, 185-km training swim couldn't extinguish.

~

It's 7.00 p.m. on 3 August 2018 and we're 63 days (and over 800 miles) into the Great British Swim. We've reached the Gulf of Corryvreckan, a narrow strait between the islands of Jura and Scarba off the west coast of mainland Scotland. There is no doubt this is the wild, wild west of Great Britain. In the summer, the towering mountains plunge into the glens below among scattered collections of pine trees. But in the winter, those same mountain ridges become shrouded in white as Arctic blizzards leave a crystalline layer of shimmering snow on their peaks.

At the moment, we are somewhere between summer and autumn. Mile after mile of gnarled, wet heathland across the firths and fells is turning a golden brown in the ever-weakening sun. All of which you can enjoy as an incredible and unique spectacle if wrapped in a thick coat, woollen hat and warm thermal gloves.

None of which you can enjoy if you find yourself submerged in 8°C seawater, midway through an attempt to become the first person to swim around Great Britain, the ninth-largest island in the world.

Which is exactly where I currently find myself. Some 856 miles into what will be known as the Great British Swim. Far from happy and far from healthy.

After swimming through treacherous storms, pounding waves, constantly changing tides and polluted shipping lanes, my lungs and limbs no longer function like they used to and have been plagued by fatigue for twelve hours a day for the past two months straight. But this was a fatigue unlike any I'd experienced before ...

Exhaustion was essentially deep-rooted within my ligaments and tendons. What's more, my tongue was shedding layers from chronic salt water exposure as I gasped for air with every stroke. (This was a condition known as 'salt tongue' where all moisture from the mouth is lost and the first few layers of your tongue begin to erode away.) To top it all off, the Scottish waters were showing no mercy as the very tides themselves felt angry and venomous.

As for my other body parts, my shoulders had been relentlessly contorted by the waves for so long, while my skin had been tormented by chafing, sea ulcers and the bitter cold. In fact it was so rough, discoloured and a strange blend of blue, purple and grey that I no longer looked like I belonged to this world. Finally, my nose and cheeks had swollen so much from the constant battering of the waves that I struggled to fit my goggles over my increasingly painful eye sockets.

But despite my long list of ailments I did consider myself lucky to still be on the surface of the water (rather than below it). The local coastguard had told us that the waters are so treacherous and the death toll so high, its place is forever cemented in Scottish folklore. Local fishermen speak of a mythological Hag Goddess who governs the lochs and pools of Scotland.

I must point out that, before arriving at the Corryvreckan I would not have considered myself very superstitious, but that would quickly come to change. As the howling winds funnelled through the islands, the haunting sound which seemed to echo across the coast led me to believe that something in Scottish mythology was insulted that I would even attempt this.

The wildlife of Scotland seemed to agree too. Gathering to enjoy the spectacle, birds began to circle overhead and a lone seal watched from afar – none of them were quite sure what they were witnessing. That's because my shoulders had been relentlessly contorted by the waves for so long, my swim stroke was dogged and cumbersome and I didn't look like most humans they'd seen before.

Keeping a safe distance from this half-man half-beast, the crew on our support boat, the *Hecate*, decided it was time to prepare me for more torture ahead. Matt (the captain of the Great British Swim) and Taz (Matt's son and chief crew) shouted clear and precise instructions from aboard the deck.

'You're going to have to sprint at full pace for the next three hours,' Matt said with a hint of empathy, knowing he was asking a lot from my bruised and battered body. 'If you do that, we'll be clear of the whirlpool.'

Given the current state of my body, a three-hour sprint was ambitious. Unfortunately, I knew he was right; this was the only way to swim through this seething stretch of water known as the Corryvreckan whirlpool. At this moment in time, pacing strategies, rest and recovery simply didn't exist. You either swam hard or you didn't swim at all.

I signalled to Matt and Taz that I was ready. Carefully positioning my goggles around my swollen eyes, I set the three-hour countdown timer on my watch and promised myself I wouldn't stop swimming until I heard the alarm. Neither whirlpool nor fabled water spirits were going to distract me from the task at hand.

Stroke after stroke I battled between the extremes of bravery and common sense. My arms ached and my lungs complained, but I knew this was better than the alternative fate that lay at the bottom of the ocean bed, so for the first 40 minutes I pleaded with my body to keep the impossible pace as we continued our attack on the Corryvreckan. But after an hour or so, the Scottish waters – also known as the mystical washtub of the Hag Goddess – had other ideas and delivered a 'curve ball' I never saw coming ... a giant jellyfish swimming straight into my face.

There was not just one, but a whole army of them in the water. Known as lion's mane jellyfish, their tentacles can grow up to 6 ft long and they can weigh up to 25 kg. But while I had been hit in the face by jellyfish tentacles many times before, this particular group was different. That's because, despite trying to swim through their initial stings, I could still feel a burning sensation across my nose and cheeks.

After two hours, the pain was excruciating ... it felt as if someone was pressing a hot poker into my face that was searing into my flesh with such intensity, I could feel the blisters forming with every mile that passed.

After two hours and thirty minutes, the pain became paralysing ... I began to feel that I no longer had any control over the left side of my face as the toxins from the jellyfish seeped into my skin in the most painful form of paralysis I've ever experienced. No longer the manager of my own mouth, I was dribbling, but thankfully still not drowning.

After two hours and forty-five minutes, the pain became blinding ... the paralysis had spread to my eyes and was now causing tears to fill my goggles and impair my vision. Trying to adjust my goggles mid-stroke, I quickly discovered this final jellyfish blow had stung my face so badly that my eye sockets had become inflamed and the seal of the goggles to my face was no longer watertight.

'Keep swimming!' Matt shouted from the boat.

With 40 years' experience of sailing, he knew better than anyone that we were still uncomfortably (and dangerously) close to one of the world's largest and most deadly whirlpools.

As my vision became increasingly impaired by my own tears and the salt water, I was now semi-blind ... in the sea ... with no sense of direction ... so in desperation I punched the goggles into my face. Somehow (painfully) securing a watertight seal around the rims again, I regained some vision and was able to sprint in whatever direction Matt told me to.

After three hours, the pain became worth it ... the alarm on my watch had never sounded so sweet as it signalled I had swum clear of the whirlpool. But with no time to celebrate, my focus immediately shifted to the pain of the jellyfish stings now plaguing my face, neck and arms.

'I've been hit by a jellyfish!' I shouted to the crew.

Taz rushed over to the side of the boat to assess the situation.

'My skin's still burning,' I said wincing from the pain.

As Matt focused on maintaining a strict course through the perilous waters, Taz looked down at my face and saw immediately what was wrong.

'Yes, I know,' he said now visibly wincing too. 'I can see the tentacle still wrapped around your face.'

Unbelievably, I had been WEARING A JELLYFISH TENTACLE all through the Corryvreckan.

I unpeeled the fat, thick, toxic tentacle that had somehow threaded itself through the goggle strap and around my face, and felt a momentary sense of relief as the bitter Scottish breeze cooled my skin. Now free to continue the swim, I covered three more miles before I was clear of the Corryvreckan's clutches.

Climbing into the boat I collapsed onto the deck, mentally and physically spent. I now understood that the rules of conventional sport didn't apply out here. In this wild and untamed corner of Britain, swimming technique was not going to be the limiting factor. Instead, adventures such as this one would be won or lost based on a person's ability to summon every ounce of physical and mental fortitude they have in their arsenal and overcome chronic, crippling fatigue.

That night I came to realise this was much more than a swim ... it was a form of extreme research into the art of resilience.

It's 7.45 a.m. on 13 August 2018 and we're (still) among the Inner Hebrides of Scotland.

'Once you go under that bridge everything changes,' said the fisherman in a thick Scottish accent that made everything he said sound even more ominous.

He was old, maybe north of 70 years old, and had been sailing these waters for more than half a century. You could almost see the wisdom and seafaring expertise etched into every line of his heavily wrinkled and weathered face, and the years spent hauling in the daily catch frozen into his deeply callused and hardened hands.

'Up until now Scotland has been gentle with you,' he said.

'Really?' I exclaimed.

I pulled down the neckline of my jumper to reveal my battle wounds that consisted of sea ulcers from the wetsuit chafing and jellyfish stings and scars from my time spent in the Corryvreckan with the Hag Goddess.

'If that's gentle, do you want to tell me what you'd classify as rough?' I asked.

'Oh, lad,' he said with a concerned smile. 'You've been swimming in the Inner Hebrides between the islands off mainland Scotland. These are close together, sometimes only a mile apart, and so offer some shelter from the wind and waves. If a storm comes in you can easily pull into a harbour for food and supplies and maybe even sample some famous Hebridean hospitality and a local single-malt whisky.'

As he said this he turned towards Kyle of Lochalsh, a place where you could hear the ancient Gaelic language being spoken and sung by folk musicians in the local pub.

'You won't find any of that once you swim under the Skye Bridge,' he warned. 'Once you pass under there, you're heading to the Outer Hebrides and beyond. With nowhere to hide or shelter from a storm, it's over 30 miles wide. You won't be welcomed with whisky up there. Instead you'll find 50-knot Arctic storms and 20-ft waves. Jellyfish might be the least of your worries.'

We all stood in silence for a moment and looked at the Skye Bridge. Spanning less than a mile across, it connects the island of Skye with mainland Scotland and the village of Kyle of Lochalsh over water that, prior to 1995, was only crossable by boat. Now it would become a pivotal landmark in the Great British Swim.

I had been on our boat this morning doing a round of interviews with the media along with some local fishermen intrigued about my round Britain adventure. The tide had begun to turn, which signalled the media interviews were over and another swim was about to begin. As the journalists and fishermen left the boat, I sat in silence with Matt as I delicately attempted to put on my cold, clammy wetsuit over my tender and raw wounds. As I did, one lone writer lingered on deck and plucked up the courage to ask three final questions that would become integral to both the swim and this book:

- 'Why are you doing this?
- 'Why doesn't your body break?'
- 'How does your mind not quit?'

In truth, I was still trying to answer these questions for myself.

Fatigue and pain were deeply entrenched in each and every cell of my body, and as I sat there they were threatening to bring a stop to the swim. In front of the journalist, even though I was still not 100 per cent sure of the answers, I tried my very best to articulate the conclusion I'd come to so far after 74 days at sea.

'I think the reason my body hasn't broken and my mind hasn't quit (yet) is because I've been able to fuse the teachings of ancient Greek philosophers with modern sport scientists to form my own form of philosophy called Stoic Sports Science.'

The journalist appeared puzzled at first but then nodded with his pen and notepad poised as if eagerly anticipating my next answer, hoping I was about to dispense some profound, deep and spiritual seafaring wisdom. But unfortunately, I had nothing else for him.

Since I still had over 900 miles left to swim, my newly found philosophy was far from proven. But I told him if I completed the swim, I would finish my study and the book.

'Then I'll have to wait to buy a copy,' he said laughing.

I smiled as we sat there taking in the vast expanse of our surroundings while pondering what had brought us together in this unlikely gathering.

'Okay, why *are* you doing this then?' he asked.

I looked at Matt. He looked back at me with knowing eyes. Nothing needed to be said.

The memory of the start of this journey (and life back on land) seemed like a lifetime ago. Many miles, tides and sunsets had passed since that day. But to understand why we were doing this, you must understand we as humans have been practising the art of resilience for centuries. It's the one key trait we possess over all other species. Therefore, in many ways, what began on 1 June 2018 on the sands of Margate beach in southeast England was just an exaggerated expression of our unique human ability to find strength when suffering.

PART 1 |
LIFE ON LAND (*BEFORE THE SWIM*)

CHAPTER 1 | WHY DID I DO IT?

LOCATION: Margate
DISTANCE COVERED: 0 miles
DAYS AT SEA: 0

Margate

It's 7.00 a.m. on 1 June 2018 in the small coastal town of Margate. Tucked away on England's southeast coast, this seaside resort has down the years served as a magnet for Londoners, with its sandy beaches less than 80 miles away from the capital. In fact, Margate has an old-world charm that makes the ice cream parlours, pie and mash shops and amusement arcades seem almost timeless. Yet the town's history is also closely tied to the sea and the absence of their once great Victorian pier, destroyed after a storm in 1978, is a constant reminder to the locals (and all who visit) of the ocean's power.

This is why the British coastline was the ideal 'testing ground' to research *The Art of Resilience*. Known around the globe for having some of the world's most dangerous tides, waves and weather, every menacing whirlpool, rugged headland and North Sea storm would become a tool for me to sharpen my mind and harden my body.

But why Margate to start? When planning for the swim, we decided we needed to swim clockwise around Great Britain because the prevailing winds affecting our island are from the west or south-west. So we would be facing the 'harder' half of the journey – if we made it down the south coast, around Cornwall and up the Irish Sea towards western Scotland – during the summer months. The 'easier' half of the swim would theoretically be over the top of Scotland and down the east coast of Britain where we would be more sheltered from the southwesterlies by the topography of the coastline. Speed was of the essence, however, in order to complete our mission before the onset of winter.

But this morning, standing on the beach looking out to sea, I had absolutely no idea what lay ahead. Many people considered this 'swimming suicide', believing it was an impossible swim that was foolish to even attempt. But to quote the award-winning novelist Pearl S Buck, 'The young do not know enough to be prudent, and therefore they attempt the impossible – and achieve it, generation after generation.'

Which is why my plan was simple. Using myself as a sea-dwelling, human guinea pig I would attempt to complete the first 1,780-mile swim in history all the way around Great Britain, while putting to test the science behind strength, stoicism and fortitude. As I researched the intricacies of resilience on this swim, my goal was to fully understand what makes the human spirit so unbreakable.

The regulations governing the swim were pretty straightforward too. It would be classed as 'the world's longest staged sea swim' (where the distance of the individual stages can vary each day, and the start point of each stage begins at the finish point of the previous stage) and would abide by the rules of the World Open Water Swimming Association (WOWSA) and the *Guinness Book of World Records*. I would be fitted with an electronic GPS tracker and my location recorded with WOWSA at the end of each day's swim. I would also tow an inflatable buoy during every swim for safety (especially at night, since it contained a flashing light so I could be seen). I myself insisted that I would not set foot on land during the entire swim, but would take my rest periods out on the water on a support boat.

Of course, this wasn't a solo endeavour. To even contemplate a swim of this magnitude I needed a boat captain equipped with iron-clad fortitude and years of experience sailing in the most adverse conditions Mother Nature could conjure up. Then I needed a crew with unwavering faith who would sail day and night alongside me, through hell and high water, to make this mission a success.

But instead of finding a team, I found something far better. I found a family.

The Knight family were a committed band of sailors and big-wave surfers who had the (joint) dream of sailing around Great Britain for many years. With a love of adventure and penchant for the impossible, dad, husband and captain Matt Knight was recommended to me by a mutual friend as the ideal man to lead my crew. When we first met down in Torquay to discuss the mission, he was struck by my enthusiasm and didn't need much convincing to adopt an utterly naive and wildly optimistic swimmer and mastermind the first circumnavigation swim around this big rock we call Great Britain.

As a personality and a character Matt's hard to explain, but let me try. Standing just over six foot, he was 60 years old but had a physique that resembled an elite triathlete. With not an ounce of body fat, he had giant, cartoon-like forearms that rivalled Popeye's and skin like hardened leather from years of battling wind, waves and salt water. But these features were purely a physical representation of his deep connection with the sea, which all began in the 1980s when, as a young boy, he left his hometown in search of adventure and sailed across the Atlantic employed as a deckhand.

Hardworking and with an insatiable love of the sea, he moved through the ranks; years later he gained his Yachtmaster qualification and skippered boats across the Atlantic, Pacific and Indian oceans.

Which is when he met mum, wife and chief cook, Suzanne, a petite, blonde Devonshire lady whose maternal instinct only seemed to be fulfilled when cooking for the family and crew while battling 20-ft waves somewhere across the high seas. In tandem with Matt, they sailed the coastlines of France, Cornwall, Devon, Wales, Ireland, Portugal and Madeira and explored some of the most remote islands in the South Pacific and Indonesia.

They even found time to produce four incredible children along the way, who would become the crew and my newly adopted brother and sisters: Taz, Harriet, Peony and Jemima. With no hierarchy, each one of my 'sea siblings' would do anything and everything possible to ensure we could continue making progress around the coast, from guiding me past lobster pots, jagged rocks and dangerous shipping lanes to guarding me from sharks, killer whales and seals during mating season.

Finally, I must mention my 'home' for 157 days. *Hecate* was a 53-ft (16-m) long and 23-ft (7-m) wide specially designed catamaran (known as a Wharram after its designer). Comprised of two parallel hulls that are essentially held together by rope and rigging, the entire boat bends, moves and contorts with the waves thanks to this form of traditional Polynesian boat-building that's remained unchanged for thousands of years.

The idea for us on the swim was for *Hecate* to progress under sail as often as possible, but there would be times when travelling through rough seas or difficult tides that we would have to rely on her engine.

But the best part of *Hecate*? The galley. Serving as the kitchen and library, it was where most of this book was written. After swimming up to 12 hours per day, the remaining time I would spend eating, sleeping (dreaming) and writing about theories and philosophies in resilience that I'd been thinking about when staring at the bottom of the seabed. In fact, during the entire 157-day swim, we calculated I spent over 1,500 hours (over 60 days) swimming with my face down looking into the dark blue abyss, writing the chapters of this book in my own head before the words ever appeared on paper.

This is why the contents of this book have become a blend of:

- Real-life events from the swim.
- Stories from my past that influenced the swim.
- Tales from the strange world of sensory deprivation that occurred in my head.

The one common theme that runs throughout is resilience. This was also inspired by research in the *Journal of Personality and Social Psychology* which found, 'The importance of intellectual talent to achievement in all professional domains is well established, but less is known about the importance of resilience. Defined as perseverance and passion for long-term goals ... resilience did not relate positively to IQ, but demonstrated incremental predictive validity of success measures over and beyond IQ. These findings suggest that the achievement of difficult goals entails not only talent but also the sustained and focused application of talent over time.'[1]

Essentially, intelligence is great and being genetically gifted physically is an advantage. But one of the most underrated, yet powerful virtues a human can possess is resilience – which is exactly why I wanted to embark on this swim.

I wanted to follow in the footsteps of my hero Captain Matthew Webb, who, on 25 August 1875 achieved what many believed was impossible: the first crossing of the English Channel (swimming 21 miles from Dover in England to Calais in France). At the time, sailors claimed this was swimming suicide because the tides were too strong and the water too cold. But Captain Webb, in a woollen wetsuit and on a diet of brandy and beef broth, swam breaststroke (because front crawl was considered 'ungentlemanly-like' at the time) and battled waves for over 20 hours to make history.

I loved this story. It was one of grit, resilience and defying all odds as his dogged persistence and self-belief captured the spirit of the times and cemented Webb as a hero of the Victorian age.

Therefore, for me, circumnavigating Great Britain would serve as a way of reconnecting with these powerful and primitive human traits. Looking at the anthropology of us humans (and earth's 4.5 billion-year history), it's the reason we're all here today sitting firmly at the top of the food chain, as we compete in the game that Charles Darwin and Herbert Spencer referred to as the survival of the fittest.

How did we do that? Well, our strategy has been simple. Around 100,000 years ago our ancestors developed these huge brains and amazing ability for endurance and physical labour and ever since have been able to outsmart, outhunt and outlast the bigger, stronger and faster members of the animal kingdom.

To them, bravery and tenacity weren't rare and respected virtues. They were daily habits that people possessed solely in order to survive when everything outside of the comfort of their cave wanted to eat them.

Fast-forward to the era of modern (civilised) man and the same attributes of grit, determination and fortitude that saw us survive, now see us thrive. From the first ascent of Everest by Sir Edmund Hillary and Tenzing Norgay in 1953 to Captain Matthew Webb's first crossing of the English Channel, it seems this idea of persistence, valour and intestinal fortitude is what bonds great feats of human endeavour throughout history.

But today we are in danger. We are ignoring these key attributes that made us great as a species and are losing our ancient, age-old abilities for mental and physical robustness. Living between our desks at work and sofas at home, we would be almost unrecognisable to our intrepid forefathers who 70,000 years ago had dreams beyond their horizons as they left East Africa to explore the world. Which is exactly why I decided to swim around Great Britain and to write this book.

To show that we modern humans are capable of the same superhuman resilience as our intrepid ancestors.

CHAPTER 2 | WHY THE BODY DOES *NOT* BREAK?

LOCATION: Margate
DISTANCE COVERED: 0 miles
DAYS AT SEA: 0

Margate

The clock strikes 2.00 p.m. on Margate beach and signals my final three hours on land.

I spent these last precious moments bouncing between the local patisseries and pizza parlours along the seafront, as a generous portion of scones, doughnuts and an 18-inch stuffed crust helped to calm my nerves. Not knowing when I might get a freshly cooked pizza again, I ate what I could and then put the rest in my pocket as I headed to the beach to meet the Mayor of Margate who'd kindly agreed to say a few words to me and the local media before we set sail.

Her name was Julie and she was lovely. Impeccably dressed and wearing a huge traditional gold medallion (known as a chain of office), she and her husband Ray had already met my mum and dad who'd arrived earlier that day. So, we skipped the formalities and instead spoke about scones and swimming and I ate pizza out of my pocket as they proudly told me about the history and heritage of their beloved town.

'How long do you think it will take you?' Julie asked.

I paused for a moment, since I really had no idea. All I knew was the waves, wind and weather would decide *if* and *when* I would finish. But as a very rough guess I replied, 'Maybe a hundred days, but likely more.'

'Oh dear,' she said disappointed and looked at Ray with concern. 'He'll miss our food festivals in August if he doesn't hurry.'

That one moment is why I will forever love Margate.

Marvellous Margate. Traditional and welcoming, but entirely unpretentious and down-to-earth. Whereas everyone else was concerned with the start, Julie was already (ambitiously) planning the finish to coincide with scones and jam at her local food festival. This is why I will be forever grateful to the town who waved me goodbye on my voyage.

But worth noting is that not everyone shared Julie's optimism and there weren't many people in attendance that day other than those who lived locally. Sponsors had tried their very best to get the national media to report on the start, but few were taking it seriously. Just months before, another swimmer had attempted the swim but quit after a week due to bad conditions. As a result, most journalists believed this was an equally ill-fated attempt at an impossible adventure.

Also, social media was rife with people posting why they thought this would fail.

Many believed the mind would quit ...

Others believed the body would break ...

But of all the naysayers, the most vocal were sports scientists within the swimming community who were quick to point out that my chunky five foot eight, 88 kg frame would *never* make it around; that with such short, stubby arms and legs it was obvious that the laws of hydrodynamics (the study of objects moving through the water) were not in my favour.

I was well aware of this, too. Months before arriving in Margate, I visited a sports laboratory for a full medical examination to see if my body could survive a swim of this magnitude. After hours of being prodded and probed I was told in no uncertain terms that I had 'no physical attributes to be an elite swimmer'. They also added, I would likely, 'sink like a stone' if I embarked on this ill-fated swim.

But it gets worse ...

Entering the room that day, the chief sports scientist picked up the clipboard containing my scan results. Looking me up and down he said, 'You're very heavy ... but also very short.'

Harsh, but true, I thought.

'That's not good,' he continued, now frowning as if the stubby statistics of my body were offending him and his laboratory. 'But if I can be honest with you, it's your body composition that concerns me the most. Since fat is buoyant and insulating, and you have very little, and muscle sinks, and you have a lot. Basically, floating and keeping warm is going to be an issue for you, never mind swimming.'

I nodded and thought this must be the most brutal assessment of a body in the history of swimming. But I wasn't out of the woods yet. His confidence-crippling critique of my body continued and this time he had an issue with specific body parts.

'Also, it's your head,' he continued.

'What about my head?' I said, now feeling a bit self-conscious.

'It's big and dense,' he declared bluntly.

'I know I've a big head, but—' I was interrupted before I could defend my oversized cranium.

'Yes, but it's not just big. It's very *dense*,' he said gesturing with his hands. 'In fact, all your bones are dense, but my concern is when swimming, because of the position and size of your head, you're basically turning yourself into a human submarine, as the weight of your massive skull plummets you into the ocean bed.'

He then continued to flick through the pages of notes, surveying the metrics while continuing to tell me I had one of the densest skulls he'd ever seen. Moments later (and five pages in) we found a statistical silver-lining.

'Oh wait,' he said. 'There might be some good news.'

I breathed a sigh of relief.

'You have brilliant ... fat ... chunky ... child-bearing hips.'

'WHAT?' I had no idea how this was good news, but decided it was better than a massive submarine skull so decided to listen.

'You carry your fat around your thighs like a woman,' he said, again gesturing with his hands. 'What this means is despite your big heavy head sinking, your fat thighs will float ... almost like a duck's bum.'

He paused to consider his final diagnosis. 'If you want my advice, I'd stop strength training. Lose muscle. Obtain a body that more closely resembles that of a swimmer. Then try and swim around Great Britain in a few years, because right now I'm not sure you could walk around never mind swim around.'

Sitting there, I agreed with everything he said apart from this hips 'prescription'.

I do have a heavy head and child-bearing hips, but – completely contradictory to conventional sports science – I would argue that despite being a super-sized sumo-swimmer, these would uniquely equip me to swim around Great Britain.

Why was I so sure? Because his diagnosis was based on an elite swimmer competing in a 100 m or 10 km race and not someone attempting to swim 1,780 miles around several countries. This was the fundamental difference, since I was aware that being a leaner

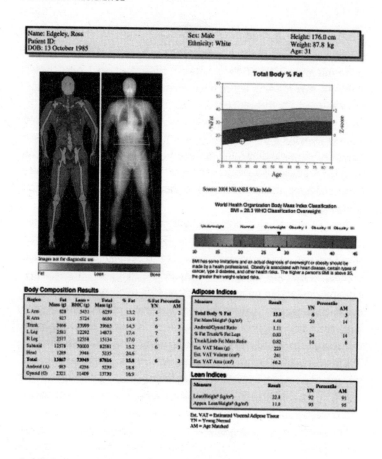

and lighter swimmer would make me faster, but I was also aware that being heavier and stronger would make me more robust.

Studies in strength agreed, too. Research from the National Strength and Conditioning Association (NSCA) stated, 'When considering sports injury prevention strategies, the role of the strength and conditioning coach can extend beyond observing exercise technique and prescribing training to develop a *robust and resilient athlete*.'[2]

This is true in swimming and other sports. As early as 1986, research published in the *Journal of Sports Medicine* found that, 'The incidence of various types of overuse injuries, such as swimmer's shoulder and tennis elbow, may be reduced by the performance of resistance training activities.'[3] How? Scientists added, 'Resistance training promotes growth and/or increases in the strength of ligaments, tendons, tendon to bone and ligament to bone junction strength, joint cartilage and the connective tissue sheaths within muscle. Studies also demonstrate resistance training can cause increased bone mineral content and therefore may aid in prevention of skeletal injuries.'[4]

Now every athlete is, of course, different. Equally, there are thousands of incredible (and specific) treatments performed by world-leading physiotherapists, osteopaths and injury prevention specialists that are being used to treat thousands of specific intricate injuries, and in no way am I attempting to gloss over these. But evidence suggests – as you will see in a later chapter – that on a large scale across sports, countries, age groups and gender, strength training could hold the key to creating *robust and resilient humans.*

This (I believed) would be a deciding factor of the swim, because if I was to miss just a few days of perfect swimming conditions due to injury, I could also miss up to 100 miles of progress. Therefore, speed was an advantage, but physical resilience was a necessity.

Of course, many disagreed with this theory. But do you know who agreed with me? Barry. Yes, Barry always believed in me. A local fisherman from Margate, he was 65 years old and had lived here all his life. When news reached his local pub that someone was about to attempt to swim around Great Britain, he and his friend George came down to the harbour to watch the start of the swimming spectacle unfold.

Looking me up and down (like a short racehorse) Barry and George decided that there might be money to be made out of my little adventure. As they sipped their pints of locally brewed ale, they considered the terms of their wager and each gave their verdict on what they thought the outcome of the swim would be.

George approached me first. Very polite, but also very sceptical. He agreed with sports scientists from the swimming community and thought I might get 100 miles down the coast before my body broke or my mind gave up.

'Young man, please don't take offence,' he said, looking up and down at my height (or lack of), 'but based on how rough the sea gets on the south coast, I think you've just won me a hundred quid.'

Barry shook his head and disagreed, putting his arm around me as he said, 'Go on, lad. I'll get the beers in when you're back.'

I laughed and gave Barry a big hug.

Again, this is why I love Margate. I thanked them both for coming as, regardless of the bet, they both showed up to wave me goodbye. But my parting words to Barry were, 'I prefer cider to beer, but see you in a few months.'

It was late afternoon and the tide was beginning to turn. Once it did I would be swimming out of the harbour and heading east towards the famous white cliffs of Dover on the south coast of England, only returning to Margate after I had swum all the way around Great Britain.

To be successful, I would have to ensure my body wouldn't break and my mind wouldn't quit; and to do this I knew I couldn't defy the laws of sports science. Many of the rules that govern our psychology and physiology are infallible and as a sports scholar I knew I couldn't ignore them.

Instead, over the next 157 days, I had to learn how to bend them.

CHAPTER 3 | WHY THE MIND DOES *NOT* QUIT?

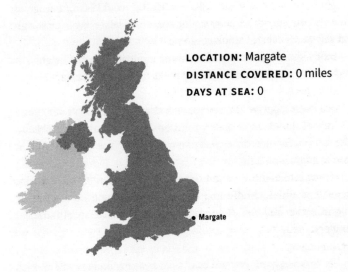

LOCATION: Margate
DISTANCE COVERED: 0 miles
DAYS AT SEA: 0

Margate

The time is 5.00 p.m. and I'm standing on the beach barefoot looking out to sea.

I knew my feet and toes would come to forget the feeling of sand and solid ground. Once I left Margate harbour that day via the south-facing entrance, I vowed to myself I wouldn't touch land again until I'd swum 1,780 miles around Great Britain and arrived back into the same harbour via the north-facing entrance. Trying my best to enjoy the feeling of terra firma as much as I could, I wedged my toes into the ground and began wiggling them around.

Moments later I was joined by my mum, dad and girlfriend.

Usually, I like to be on my own before any athletic adventure because I get so nervous, but these three were an exception. That's because my dad always had some profound words of wisdom he would share that would help calm my nerves. My mum would typically arrive equipped with her homemade lemon and blueberry cheesecake which would temporarily distract me from any worries I might have had. Then my girlfriend Hester would bring a sense of normality to the occasion by saying something like, 'Well, this is an odd way to spend the summer, isn't it?'

I took a giant slice of cheesecake and couldn't help but laugh.

'Couldn't we just go on holiday like a normal couple?' Hester asked.

We'd been together for five years, so she knew I wasn't very good at 'normal' holidays. I once promised her a romantic Caribbean holiday only to then do a triathlon carrying a tree (for charity) in what would become the world's first tree-athlon. But all jokes aside, Hester was incredibly patient and knew my athletic adventures, where I so often blindly and enthusiastically took on events far beyond my capabilities, stemmed from a supportive, sport-fanatical family.

Growing up, I played each and every sport. My brother Scott, who is two years older than me, would take me everywhere with him, from football and cross-country to athletics and tennis. As a result, I was always younger and smaller than everyone else and would substitute my lesser stature and lack of skill for stubbornness and speed.

My dad was always keen to encourage this too. After football training on a Sunday, I'd ask him to stop the car at the bottom of our road so I could get out and race the car home. Of course, he'd only be driving at 5 mph and would always let me win. Slowing down just enough for my tiny legs to take me to the finish line (our house) first, he'd celebrate my victory over a family Sunday roast dinner as I proudly (and naively) told my mum I was faster than a car. She would then honour the occasion by giving me an extra Yorkshire pudding with my dinner followed by several servings of her home-made rice pudding (mine and my brother's favourite).

A year later, I'd want to add strength to my skill set so I developed a love of wrestling. In any form, it didn't matter. I remember watching old sumo wrestling tournaments on TV with my grandad on Sundays, and when Dad came home from work he would re-arrange the furniture in the lounge and we'd host our own tournament. Mum was usually knitting, but would cheer and move her legs out of the way to make the arena bigger.

Then me, Scott and Craig, my younger brother, would take it in turns to try and beat Dad who was the reigning sumo champion of the house. We never did. To this day I think he remains the highest rank in sumo within the Edgley family.

But from an early age, my mum and dad had created a love of sport in our family. So much so, that by the age of 10, I was obsessed with training. I was always trying to make myself bigger, stronger and fitter so I'd be able to compete with Scott and his friends. I would put weights in my backpack when walking to school and would pester my dad for exercises that would give me 'stronger arms' or 'faster legs'.

I was completely clueless, but utterly keen. I remember finding a very basic military circuit training routine in an old book that consisted of push-ups, lunges, sit-ups and shuttle runs: exercises it said would 'build character'. So, I took it downstairs and asked Dad which muscle that was since I couldn't find it on any anatomy chart.

Fast-forward three years and I was a 13-year-old schoolboy playing water polo against men. Getting beaten, drowned and wres-tled underwater seven times a week at training just became normal, until I came out the other side of puberty and was able to win a few more fights than I lost.

This then continued for over 20 years as the inherited work ethic from my mum and dad formed the basis for my belief system and the following motto governed every training session I ever had for two decades:

> 'Hard work is so often the answer.
> The question is so often irrelevant.'
> ROSS EDGLEY

It also had a profound impact on the entire swim that lay ahead. This is because in many ways the wiring of my brain and construction of my body was the result of the unbridled support of my family and the constant pursuit of what many thought were either impossible or improbable adventures.

But at 5.15 p.m., I embarked on my biggest challenge to date. Putting on my goggles and wetsuit I hugged my mum, dad and Hester. It wasn't an emotional goodbye, since they'd already plotted and planned where they could come and see me around the coast and had Matt on speed dial, so I'd be seeing them soon enough.

Instead, my main concern was now safely entering the water and successfully exiting the harbour as a small group of people (and local media) had gathered on the old pier to wave me goodbye. There was probably only about fifty in total (including owners of the pizza place) but their cheers reverberated across the water and sounded like an army of support.

Wading into the water up to my waist, I then turned and thanked Barry, George, Julie and Ray before diving in and swimming towards *Hecate* that was setting the course a few hundred metres in front. As my face hit the water, I felt a huge sense of relief wash over me. All the planning and preparation was over. Now it was just me versus the sea, in a battle of wind and waves versus swimming and sports science.

Trying my best to keep my emotions in check, I stopped by the pier to thank the people of Margate for attending the start and told them I hoped to be back before Christmas. They all laughed (since this was six months away), but unfortunately I was being serious.

The first few miles were then fuelled by pizza, cheesecake and pure adrenaline. Captain Matt held a steady course and I used *Hecate* to sight off as we made our way towards the port of Dover. Swimming long into the evening and then again in the morning, we covered 21 miles in less than nine hours of swimming. That's the equivalent of the English Channel, so by most swimming standards it could be argued progress was good.

But this was an entirely different swim on an entirely different scale. For us to complete a circumnavigation swim around Britain made for some pretty depressing maths. We had to repeat this ... UP TO 100 TIMES.

Already my eyes were sore, my arms were tired from repeatedly battling the waves and my tongue was fatigued from the salt water and copious amounts of calories needed to fuel the swim that lay ahead.

Even at this very early stage, I knew this was no longer a swimming expedition. My head position, hand placement and stroke rate would not determine whether I circumnavigated this big rock called Great Britain. Instead it would be a 157-day fight with a very different kind of enemy: fatigue in all its forms.

Which is why in *Hecate's* galley-cum-library, there was a copy of a book that I had been studying ever since I had the idea for the swim: *The Facts of Fatigue.*

FATIGUE: THE FACTS

Sports science hasn't always fully understood fatigue. We knew it was the result of something within us failing,[5] but historically psychologists and physiologists have debated whether fatigue manifests itself in the brain or in the body. This is why the *Journal of Neuromuscular Fatigue in Contact Sports* said that, 'Fatigue has been defined in accordance with the varied sub disciplines associated with sports science, namely the divisions of physiology (the body) and psychology (the mind). At one extreme, physiologists may consider fatigue as failure or dysfunction of a particular physiological system (occurring in the body). At the other extreme, psychologists may view fatigue as an uncomfortable perception or sensation (occurring in the mind).'[6]

But I was being physically bruised and mentally battered by the sea.

Fatigue was plaguing both my mind and body and I would need to consult the teachings of both psychologists and physiologists to nurse me around Great Britain. Hundreds of pages into my research and it became clear that more recently sports science has come to understand fatigue as a fusion of the two schools of thought (psychology and physiology).

To quote researchers from the Institute for Movement and Neurosciences at the University of Cologne, Germany, 'Multiple symptoms of fatigue can occur simultaneously. The underlying mechanisms (both *biological* and *psychological*) overlap and interact.'[7]

Hence the reason why modern scientists developed the Psychobiological Model of Fatigue and acknowledged fatigue is a combination of many complex factors that are both physical and mental.

FATIGUE: A MODERN HISTORY

We didn't always think of fatigue like this. In the early twentieth century we believed exhaustion was the body breaking down. To test this theory, back in 1907 the Nobel Laureate Frederick Hopkins and his team cut off the hind legs of frogs and electrically stimulated the muscles over and over until they couldn't contract anymore. He discovered the depleted frog muscles were bathed in lactic acid and unable to continue moving.

As a result, scientists believed exhaustion resulted from your body being unable to pump oxygen to the working muscles, with the acidity of your blood going through the roof along with many other physiological failings, meaning you hit the wall, tap out and surrender.

This is partly why in 1954 many people believed running a 4-minute mile was impossible. Runners in Australia, Europe and America had got agonisingly close. In the USA, Wes Santee ran 4 min 2.4 s in a widely publicised mile event. In Australia, John Landy was getting even closer and ran four separate mile races around 4 min 2 s. But in reality, nobody looked like beating the existing world record of 4 min 1.4 s set back in 1945 by Sweden's Gunder Hägg, which is why sports scientists of that era believed (supported by their frog research) that the legs and lungs of a human couldn't run a 4-minute mile.

But a 25-year-old medical student by the name of Roger Bannister thought otherwise.

FATIGUE: ROGER BANNISTER'S 4-MINUTE MILE

Bannister, who used his knowledge of medicine to hone the mechanics of his running and devise his own training regime, began his record-breaking quest by recruiting the most elite pace-making squad ever assembled.

This consisted of Christopher Chataway (who that summer set the 5,000 m world record) and Chris Brasher (the 1956 Summer Olympic steeplechase champion), two men uniquely capable of pacing the greatest mile ever run. On 6 May 1954, on Oxford's Iffley Road track, that's exactly what they did.

Brasher led for an impeccably timed, metronomic two laps before handing over to Chataway. Bannister, following closely behind, had to run the final quarter-mile in 59 seconds. Collapsing over the finish line he heard the statistician Norris McWhirter, announce over the public address, 'A track record, English Native record, British National, British All-Comers, European, British Empire and World record; the time: three ... [the rest drowned out by cheering] ... minutes, 59.4 seconds.'

But the breakthroughs in sports science and psychology didn't stop there. Just 46 days after that fateful day on the Iffley Road track, John Landy broke the barrier again with a time of 3 min 58 s. Then, one year later three runners broke the four-minute barrier in a single race. Now over the last half century more than a thousand runners have conquered a barrier that had once been considered hopelessly out of reach.

So, what happened? Was there a sudden leap in human evolution? Was there an abrupt advancement in shoe technology or nutritional science? No. The proverbial bar had been raised and the collective mindset of runners had changed. Once people saw the four-minute mile was possible and that perceived limit of human performance was broken, more people ran it.

Bannister essentially helped re-write every theory of fatigue and showed it cannot be fully explained by electrically stimulating severed frog legs. Instead, we must take into account the key role the mind plays, which is exactly what Professor Tim Noakes did in 1996.

Expanding on the work of Archibald Hill in 1924, Noakes developed the idea that the brain will override your physical ability to run, swim, cycle or fundamentally continue any activity and 'shut the body down' before you're able to do (what the brain believes is) serious damage to yourself.

This became known as the Central Governor Theory and this is why Noakes believes that the point when you think you cannot go on is actually a response from the brain to slow down to preserve health, rather than a physiological reality.

Basically, the brain quits before the body.

But why does this happen? Well, for good reason. If your brain didn't regulate physical exertion in this way you could quite literally run yourself to death, by either destroying skeletal or cardiac muscle or by starving the nerve tissue of sugar and oxygen.

This is why Noakes believes the brain is inherently selfish and only really cares about itself. It will do anything necessary to maintain balance within the body, a state of equilibrium which we call 'homeostasis'.

HOMEOSTASIS: A BRIEF HISTORY

First discovered way back in Ancient Greece, the famous physician Hippocrates (considered the founder of Western medicine) maintained that health required the proper balance of elements that make up the human body; imbalance resulted in disease. Therefore, in a sense, Hippocrates and the school of medicine that followed him can be considered the originators of the notion of 'homeostasis'.[8] But years later and the theory and idea of harmonic equilibrium was converted into more measurable medical science.

In 1915, an American physiologist by the name of Walter Cannon and French scientist Charles Richet found, 'The living being is stable. It must be so in order not to be destroyed, dissolved or disintegrated by the colossal forces, often adverse, which surround it. By an apparent contradiction it maintains its stability only if it is excitable and capable of modifying itself according to external stimuli and adjusting its response to the stimulation. In a sense, it is stable because it is modifiable – the slight instability is the necessary condition for the true stability of the organism.'

It sounds complicated, but it's not. You know when your body temperature is good? Your immune system is okay? And millions of other internal mechanisms are running like clockwork to keep you healthy? All without you consciously having to lift a finger? This is homeostasis at work. It's that easy.

Now Noakes believes our brain is dedicated to maintaining internal homeostasis in the body during exercise and its biggest fears are that during prolonged and strenuous exercise:

- Muscle glycogen (stored carbohydrates) are entirely depleted.
- Heart rate rises too high and results in cardiac failure.
- Body temperature rises too high and you develop hyperthermia (failed thermoregulation).
- The brain is damaged if blood glucose concentrations are low.

In many ways, the brain is a hypochondriac that babysits the body. It serves this preventative and precautionary role that fears the worse-case scenario for every body part and every sense in the body, as pain and fatigue signal that homeostasis is under threat, so it tells our body that we should probably stop whatever we are doing.

According to Noakes, when exercise intensity and stress to the heart, skeletal muscles and nervous tissue reaches 'the limit of what is safe, the brain's motor cortex, which recruits the exercising muscle, is informed, and it stops recruiting additional muscle'. What this means is the sensation of fatigue (and accompanying pain) and a slowing of pace are pre-emptive and protective, yet extremely powerful actions taken by the brain to avoid real physical trauma to the body.

This is understood by all of us athletes who have experienced those workouts when midway through it feels like your lungs are on fire and you're going to die. At this point, homeostasis is completely out of balance.

Yet once the workout is over (or you stop), you miraculously feel fine. This isn't because you have superhuman healing powers and the damage caused to the body is instantly repaired, but is because the body is returning to its normal state of homeostasis. As a result, the brain knows the threat of exertion has passed which means it stops sensations of pain and fatigue.

This is why Noakes summarised the concept of the central governor when he said, 'Fatigue is merely an emotional expression of the subjective symptoms that develop as these subconscious controls wage a fierce battle with the conscious mind to ensure that the conscious ultimately submits to the superior will of the subconscious.'

This means that each race, adventure and training session is just a battle within ourselves, and the best athletes and adventurers in the world are the ones who consistently win those battles. Today, many researchers claim the term 'central governor' has fallen from favour since there is not one physical area in your brain that is solely responsible for this effect. The preferred name is now the Psychobiological Model of Fatigue.

But as an athlete adventurer and someone who's on the 'front line of fatigue', I'm not interested in studying terminology, the concept is the same. This is why the US Navy Seals don't refer to it as the psychobiological model of fatigue but rather, the Forty Per cent Rule. Put simply, they believe when your mind is telling you that you're done, that you're exhausted, that you cannot possibly go any further, you're only actually 40 per cent done.

Finally, this isn't to say that the physiological demands aren't real. There is no doubt that improving your physical fitness will help you run faster, swim further and cycle harder. But the psychobiological model of fatigue posits that to truly excel in extreme physical activity, you must train both the body and the mind.

That's something I soon came to learn while dodging ships across the world's busiest shipping lane, with a philosophy I developed called Stoic Sports Science.

PART 2 |
LIFE AT SEA (*DURING* THE SWIM)

LESSON 1 | STOIC SPORTS SCIENCE IS PHILOSOPHY FORGED IN BATTLE

LOCATION: St Margaret's Bay
DISTANCE COVERED: 20.5 miles
DAYS AT SEA: 1

St Margaret's Bay

It's 7.10 p.m. on 2 June 2018 near St Margaret's Bay. Located on Kent's south coast, this quiet and peaceful coastline is just miles around the corner from one of Britain's most famous landmarks: the White Cliffs of Dover. Made of a very pure form of limestone and towering 106 m (347 ft) above the sea, they owe their striking appearance to a composition of chalk accentuated by streaks of black flint. They were also witness to some of the most dramatic moments in English history, from the arrival of the Romans to the return of the British forces from the battle of Dunkirk during World War II.

But that evening they bore witness to the most ambitious swim the coastline had ever seen. That's because we had been swimming for just over 24 hours and were only 20 miles into our planned journey and already I was in trouble as the salt water and my wetsuit had fallen out with the skin around my neck, and the subsequent chafing had opened up a raw and perfectly circular wound around my neck.

I must stress this was entirely my fault. For I (foolishly) picked a brand-new wetsuit for the start and hadn't properly worn it in, or trialled it. As I noticed the lining of the collar tearing into my skin, I was too embarrassed to stop, especially in plain view of Barry, who you recall had a £100 bet on me, and my mum and dad who would only drive back home worrying the entire time.

Now I was instantly regretting it. To make matters worse, I was about to attempt to swim across one of the busiest shipping lanes in the world: the Port of Dover. Famous for being the nearest English port to France, up to 12 million passengers, 3 million lorries, 2 million cars and 80,000 coaches pass through here each year. But today, they'd add one strange swimmer to that list.

As we approached, Matt called the port authority over the radio to inform them of our plans. He had emailed them weeks in advance and provided a full breakdown of all the necessary safety protocols we had in place. Safety was paramount, especially as we could see two giant cargo ships on the horizon coming from France. Possibly 200 m (656 ft) in length and 25 m (82 ft) in width, they were travelling at 20 knots which meant any sort of collision would not end well for me.

I was no stranger to the Vessel Traffic Service (VTS) Officers of Dover either. That's because I had spoken to them months before about my plans to become the first person to swim the length of the English Channel (531 km from Dover to Land's End) followed by a gentle swim around the entire country. But it wasn't until I visited the harbour for the umpteenth time that they knew I was serious.

So, eventually (and politely) they advised me that although there's a million logical reasons why this couldn't be done, there wasn't a single legal reason why it couldn't be done. Which was the glimmer of hope (and atom of approval) I needed.

'Good to see Ross back again.' You could almost hear the harbour master smiling down the radio. 'Are you swimming the right way [21 miles] *across* the English Channel from England to France today, like most normal folk?' he asked. 'Or the wrong and long way [330 miles] down the *length* of the English Channel to Land's End?'

'Land's End, Cornwall,' Matt assured him in a serious tone that showed, as ambitious as our plans might have seemed, we were 100 per cent sincere and committed to our intended mission.

With the cargo ships ever visible on the horizon the tone of the conversation became more business-like as the VTS Officer then asked, 'How fast will the swimmer be travelling? If you're able to maintain four knots, you can go now before the cargo ships arrive from France and we can grant you safe passage. If you can't, you will have to wait, I'm afraid.'

I was treading water close to the boat when Matt asked me, 'Can you give me four knots now? If not, we'll have to wait.'

Even at this early stage of the swim I knew delays were a bad idea and waiting should be avoided at all costs, so despite the wetsuit chewing at the increasingly raw open wound around my neck, I signalled I was ready and awaited further instructions.

Matt informed them we were ready and then stood poised at the radio. Moments later, we were given the green light. I put my head down and took six powerful strokes to begin my crossing. Once up to speed and travelling at 4 knots (4.6 mph) I settled into a rhythm and began breathing bilaterally every three strokes. Looking to my left I could see Matt had positioned *Hecate* between me and the cargo ships still motoring towards us from France. To my right were the impressive giant concrete walls of the Admiralty Pier Turret. Built in 1882 and made entirely from granite, it's an enclosed armoured turret on the western breakwater of Dover harbour and contains two 80-tonne guns (the biggest installed in the United Kingdom) that were declared obsolete in 1902.

I felt privileged to be a strange kind of sea tourist. But my enjoyment was short-lived. Now with each stroke I could feel the wetsuit ripping into my skin as the salt water sharply stung my chafing wounds that were becoming deeper and rawer with every metre I swam. The water tasted as you'd expect from the world's busiest shipping lane: industrial. As my taste buds complained I tried my best to only breathe through my nose, but the synthetic substances floating on the surface of the water were plaguing my nostrils as much as they were my mouth.

'Faster! Faster! Faster!' Matt shouted from the boat while holding up four fingers to signal we had to maintain 4 knots at all times.

Dutifully, I did my best to give him and the team the speed we needed. After thirty raw and painful minutes, we crossed the entrance to the harbour and were safe. No longer in the firing line of the cargo ships, I turned to the watchtower and waved to thank the service officers for their support as Matt verbally did the same over the radio.

Taking a deep breath, relief then washed over my body along with a wave of lactic acid from the impossible pace I had just set.

But there was no time to celebrate. On leaving the shelter and safety of the Admiralty Pier Turret, I was no longer shielded from the wind and waves and was instantly served my first dose of seasickness. For those not familiar, motion sickness is what happens when there's a conflict between what your eyes see and what your inner ears (which help with balance) sense. If there's a mismatch of information between these two systems, it's very likely you will feel nauseous and struggle to keep your breakfast in your belly ... something I was about to discover.

SEASICKNESS STRIKES

It was 9.10 p.m. and things were about to get worse. The sun was setting and night was creeping in, which meant swimming in the dark among choppy waves and six-foot swells felt like I was in a giant washing machine with the lights turned off. Trying my best to put on a brave face, I continued to battle the sea, my stomach and my gag reflex heading into the night, but Matt could sense something was wrong.

'Are you okay, Ross?' he asked genuinely concerned.

He had every reason to be too. We'd been swimming just over 24 hours and already he could see I was a strange shade of grey and green. Too polite to admit I was in a bad way, I tried my best to smile through the seasickness as I didn't want Matt to worry at such an early stage.

'Yes, all great down here.'

'I think I ate too much pizza before we left though,' I confessed.

Standing on deck, Harriet smiled sympathetically. She was my newly adopted sea sister and had left her apartment, work and life back on land to be with her family and support the swim, so I really didn't want her to see me struggling either. Which is why, while breathing bilaterally (every five strokes), I decided I'd be sick underwater to conceal the evidence. Without barely breaking stroke I thought I'd got away with it too ... but there was a problem.

That night we were swimming with a tailwind which meant the chunks of pizza and porridge were now being swept along in my direction. What's worse is the tides around Dover are pretty fast, which meant my own sick was travelling at an impressive speed and I was forced to either swim harder or to bathe in it; not a dilemma you ever want to find yourself in.

So, there I was, locked in a race with my own sick at sea. An hour passed and I continued to throw up around the southeast coast, concealing the evidence under the night sky. I thought to myself this couldn't get any worse. I was wrong.

'It's getting dark,' Matt shouted to the crew. 'Harriet, [for safety] can we get a spotlight on Ross.'

Moments later Harriet was shining a high-powered, 500-watt light in my direction that illuminated the entire ocean surrounding me ... along with the chunks of sick. Any attempt to maintain my dignity had now failed as Harriet alerted the crew.

'He's been sick.'

As Matt continued to maintain a steady course, Suzanne responded from the galley.

'Just sick? Or has he pooed himself?' she asked.

'No, no, it just looks like sick.'

Pots and pans then rattled around the galley followed by the sound of a kettle boiling. Eventually, Suzanne burst through the galley doors heroically equipped with an ancient sailing recipe. The weapon she was wielding? Freshly made ginger root tea which she served to me from the back of the boat as I did my best to tread water among the waves and avoid getting seawater in my tea.

Suzanne later told me this particular remedy was based on a study published in the National Centre for Biotechnology Information in the USA where 80 naval cadets, unaccustomed to sailing, were given ginger root to monitor its impact on motion sickness.[9] What they found was, 'fewer symptoms of nausea and vertigo were reported after ginger root ingestion'. While modern science still doesn't fully understand how it does this, at the time I didn't care because it was working: my stomach and I were now cooperating again.

But what happened that night and during that tide is so often overlooked in endurance events and expeditions. This is despite research showing gastrointestinal distress (in many forms) being one of the main reasons ultra-marathon runners (and many other athletes) quit. According to an article in the *International SportsMed Journal*, 'Gastrointestinal distress problems are frequent in endurance athletes. The prevalence of such symptoms has been reported to be 30–50% among marathon runners.'[10]

The embarrassment of racing my own sick down the south coast in front of my team was strangely liberating. It was like the opening day's swim set the tone for what was socially acceptable, and if bathing in sick and seawater while sipping tea was deemed okay, then any other swim was going to seem like a walk in the park.

But putting regurgitated pizza to one side, it was in this moment I realised the open sea simply didn't care about pacing strategies, rest and recovery. Neither did it care about the state of my delicate stomach.

It was clear to me that studies in sports science would become less useful the more this swim progressed, as wetsuit wounds, lacerated skin, shipping lanes, storms, whales and sharks all exist outside of the realms of conventional sport.

Instead, when venturing into the unknown I needed a framework to think. Almost like an operating system to ensure the mind and body could work in harmony despite seemingly insurmountable pain, hardship and adversity. I basically needed a philosophy, a theory that could act as a guiding principle for behaviour.

My quest for answers led me to the philosophy of the Ancient Greeks.

THE PHILOSOPHY OF RESILIENCE

Too often, the mind and body are seen as separate. In fact, so too is our mastery of them. You're either a library-dwelling genius or a sporting specimen found in the gym, but rarely is it considered possible to be both. Yet, to truly build bulletproof resilience in the face of adversity it requires an in-depth understanding of the two.

That's because you can be mentally durable, but if you're not physically fit your body will simply lose to the tides and waves and be found at the bottom of the seabed. Conversely, you can be the world's most physically gifted swimmer, but if you're not mentally strong your mind will break in the cold Arctic storms that often plague the top of Scotland.

The Ancient Greeks understood that both the mind and body must be exercised. This is why the great Greek historian of Athens, Thucydides (460–400 BCE) famously once said, 'The nation that makes a great distinction between its scholars and its warriors will have its thinking done by cowards and its fighting done by fools.'

It's also why a 'gymnasium' in Ancient Greece functioned as a training facility for competitors in public games such as wrestling, but was also a place for socialising and engaging in intellectual pursuits. It was a place that produced many a great Greek.

Take Plato for example, widely celebrated – along with Socrates and Aristotle – for laying the philosophical foundations of Western culture; he was also an accomplished wrestler and skilled gymnast. He reportedly competed at the Isthmian Games (comparable to the Olympics) and his actual name was Aristocles, but 'Plato' was given to him by his wrestling coach because of his broad shoulders (in Greek, 'Platon' means broad).

But it was in the gymnasium where he began work on *The Republic*, which he wrote in around 380 BCE. Within it, he spoke strongly on behalf of the virtues of physical education. He felt that one should balance physical training with 'cultivating the mind', exercising 'the intellect in study'. He wrote, 'In order for man to succeed in life, God provided him with two means, education and physical activity. Not separately, one for the soul and the other for the body, but for the two together. With these means, man can attain perfection.' He also said, 'He who is only an athlete is too crude, too vulgar, too much savage. He who is only a scholar is too soft, too effeminate. The ideal citizen is the scholar athlete, the man of thought and the man of action.'

I needed to become that scholar athlete. Put simply, I needed to study mental fortitude and physical fortitude in equal amounts, if I was to do battle with the obstacles in front of me. So (inspired by Plato) I continued my research, which led me to the work of the ancient stoics.

Fusing their teachings with a decade of my own within the field of sports science, I hoped to better understand the science and psychology of unbridled human resilience.

'Wrestle to be the man philosophy wished to make you.'
MARCUS AURELIUS

WHAT IS STOICISM?

Stoicism was founded in Athens in the early third century BCE. Although it's over two thousand years old, what most appealed to me was that this timeless school of thought teaches you to become steadfast, strong and in control of yourself even in the most adverse and unpredictable conditions.

Founded by Zeno of Citium, stoicism sets out to remind us of how unpredictable the world can be. Its central teachings include:

- How we don't control and cannot rely on external events, only ourselves and our responses.
- How our perception shapes how we see the world around us.
- How the source of our dissatisfaction lies in our impulsive dependency on our emotionally charged reflexive reactions rather than logic.

Finally, stoicism doesn't concern itself with complicated theories about the world, but with helping us overcome destructive emotions and act on what can be acted upon. It's built for action, not endless debate, and its three principal leaders used it as a tool to serve their specific actions:

- Marcus Aurelius was the emperor of the Roman Empire from 161 CE to 180 CE. Considered the most powerful man on earth at the time, he would sit down each day to write himself notes about restraint, compassion and humility. He used stoicism to create an empire.
- Epictetus was born a slave, but endured the horrors of slavery and founded his own school where he taught many of Rome's greatest minds. He used stoicism to create an academy.
- Seneca was a stoic philosopher and rhetorician whose written work is considered timeless by many as it's been passed down through the ages. His thoughts famously influenced historical figures such as Pascal, Francis Bacon and Montaigne. He used stoicism to create a timeless teaching manual for many.

Then you had me. I would use stoicism to swim around Great Britain.

Sports science alone wouldn't be enough to battle mile upon mile of physical and mental obstacles on my journey. Instead, I needed to combine a decade of research at Loughborough University School of Sports, Exercise and Health Sciences with this ancient philosophy of adversity. I came to call it Stoic Sports Science because it represents an evolution in thinking, from an *athlete* to an *athlete adventurer*.

WHAT IS STOIC SPORTS SCIENCE?

The Great British Swim was one giant aquatic athletic adventure. It required me to take the principles of swimming, extend and exaggerate them and then apply them outside of the realms of conventional sport in an adventure setting. This is the fundamental difference between being an *athlete* and an *athlete adventurer*.

Let's take swimming as an example. As an *athlete* you perform in swimming pools, lakes or at sea just a few miles off the coast and it can last between twenty seconds to two hours. Basically:

Athletes: Apply principles of sports science under controllable, safe conditions.

As an *athlete adventurer* attempting to swim around Great Britain, you perform in waves, across headlands, through seasickness with sharks. So:

Athlete Adventurers: Apply principles of sports science under uncontrollable, dangerous conditions.

This means you have a greater degree of pain, stress and uncertainty to endure and therefore a greater need for cognitive clarity and resilience under extreme physical and mental exhaustion. But since no one had ever completed a sea swim of this scale before, there was no blueprint ... therefore I had to be the one to write one.

Tucked away in the *Hecate* galley, I began writing my own philosophy. My own operating system to ensure the mind and body could work in harmony. My own theory that would act as a guiding principle for behaviour, no matter how rough the sea was or how sick my stomach became.

HOW TO CREATE A STRONG BODY, STOIC MIND, STRATEGIC PLAN

Under conditions of extreme fatigue and stress, your risk of injury is increased and your physical and mental capacity to apply proven principles of sports science is reduced as the body's innate, inbuilt self-preservation system and desire to maintain safe homeostasis increases your perception to fatigue and your desire to stop. Stoic

Sports Science is related to your physical capacity and mental clarity to apply proven principles of sports science and psychology, under conditions of extreme exhaustion, stress and adversity.

It's essentially sports science and philosophy that's been forged in battle. But to succeed you need three things:

- Strong Body
- Stoic Mind
- Strategic Plan

Your body only determines your (theoretical) physical potential: essentially your lung capacity, strength, biomechanics, ability to coordinate and activate muscle fibres, joints and ligaments and many other factors that will determine how fast you run, how far you swim or how much you lift.

This (theoretical) physical potential will lay dormant unless your brain consistently triggers the necessary electrical impulses through the body to run, swim and lift to your full physical potential. Equally, the mind must continue to operate when confronted with fatigue and must work hard to logically override the body's innate, inbuilt self-preservation mechanisms and desire to slow down or stop (to maintain safe homeostasis).

But this is just your (theoretical) physical and mental potential. This is doomed to fail unless your strong body and stoic mind has a strategic plan. This allows you to research restrictions (like excessive pain, fatigue or lack of sleep and food) and limit limitations by practising cognitive clarity and logic rather than relying on your emotionally charged reflexive reactions that are amplified by fatigue, pain and discomfort.

Ultimately, as I made my way around the coastline of Great Britain, this is how I ensured my body wouldn't break and my mind wouldn't quit, as Stoic Sports Science served as a mental map that segmented limitations and systematically looked to offer possible solutions.

DON'T READ IT, LIVE IT

It is not enough to read about Stoic Sports Science; you *must* practise it. This is why Epictetus once told his students, 'A carpenter does not come to you and say, "Listen to me discourse about the art of carpentry," but he makes a contract for a house and builds it ... Do the same thing with yourself. Eat like a man, drink like a man ... get married, have children, take part in civic life, learn how to put up with insults and tolerate other people.'

Basically, it's not about learning a lesson, it's about practising a lesson. How? Well, one of the best ways is through the art of journaling. This is the one shared habit that all the stoics had in common, because although Epictetus was a teacher, Marcus Aurelius an emperor and Seneca a playwright, they all took time to document their daily thoughts, feelings and theories.

Epictetus would constantly remind the students of his school that philosophy was something they should 'write down day by day,' and that a written diary was a way they, 'should exercise themselves' with constant and continual reflection and self-improvement.

For Seneca, journaling was a more solo endeavour and his favourite time to write was in the evenings when his wife had gone to bed and he was left alone with his own thoughts. He explained to a friend, 'I examine my entire day and go back over what I've done and said, hiding nothing from myself, passing nothing by.' He would then go to sleep finding that 'the sleep which follows this self-examination' was always better.

Finally, Marcus Aurelius was renowned for his writings, but it's unlikely he ever intended for them to be published as his work had no official title and often came in the form of quotations varying in length from one sentence to long paragraphs. But in 1558, Wilhelm Xylander translated his work and it's since been put into book form (entitled *Meditations*) with millions of copies sold around the world.

How do you start? Well, in a letter to his older brother Novatus, Seneca describes a beneficial exercise he borrowed from another prominent philosopher. At the end of each day, he would ask himself variations of the following questions:

- What bad habit did I curb today?
- How am I better?
- Were my actions just?
- How can I improve?

In summary, understand that in stoicism the act of journaling is more than keeping a diary. It's a daily practice in philosophy as you reflect on the days that have passed and prepare for those ahead. In this way, journaling *is* stoicism. You cannot have one without the other and it's important that you:

- Meditate on the lessons learned from past events.
- Repeat and remind yourself of past teachings from mentors.

Which is what I did throughout the entire swim (essentially this very book). Mostly journaling alone from the comfort of the galley, I would also talk theories and philosophies of the sea and sports science with Matt over cups of ginger tea. In many ways, they became mini Stoic Sports Science Sea Seminars and just two days into our swim we hosted the first of many in the Kent port town of Folkestone.

FIRST STOIC SPORTS SCIENCE SEA SEMINAR

LOCATION: Folkestone
DISTANCE COVERED: 33 miles
DAYS AT SEA: 3

It's 3 June 2018 and approaching midnight.

Swimming past one of Kent's many seaside towns, I always felt that Folkestone was very different to the others. While Whitstable is renowned for its candy-coloured beach huts and genteel clientele and Broadstairs comes equipped with its sweeping sandy beaches seemingly borrowed from across the channel in France, Folkestone radiates a unique quality. Dour and stoic, it's the type of aura you only acquire when you've spent centuries being battered by storms and icy salt water; even the German bombers used to dump their unused payload over the town on their way back home from bombing London during World Wars I and II. But there it stood, under the night sky, defiant and immovable. It seemed a fitting setting for our first Stoic Sports Science Sea Seminar, as I drew inspiration from the indomitable spirit of Folkestone and the people who lived there.

I was grateful that me and my digestive system were now friends as the headland up ahead known as Dungeness offered some valuable shelter from the southwesterly wind and waves. But although my stomach was fine, my skin was not.

Climbing onto the back of the boat at the end of that day's swim, I slumped in a seat and removed my goggles and hat as a mixture of salt water and blood dripped down my neck and formed a puddle at my feet.

'It looks like you got kissed by a shark,' Matt said smiling.

'I know ... and they didn't even buy me flowers,' I replied laughing.

As funny as this was, it was actually a good way of describing it, since the pain wasn't debilitating or paralysing at this point, but instead incessant and raw.

'So how bad is it?' I asked, turning my neck so Matt could assess the damage.

'Hmm ... with every swim the wounds become wider and deeper. If that happens it could turn into a severe collection of sea ulcers.'

'What's that?' I asked, since I didn't know what a sea ulcer was, but was pretty sure I didn't want a collection of them.

'These are basically lacerations to the skin that will never dry or heal since you're constantly in and out of the water swimming twelve hours a day, in six-hour intervals. Each time you get in the water, the scab (protective tissue) is removed and the wound gets deeper and deeper.'

'Then what happens?' I asked, now a little worried.

'There's medical reports of this type of injury getting so bad the lacerations can get as deep as the tendons, muscles and bones.'

In that moment, we both knew the only real and effective treatment would be to stop swimming so the wounds could heal, but we both refused to say it out loud. Not even wanting to entertain the idea, we were three days into the swim and far too stubborn to stop (or even pause).

'The best thing we can do now is clean the wound, bathe it in disinfectant and then let's get some sleep. The tide changes and runs in our direction again in six hours, so we need to be ready to go by 5 a.m.,' he said.

Our swimming schedule was relentless; relaxation, recovery and proper medical treatment were not luxuries we had. But what was worse, I knew 'bathing it in disinfectant' was going to do more than tickle. Reaching into the boat's medical supplies and pulling out a giant, industrial-sized 500 ml bottle of disinfectant solution, Matt then unscrewed the top.

'You ready?' he asked.

Bowing my head so he could bathe the entire wound, I said, 'Yes, pour away,' trying my best to smile, purse-lipped, through the pain.

As Matt generously applied most of the bottle's contents to my open (and bleeding) wounds, I thought about a central theme of stoicism. 'It's not about learning a lesson, it's about practising a lesson.' Which is why as I was sitting there with my skin feeling like it was on fire, me and Matt then found ourselves talking about Marcus Aurelius.

Aurelius always spoke about viewing rough or smooth sensations that impose themselves on the mind with detachment. He noted that unpleasant sensations were bound to impinge upon our aware-ness because of the natural sympathy between body and mind (our mind–body connection), but we should refrain from calling them either good or bad. Rather we should accept the presence even of these 'rough' sensations with total indifference.

For me, it was like rubbing sandpaper on an open wound and then soaking it in salt water and vinegar, every day, four times a day, but this daily practice ensured that my injuries never became infected and that we continued with the swim and made progress.

'Okay, time to sleep,' Matt said after finishing the treatment.

So that's what I did, knowing that in six hours me and my raw and sore skin would again be swimming in salt water and disinfectant solution as I continued to practise Stoic Sports Science.

> 'Make sure that the ruling and sovereign part of your soul remains unaffected by every movement, smooth or violent, in your flesh.'
> MARCUS AURELIUS

LESSON 1

- Stoicism teaches us that virtue is happiness and judgement is based on behaviour rather than words. **We don't control external events, only ourselves and our responses**.
- The best way to practise it is through journaling (writing down your thoughts day by day). **Don't read It, live it**.
- Stoic Sports Science is an evolution of stoicism and teaches us that under conditions of extreme fatigue, your risk of injury is increased and your physical and mental capacity to apply proven principles of sports science is reduced.
- Stoic Sports Science is therefore related to your physical capacity and mental clarity to apply proven principles of sports science and psychology, under conditions of extreme exhaustion, stress and adversity. It's essentially sports science and philosophy that's been forged in battle.
- It ensures your body doesn't break and your mind doesn't quit and is based on three things: a **Strong Body**, a **Stoic Mind** and a **Strategic Plan**.

LESSON 2 | LEARN THE POWER OF SPIRITUAL SPORTS SCIENCE

LOCATION: Dungeness
DISTANCE COVERED: 48 miles
DAYS AT SEA: 4

Dungeness

The time is 6.00 a.m. on 4 June 2018 and the sun is rising on the boat.

The white cliffs of Dover were now in our 'rear-view mirror' and Margate a distant memory as we continued to make our way down the south coast of England. But utterly exhausted from last night's brutal swim, I failed to wake up despite the beams of light shining through the small porthole window and the sound of my alarm clock. So Harriet opened my cabin door and (kindly) placed a cup of coffee on the step, hoping the smell of freshly brewed beans would lure me out of bed.

'Thank you,' I managed to mutter from beneath my bedding.

Lifting my head up from my pillow, I immediately knew something was wrong. Although Matt had done a brilliant job sterilising my wounds from last night's swim, I had failed to consider the consequences of resting my head on my pillow when those wounds weren't dry yet. As a result, the blood from cuts, tears and lacerations around my neck had fused to the bedsheets leaving me with no other option but to rip them from my neck before I could get ready for the day's swim.

I counted, 'Three ... two ... one ... f*ck!' and in one swift movement, I removed the bedding from my neck (along with a few layers of skin) and then headed to the cabin bathroom to assess the damage. Taking a sip of coffee along the way to help numb the pain, I tried my best not to bleed all over the boat which was already beginning to look like a murder scene from the night before.

Looking in the mirror, my worst fears were realised. The wounds were already getting deeper and were maybe a few swims away from becoming an impressive collection of sea ulcers. What's worse, the skin was torn in the exact position that my shoulder rubs against my neck when I reach to take a stroke. This means every time I swim I tear the skin, deepen the wound and increase my chances of infection.

Deciding it was best to consult Matt, I went on deck to find him sitting in the galley looking at maps and sipping coffee. As I sat down next to him, I didn't have to say a word since it was clear from the trail of blood tricking down my neck that I wasn't having a great morning.

A few moments later Matt said, 'It looks like you cut yourself with a pillow,' while taking another sip of his coffee. I couldn't help but laugh. It must have looked like one of the strangest injuries to have ever occurred at sea.

We sat there again in silence. Both very aware that the most effective treatment would be to stop swimming to let my neck heal, but (even at this early stage of the swim) both realising this would mean losing precious progress that might come to haunt us later.

We knew this swim *had* to be finished before the British winter arrived. When it did, storms at sea would become more frequent and create unsafe and unswimmable conditions, meaning our swim would come to an abrupt end. This is why in that moment, we chose to forgo sensible solutions for stubborn ones instead.

Fuelled by a sense of defiant optimism, we began looking around the boat for a solution, only to find rolls of duct tape, tubs of Vaseline lubricant, plasters and bin bags instead. Now it must be said, our invention wasn't perfect. Nor would you find it in any swimming or sailing textbook. But we worked out that by wrapping this combination of kit around my neck, we could create a (semi) watertight, anti-chafing, prototype 'sea scarf' that would hopefully keep the wounds dry and prevent them from getting worse. That was the theory anyway.

We began with a generous application of sterilising solution to any patch of skin that was red, sore, swollen or ripped, ridding my open wounds of the bacteria and infections found lurking in the shipping lanes of Dover. This was followed by a large, oversized plaster, which we cautiously positioned over the wounds, being careful not to create any creases that may have added more chafing points to my already dishevelled, chewed up neck. With this in place our next challenge was making it watertight so the broken skin had a chance to heal.

So we applied rolls of thick duct tape onto my 'good skin' in order to keep the plasters and dressing in place over my 'bad skin' and to keep it dry. This wasn't ideal since adhesive tape and human skin don't usually cooperate very well, and in time (if we kept using it) would mean I had very little 'good skin' left. But for now, this was our only option.

Trying to minimise any further friction, we then applied lubricating petroleum jelly to any crease and crevice that could be found around my shoulders and arms.

In many ways, this moment again epitomised Stoic Sports Science. To quote Epictetus, 'Difficulties show a person's character.' Now, more than ever, I knew I had to learn to 'apply proven principles of sports science and psychology, under conditions of extreme exhaustion, stress and adversity'.

Carefully zipping up my wetsuit over my newly formed 'armoured' neck dressing, I once again began thinking of Marcus Aurelius ... a Roman Emperor who was sick, but never stopped.

SICK BUT NOT STOPPING

From what we know, Marcus Aurelius was not a well man. He suffered from chronic chest and stomach pains, problems sleeping and poor appetite, among other symptoms. While it's not clear what illness he suffered from, modern scholars have speculated he may have been exhibiting the symptoms of stomach ulcers, which could have been caused by a collection of other illnesses.

In fact, such was the extent of his declining health that many people thought he had died. This included one of his most senior generals Avidius Cassius, who decided to claim the title of emperor for himself. This forced Aurelius to travel to the East to regain control – but he did not have to fight Cassius, who was murdered by his own soldiers.

But what continually inspired me was the remarkable physical resilience that Aurelius showed despite crippling physical frailty. He lived to be nearly sixty, at a time when war or plague claimed many of his contemporaries at a younger age. For example, his adoptive brother Lucius Verus, despite being a stronger, fitter man, dropped dead aged thirty-eight, and Marcus' son Commodus was assassinated at thirty-one.

So how is it possible that Marcus Aurelius defied the odds? The answer is sheer mental fortitude. As he was famous for saying, 'Nothing happens to any man which he is not formed by nature to bear. The same things happen to another person, and either because he does not notice that they have happened, or because he wants to show off his strength of character, he is firm and remains unharmed.' He basically believed that any challenge could be overcome by a person if they cultivated their fortitude and virtuous nature.

He also believed that unpleasant physical sensations, such as pain, were natural and inevitable in life, but that our conscious mind should not 'add to the sensation the opinion that it is either good or bad' as he reminded us of the futility of struggling against suffering that was beyond our direct control: 'Imagine every man who is grieved at anything or discontented to be like a pig which is sacrificed and kicks and screams.'

He added that we commonly intensified our emotional suffering by struggling against events in futile ways and growing frustrated with life. On my swim, as I struggled to breathe while wrapped in duct tape, I would constantly remind myself of Marcus Aurelius. A man who ruled an empire, survived wars and plagues and outlived his family.

This is why every time I turned to breathe, I would remind myself, 'If it's endurable, then endure it. Stop complaining. If it's unendurable ... then stop complaining. Your destruction will mean its end as well. Just remember: you can endure anything your mind can make endurable, by treating it as in your interest to do so. In your interest, or in your nature.'

In short, Marcus Aurelius was the reason I jumped off the back of the boat and got into the water that day to trial Matt's newly modified, watertight, anti-chafing technology.

SORE SEA SKIN AND MURKY WATER

'How does it feel?' Matt asked.

I tried my best to remain still so I could sense if there was any water leaking through the metres of duct tape I was currently wearing around my throat.

'I can't really turn my head to breathe,' I replied.

This might have been an issue on account of me needing oxygen when swimming. Also, it was quite tight so I don't think I would be breaking any speed records that day. But despite all that, I was feeling optimistic.

'It does feel watertight, though, and there's a chance this could work,' I said.

Matt smiled proudly. Amazingly it was working. Granted, I had to awkwardly twist and contort my entire body to breathe. Also, turning to the right was proving harder because the cuts around my neck were deeper on that side. This meant I was unable to 'sight off' the land and coastline and instead had to constantly get my bearings from the boat. Lastly, I wasn't able to fully reach forward during each arm stroke and instead had to place my hands unnaturally wide to ensure my shoulders didn't rub against my neck. But with this heavily modified stroke (that only faintly resembled front crawl) I was moving forward and making progress past the shingle beaches of the Dungeness headland.

After swimming another few miles, my taste buds began picking up on a change in the consistency of the water. I also noticed it was turning a murky, grey and brown colour. Popping my head up from the water, I shouted to the crew on the boat.

'Why does the water taste funny?'

Harriet came to the side of the boat and was trying not to laugh. She knew I couldn't turn my head to the right so I'd missed noticing the giant nuclear power station housed on the headland of Dungeness that I'd been swimming past for the last hour.

'That might have something to do with it,' she said, pointing at the huge concrete fortress.

Now I'm not saying it had polluted the water, but it definitely hadn't helped. So I decided it was best to swim as fast as my sore and raw shoulders would let me in an attempt to reach clearer and cleaner waters. Swimming day and night, it took us three days to clear the headland and forget the taste of Dungeness nuclear power station. During this time, Matt and I continued to refine and improve our prototype 'sea scarf' while generously apply sterilising solution to my wounds.

Stoic Sports Science Sea Seminars were also part of our daily ritual. It was in one of our sessions that Matt asked me when the idea for the Great British swim began. Thinking long and hard about my answer, I told him the origins of the swim could be traced back ten years to when I lived with a group of Yamabushi warrior monks in Japan. They taught me an almost spiritual form of sport that was void of records, medals and trophies and had a much more 'pure' purpose.

'It's a long story,' I warned him.

'Oh, I'm sure we've plenty of time,' he said smiling.

So, between swims and during our Stoic Sports Science Sea Seminars, I explained how for me this swim was a modern version of an *Okugake*, an ancient practice I learned while climbing a sacred mountain in Japan.

SPIRITUAL SPORTS SCIENCE

Back in 2008, I was climbing Mount Sanjogatake, a 1,700 m (5,500 ft) peak on Japan's main island of Honshu with a team of Yamabushi warrior monks as they embarked on their annual, endurance-based pilgrimage of self-discipline and spiritual enlightenment called an Okugake. This forms a fundamental part of the Shugendo religion where the Yamabushi seek wisdom in the mountains, as it's believed the jagged rocks and perilous peaks are sacred places with 'powers unbeknownst to man'.

Now an Okugake is quite hard to describe, but let me try. The Yamabushi way of life centres around asceticism which is characterised by abstinence from sensual pleasures. Asceticism is found in many religious traditions and is often associated with a frugal lifestyle and sometimes periods of fasting while concentrating on the practice of reflection upon spiritual matters.

This is why daily practices would include waking up at 4.00 a.m. and drinking as much green tea as your bladder could withstand, but skipping breakfast. Lots of meditating. More green tea. Trekking thirty kilometres across mountainous terrain. Finally, meditating under waterfalls to test the limits of your willpower and blood circulation in your extremities. Should you have survived all that, you were granted entry into a neighbouring monastery where dinner was served, you slept and repeated it all again the next day.

The purpose? To achieve spiritual enlightenment through self-discipline by immersing yourself in the vast nature of the mountain, and to sharpen your wisdom through discipline of both the body and mind. Essentially, the Yamabushi believe you learn best when you push your mind and body to its limits, which is achieved by trekking over terrain so high and so steep it taxes both the lungs and legs.

I was of course eager to explore this idea of spiritual sports science and so joined the Yamabushi elders for dinner. Rice bowls were served and more green tea was poured as I plucked up the courage to ask my hosts and mentors about their journey.

'What's the speed record on Mount Sanjogatake?' I asked.

They looked at each other and smiled.

'Ross, it's not about speed, it's about spirituality,' said one of the elders in broken English.

Deep down I knew this too, but I was young and naive and the athlete in me still wanted to know. 'Okay, understood. What's the *spirituality* record on Mount Sanjogatake then?' I asked.

This time they burst out laughing.

I laughed too, but secretly still wanted to 'win' the spirituality test, or at least get the Mount Sanjogatake course record. Not wanting to tame my enthusiasm, the Yamabushi elders then told me the most brutal story of spirituality and sports science I have ever heard. Void of medals, it takes place over 1,000 days and 1,000 marathons and ends in spiritual enlightenment or death.

THE WORLD'S MOST BRUTAL ULTRA-MARATHON

Among the mountain ranges outside Kyoto is a sacred place called Mount Hiei. Impressive and imposing, it's also home to the legendary mountain monks of Japan. Part of the Tendai School of Buddhism, Tendai monks are celebrated in history as being one of the most extreme practitioners of 'spiritual sports science' and are famous for the *Kaihogyo*, a practice where monks run 1,000 marathons in 1,000 days in a quest for enlightenment.

What's worse is they must complete it devoid of cutting-edge sports nutrition and high-tech clothing, but instead on a modest diet of rice and vegetables and wearing straw sandals called *waraji*.

But wait, that's not the brutal part. Historically, trainee Tendai monks must qualify for the Kaihogyo by completing an initial 100 days of practice, running 30–40 km per day. Upon completing this, they must petition to the senior monks to complete the remaining 900 days, but their bid to continue comes with a warning.

This is because in the first 100 days, withdrawal from the challenge is permitted, but from day 101 onwards a monk is no longer allowed to withdraw. Tradition dictates he must either complete the course or take his own life using the rope and short sword they are forced to carry.

Of course, in contemporary times this is symbolic and the selection process ensures that those who embark on the practice will complete it. But the unmarked graves from Tendai monks of old serve as a stark reminder of the sanctity and severity of the Kaihogyo, which explains why it's very rare that a monk embarks on the spiritual quest and even rarer that he completes it.

In fact, only 46 men have completed the 1,000-day challenge since 1885. One look at the format and you see why.

Year 1	Year 2	Year 3	Year 4	Year 5	Year 6	Year 7
40 km per day for 100 days.	40 km per day for 100 days.	40 km per day for 100 days.	40 km per day for 200 days.	40 km per day for 200 days.	60 km per day for 100 days.	84 km per day for 100 days, followed by 40 km per day for 100 days.

By year 5, the Kaihogyo is punctuated by what many consider the most daunting phase of the process. The monk must go for seven days without food, water, or rest of any kind. He sits in the temple and recites mantras while two monks accompany him, one on either side, to ensure he does not fall asleep.

As the Yamabushi elders finished this story (and their bowls of rice) they asked if I still wanted to know the race record for Mount Sanjogatake. I smiled and shook my head. This was the ultimate process of self-improvement and self-discovery through self-discipline, and I now understood that spirituality is devoid of medals, records and trophies.

Essentially, the process is its own reward.

MONK-LIKE MENTAL TOUGHNESS

So, what did I learn during my time in Japan? I discovered this idea of monk-like mental toughness ungoverned by money, medals and records. Instead, they are motivated by a deeper intrinsic purpose. Sports psychologists have come to define this as Intrinsic *v* Extrinsic Motivation:

- **Extrinsically motivated:** This is when we are motivated to earn a reward (or avoid punishment). You're basically engaging in behaviour not because you find it satisfying, but because you want to get something in return (or avoid punishment).
- **Intrinsically motivated:** This is when you're engaged in an activity because you find it personally rewarding. There's no trophies, records or accolades, but rather the activity and process itself is its own reward.

Which form of motivation is best? Studies suggest that intrinsic motivation is a bigger predictor of success. In a large-scale study, researchers followed 11,320 West Point military cadets and assessed their motives for attending the academy over a 14-year period.[11] What they discovered was those who enrolled because of internal motivators were more likely to graduate, receive promotions, become commissioned officers and stay in the military compared with those who enrolled due to external motives.

Of course, both extrinsic motivation and intrinsic motivation are important ways of driving behaviour. But I knew that to swim for 12 hours a day, for 157 days, in the solitary confinement of the sea, I had to embody the same form of intrinsic motivation that fuelled a successful Okugake.

One of my favourite examples of this was mountaineer and explorer Sir Edmund Hillary. After summiting Mount Everest in 1953, he was celebrated by the media as an example of how humans had managed to stand on the roof of the world and conquered the highest peak Mother Nature could create. But upon reflection (and in an interview with the *Pittsburgh Post-Gazette* in 1998) Hillary was philosophical about his motivations and said, 'It is not the mountain we conquer, but ourselves.' Elaborating on this further he added, 'What I generally say is that it's the sense of challenge, the attempt to stretch yourself to the utmost and overcome considerable difficulties. If you can do that, you get a great sense of satisfaction.' Whether he knew it or not, what Hillary was describing here was a type of Okugake and a powerful form of intrinsic motivation very similar to the Yamabushi.

Two further examples can be found when looking at two of the greatest distance runners to have ever lived: Emil Zatopek and Eliud Kipchoge. Two men from different eras and places in the world, but both with an almost spiritual outlook on sports science.

It was Zatopek who famously once said, 'If you want to run, run a mile. If you want to experience a different life, run a marathon.' Considered to be the greatest runner of the twentieth century, he is best known for winning three gold medals at the 1952 Summer Olympics in Helsinki. He triumphed in the 5,000 m and 10,000 m, but his final medal came when he decided at the last minute to compete in the first marathon of his life.

Nicknamed the 'Czech Locomotive', in 1954 he also became the first runner to break the 29-minute barrier in the 10,000 m, having three years earlier broken the hour mark for running 20 km. But what's fascinating is that all this was achieved despite incredibly humble beginnings. The seventh child of a Moravian carpenter, he had spent his youth working in a shoe factory in Zlin. During World War II, he found that running and training offered a form of escape from the oppression of Nazi occupation – and began to train with levels of obsession and invention that no one had contemplated before. By the time of the liberation, he was the best runner in the country.

He joined the newly reconstituted Czechoslovakian army and quickly became one of the first of a new breed of working-class, Communist-friendly officers. He had grown up in great poverty, and was a firm believer in the basic ideals of socialism. Practising self-discipline, asceticism and intrinsic motivation he said, 'An athlete cannot run with money in his pockets. He must run with hope in his heart and dreams in his head.'

Years later and Zatopek's monk-like mental toughness and running ability has arguably only ever been matched by the great Eliud Kipchoge. Considered to be the finest runner of the modern era, he was also a man of immense self-discipline. A sporting hero in Kenya and a self-made millionaire, Kipchoge's way of life bore no trace of grandeur: one day he might be accepting the latest sporting accolade, the next he could be seen chopping vegetables for the team's communal meal or helping to clean the family home.

Equally as ascetically admirable was Kipchoge's unusual diet of monastic extreme. Distinctly low-tech, he consumed milk from cows that roamed the fields near his training camp and his meals centred around rice or the Kenyan staple of *ugali* (porridge), with an occasional helping of beef.

But perhaps what is most unusual is when asked about his ambitions to become the first human to run a sub two-hour marathon (a highly powerful extrinsic motivator to most people), Kipchoge replied, 'I want to run with a relaxed mind.' He added, 'To be precise, I am just going to try to run my personal best. If it comes as a world record, I would appreciate it. But I would treat it as a personal best.'

On 12 October 2019 that's precisely what he did. Running with a 'relaxed mind' (and intrinsically motivated) he achieved a personal best on the streets of Vienna, Austria, and covered 26.2 miles in a remarkable 1 hour 59 minutes and 40 seconds.

Which is exactly what I wanted to do. To embark on my own Okugake athletic adventure of self-improvement through self-discipline around the coast of Great Britain and to set a personal best.

MATT AND HIS OKUGAKE

LOCATION: Hastings
DISTANCE COVERED: 61
DAYS AT SEA: 5

Hastings

The time is 10.00 p.m. on 5 June, off the coast of Hastings. During my swim around this part of the coast, I didn't dare complain or talk about my problems. For this was an area famous for the 1066 Battle of Hastings between the Norman-French army of William the Conqueror and an English army under the Anglo-Saxon King Harold Godwinson. So much blood was shed on these shores, my various aches and pains were but a scratch compared to the injuries this coastline had seen.

It was in this moment of deep reflection (and still with lessons of the Okugake in my head) that I found myself in a form of spiritual, stoic silence. And I began to think about Matt's motives for agreeing to this swim. I knew he loved the sea and came from a family of sailors and big wave surfers who always had the dream of sailing around Great Britain, but as part of that plan I'm sure he never envisaged having a seasick swimmer bleeding all over his precious boat.

'So why did you agree to it?' I asked.

He paused to consider his response carefully.

'Because I wanted to see if it was possible myself,' he admitted.

'Sailing around Great Britain is a challenge for even the world's most experienced captains, but no one has ever skippered a boat to get a swimmer around. I suppose it was out of pure, personal curiosity ... but I wanted to see if it could be done,' he said smiling.

I loved this response, spoken like a true Yamabushi. Maybe his Okugake was sailing. Since, to quote Marcus Aurelius, 'Everything, a horse, a vine, is created for some duty. For what task, then, were you yourself created? A man's true delight is to do the things he was made for.'

LESSON 2

- For centuries, we humans have been using extreme acts of self-discipline (in the form of a pilgrimage or an **Okugake**) to learn more about ourselves as a form of self-discovery.
- Studies show **intrinsic motivation** (personal reward, without trophies or accolades) is a bigger predictor of success than **extrinsic motivation** (seeking to earn a reward or to avoid punishment).
- Combining intrinsic motivation with an act of self-discipline for self-discovery is a modern-day pilgrimage and is like a powerful form of spiritual sports science understood by some of the greatest athletes in history.

LESSON 3 | THE BODY BRUISES AND BLEEDS BUT CANNOT BE BEATEN

LOCATION: Isle of Wight
DISTANCE COVERED: 168 miles
DAYS AT SEA: 12

The Needles

It is 9.40 p.m. on 11 June and we are passing the Isle of Wight. A small island off the coast of England, renowned for its beaches and seafront promenades, in many ways it's the most quintessentially British holiday experience you are likely to find.

Unfortunately, I couldn't enjoy any of this.

Swimming for up to 12 hours per day and practically living in the narrow, two-mile-wide stretch of water that separates the island from mainland Great Britain (known as the Solent), I was instead preoccupied with not getting hit by the hovercrafts and ferries with which I was sharing my 'swimming pool'.

Day and night we continued to swim, until after 48 hours our efforts were rewarded and we could see the island's most western point, The Needles. One of the most photographed groups of rocks in the world, this row of three distinctive stacks of chalk landforms that rise about 30 m out of the sea is overlooked by a lighthouse that has proudly stood there since the nineteenth century.

This was a huge milestone that *should* have been celebrated. We had covered over 150 miles, navigated through the strong tidal streams and were almost halfway across the south coast of England. But the reason my celebrations were a little subdued was because I was mourning the casualties we'd lost along the way to salt water erosion. These included:

- 2 pairs of snapped goggle straps.
- 3 ripped swim hats.
- 1 torn wetsuit.
- A layer of skin from my tongue.

As you can imagine, I was most concerned about the last on that list.

On first noticing signs of salt tongue around the coast of Brighton, when I was losing all the moisture from my mouth from chronic salt water exposure, Suzanne prepared an incredible vegetable soup in the hope I'd find that easier to eat. Bowl after bowl was served and it was helping until I began to wonder why mine had additional chunks of meat in it.

Eventually I politely asked, 'Is this beef, pork or chicken?'

Peering into my bowl and comparing it to her own, Harriet replied, 'No, that appears to be your tongue.'

Conflicted about what to do, I ate it anyway and it actually tasted okay, albeit a bit chewy. This then continued for several days, and while I was prepared to lose (and ingest) parts of my tongue for the greater cause, I did begin to wonder how much of it I would have to sacrifice at sea to make it all the way around Britain.

Thankfully, I didn't have to wonder anymore. For the Isle of Wight had produced a solution and his name was Siggy. A friend of Harriet's who was born on the island, he was coming aboard the boat to help as crew while Suzanne visited land for a few weeks. He was a chef and knew a little about herbal medicine too.

Perhaps that's why he took one look at my degrading tongue and said, 'Take a mouth full of coconut oil and melt it on your tongue.

'The theory is this will lock in the moisture and create a barrier to protect against the salt water. Then chew on mint leaves as this will change the alkalinity of your tongue which is good "for maintaining good oral health" as you swim.'[12]

Did it work? Yes, like magic. Over 24 hours (and 20 miles) later I was storming around the coast of the Isle of Wight with my tongue still attached and my mouth minty fresh and moisturised. Siggy was a genius: like a sea-dwelling wizard he arrived on the boat, saved my tongue and returned to land a few weeks later. Although his time on the crew was brief, his contribution to the entire swim was huge and my tongue is forever grateful to him.

As a swimmer, I found I was now evolving. Mile after mile we adapted and added new tools to our arsenal, which included:

- Minty-mouth medicine.
- Coconut tongue-technology.
- Matt's newly invented 'sea scarf' (basically duct tape and lubricant).

The latter, in particular, was working brilliantly now too. Just eight days following its invention, Matt had successfully managed to stop the skin from completely eroding away, which meant the previously sore and raw skin around my neck was now (semi) healing. Becoming hardened with scar tissue and thick calluses, it formed what felt like an 'armoured neck' which wasn't aesthetic to look at ... but was functional to swim with.

I have to say that I was proud of my callused clavicles. Wearing them with pride as hard-earned badges of honour, it felt right (and royal) swimming past Cowes Castle. Originally built by Henry VIII in 1539 to protect England against the threat of invasion, it was now the club-house to the Royal Yacht Squadron, one of the most prestigious yacht clubs in the world, where seasoned sailors assemble in the summer.

But despite its long history, the clubhouse had never seen anything like my neck. A group of elderly sailors who we had met there during a rest break concluded the only other place they'd seen skin that thick was on safari in Africa and it belonged to a rhino. We all laughed, but this was perhaps the best description of my contin-ued evolution, so from that day forth sailors from the Isle of Wight said they would forever dub me 'Rhino Neck'.

I won't lie, I loved the nickname. It brilliantly summed up the swim so far. Like the term roughneck, it felt earnest.

Other physical adaptations my body was experiencing from almost a fortnight in the sea included a fuller, fortified beard, which was becoming increasingly thicker due to the salt water and my complete disregard for any grooming products or procedures. Although it looked a mess, the matted hairs offered some protection against the elements.

I might have looked like a water-dwelling werewolf but the waves continued to test the durability of my limbs, just as the shipping lanes had tested the durability of my immune system and stomach. Thankfully, salvation was about to arrive in the form of my friend and physio, Jeff Ross, who Taz was collecting from land in our smaller motorised boat.

A unique sailing–physio hybrid, Jeff was born in New Zealand and bred sailing boats. So, although he was usually tasked with caring for the physiology of elite athletes, ranging from New Zealand's Rugby League team to Premier League footballers here in Britain, he was also perfectly at home treating my bruised and beaten body in the boat's kitchen.

He also came equipped with these inexplicably big forearms and muscle-bound fingers, which meant he could effortlessly bury his thumbs into your tendons, ligaments, muscle and fibrous tissues to perform a strange kind of autopsy.

Which is what I endured for the next few hours as Jeff painfully prodded and probed before giving his diagnosis on the state of my body. As I lay face down on the treatment table that he had somehow managed to assemble in the ship's galley, with his knuckles embedded into my back and spine, Jeff made a casual observation.

'You look and feel horrendous.'

It was true, I looked like a hairy, swollen, sea pirate.

'Also, you've lost parts of your tongue from salt water exposure and those chafing wounds around your neck and shoulders might get infected.'

This was also true, I'd left a lot of skin around the coast of Great Britain.

'But weirdly … you're not injured or ill.'

I smiled. There it was, a glimmer of hope.

I then told Jeff about my visit to the sports laboratory, my submarine skull, child-bearing hips and buoyant duck bum, and that I felt years of strength training would actually uniquely equip a super-sized sumo swimmer like myself to complete this swim.

He paused for a moment and considered my theory before giving his verdict on my sea-based sports science musings.

'I believe your theory is spot on. There is no doubt in my mind that strength underpins everything we do and it is the accumulation of strength over a period of time that allows all of our body's structures to adapt and make us more able to deal with the stresses and strains that we place upon it. Whether that's bones, muscles, joints, ligaments or tendons: all of these structures have the ability to adapt to the forces that are placed upon them. If we load too quickly and have not accustomed our body and its structures to the loads that we intend to place on it, then we will almost certainly pick up some form of injury. On the other hand, if we increase the load gradually while incorporating some rest and recovery time (which allows the body to adapt further) then we become stronger and more resilient.'

I liked what I was hearing and it made the sores on my neck sting a little less. I continued taking notes on Jeff's nautical genius as he added, 'It's possible that you're able to keep going based on the foundations of years of loading your body with different forces, impacts and tension [although there was no impact load during the swim, there was still joint stress, particularly in the upper body]. This meant that muscles, ligaments and tendons have adapted to the forces placed upon them and have become stronger over time, which have allowed them to cope with the stresses of the Great British swim.

'I don't believe you could take an office worker, for example, and throw them in the water and ask them to do what you did. Even a lower limb athlete, who hasn't subjected their shoulders and upper body to the same stresses as their lower limbs, would not be able to cope with the load placed upon them by the swim.'

Jeff then explained how this entire process of building resilience takes years. 'Pre-season training has probably become seen by most people as a way of getting athletes and teams fit for the upcoming season. This is true to an extent, but it serves a much more important role of getting athletes and teams accustomed to the loads that they will have to deal with during a long season. One pre-season doesn't make a summer though, so to speak, and it is the accumulation of years of pre-seasons that make athletes more robust.'

Jeff and I then spoke about how pre-season training can serve to make us mentally more robust as well as physically more resilient. With my face buried into the foam pillow on Jeff's treatment table, I then hosted another impromptu Stoic Sports Science Sea Seminar and told him about one of the strangest stories in sports psychology that to this day helps me cope with pain.

HOW TO TRAIN PAIN: THE KALENJIN TRIBE

It was 15 August 2008, a day my legs, feet and genitalia will never forget.

I was on my travels (again). This time on the sun-bleached African plains of Namibia, tasked with documenting the life of the San Bushmen, considered to be one of the world's greatest hunter-gatherer civilisations to have ever existed.

We were midway through what would become a 50 km hunt and I was struggling. Struggling with the heat. Struggling with the lack of food. Basically, just struggling to keep up with the relentless pace and mileage my hosts could maintain all day, every day.

This is because my hosts were the Ju-Wasi tribe. Detailed analysis of African DNA reveals the Ju-Wasi are descendants from the oldest population of humans on earth. Therefore, they've been perfecting the art of endurance longer than any other civilisation.[13] Not to win medals. Not to set records. Instead, it's to secure survival in one of the harshest climates on earth. Covering a marathon a day in 39°C heat and on sand with barely any food or water, their ability to track and hunt animals into exhaustion has become legendary.

They have a name for it. It's called Persistence Hunting. This involves chasing after your dinner until it collapses to the floor and onto your dinner plate. No weapons are needed. You just need patience, years of tracking experience in the African bush and a profound understanding of Human Endurance *v* Animal Endurance.

This was something the tribe's leader had forged over years and miles. His name was Duee. He was five foot six, slim, svelte and had the largest wrinkles and laughter lines I had ever seen. Engrained into his face from years of hunting in the scorching dry seasons, they went from his eyes to his mouth; it seemed his skills as a great African hunter were only matched by his superhuman endurance.

Then there was me: I hadn't had a haircut for seven months, didn't speak a word of Afrikaans and weighed 30 kg more than their heaviest tribesman. It's possible I was the world's worst wannabe San Bushman that Duee ever had to babysit.

I was painfully aware of this too. With no physical attributes to be a good hunter, I battled the psychobiological model of fatigue to keep up. Duee could see I was struggling, but could also see I was too stubborn to stop.

Hours and miles passed and the sun began to set overhead. Duee called a meeting. As he began talking in an ancient form of communication that consisted of clicking sounds and maps drawn in the sand with a stick, I had absolutely no idea what was being said. So I stayed close to Tau, my Bushman brother, who spoke a little English and had adopted me and taken me under his wing.

Tau was taller than Duee, but just as lean and light. Standing five foot ten, his family originally came from Kenya which was 2,000 miles north of our current camp. There he had learnt to speak English and a different Afrikaans and had found a career helping linguistically challenged travellers (like myself) live and learn in the African Bush.

'We set up camp here tonight,' Tau translated for me.

I nodded and was slightly relieved, unsure how much further I could continue as my legs and lungs screamed at my brain to stop under the burning sun. Collapsing onto the floor, we then made a fire, and rations were divided up equally among everyone.

Looking around, I was struck by one thing. Yes, I was heavier and physiologically very poorly equipped to run these distances in this heat, but around the campfire not a hint of exhaustion or pain could be seen on the faces of the Ju-Wasi San Bushmen.

Strong, stoic and void of discomfort, I turned to Tau and asked how they cope so well with pain and why I'm still yet to meet an African who isn't an insanely talented endurance athlete. He laughed and translated my question to the group. A debate then erupted around the campfire, because it turns out there are many theories as to why Africans are so good at running, but each theory differs depending on which part of Africa you are in.

Most experts claim it's because of superior genetics[14] mixed with environmental factors[15] while others cite 'a motivation to succeed athletically for the purpose of economic and social advancement.'[16]

But there was one theory I was *not* expecting.

Tau was adamant that the secret to Kenyan running success can be found in your penis.

He told me that Kenyan runners are so good because their perception of pain has been modified by their ritual practice of circumcision. So, it's not because they are a few ounces lighter or encounter less wind resistance after the procedure. It has a lot more to do with the brutal initiation ceremony into adulthood that most boys endure, resulting in an indomitable tolerance to suffering.

He then went on to tell me about the Kalenjin people. A tribe in Kenya with an incredible history and heritage, they account for only three per cent of the total Kenyan population but have produced more elite marathon runners than anywhere else in the world and have dominated international middle and long-distance running for over 40 years. But what's incredible is that from a very young age boys are prepped and primed to withstand vast amounts of pain as they enter into painful (and often scarring) rituals in order to be branded brave and marriage worthy. The boys who opt out of the ceremonies are often branded a 'kebitet' (a coward) and stigmatised by the entire community.

I asked Tau just how bad it could be. His answer made a bar mitzvah look like a casual beauty treatment.

'First, you must crawl naked through a tunnel of African stinging nettles,' he said, assuring me they were much worse than the ones I would find back home in my garden.

'This will cause a rash, blisters, scars and a lot of pain. After this you must accept a beating on the bony parts of the ankles and knuckles with hard sticks. You then have the acid from the stinging nettles rubbed on your genitals, until you're then circumcised without anaesthesia or pain reliever of any kind ... with a sharp stick.'

I was already wincing just thinking about it.

'You could not make that face, Ross,' he said sternly. 'During this ceremony, your face would be covered in dry mud. This is to ensure you don't flinch from the pain during the circumcision. You must remain quiet, still and strong and any involuntary twitch of the cheek might split the mud and cause you to be branded a coward.'

Tau then argued that this extreme way of training toughness was the reason the Kalenjin runners of Kenya were so good. He said, 'You have to understand the Kalenjin have been around for thousands of years and the boys who passed this test into adulthood were more likely to be married and have children. With each succeeding generation, the lineage of those best capable of coping with ridiculous amounts of pain grew stronger. The weak ones were simply selected out.'

I sat there and thought about his logic and admit it made some sense. Darwin would be proud. This wasn't survival of the fittest, it was survival of the toughest. Tau concluded his testicle-themed theory by saying, 'Combine this ability to deal with suffering, the typical body structure of a Kenyan (thin ankles/calves with a medium to light stature), add in high altitude training, a drive to escape poverty and the hero-worship that running inspires and there you have it ... the greatest runners the world has ever known.'

Tau and the rest of the team then looked at me over the campfire.

I nodded. It wasn't conventional, but it made sense. The very fact young tribesmen could undergo such pain without flinching or showing any emotion could equip them with amazing abilities to override the psychobiological model of fatigue.

'Do you still want to run faster?' Tau asked, picking up a knife with a smile, as everyone burst out laughing.

'No, no, no. Keep your cutlery away from my manhood,' I said half-laughing, while visibly flinching and shielding my gentlemanly parts.

'I will run fast tomorrow, I promise. Just leave my genitalia intact.'

Which is exactly what I did. From that day onwards, whenever I was confronted with a painful (but endurable) sensation I would always think back to the Kalenjin tribe. On my swim from now on, thanks to them, I would think about my freshly wounded neck, the stinging of the salt water and the incessant pain as a newly circumcised Kalenjin penis.

Yes, I know how odd that sounds. But this swim was operating outside of the realms of conventional sport and so required an unconventional mindset. A mindset that was only getting more peculiar and primitive as the days went on. Visiting the boat most weekends, my (incredibly patient) girlfriend, Hester, was a witness to this necessary devolution too, watching on as her boyfriend regressed into an almost primordial form of human. Our relationship was truly tested only a few days later after I passed one of the most dangerous headlands on the south coast: Portland Bill.

TOILET TROUBLES AT PORTLAND BILL

LOCATION: Portland Bill
DISTANCE COVERED: 197 miles
DAYS AT SEA: 15

Portland Bill

It is 1.00 a.m. on 15 June as we approach Portland Bill.

Known for its limestone cliffs, rock formations and fossils that show millions of years of geological history, it also has a darker (and more dangerous) history as an area that has become the graveyard of many a vessel that failed to reach safe harbour in Weymouth due to the treacherous waters that surround this part of the south coast.

Looking up at the night sky, I joined Matt at the bow of the boat to look at the swim that lay ahead. Watching the waves crashing on the rocks, I sensed the next few miles would make the seasick swim of Dover look like a paddling pool.

'How's the stomach tonight?' asked Matt.

'Good,' I replied trying my best to reassure him. 'But let's not tempt fate. Any chance Suzanne can keep the kettle and ginger tea on standby?'

'She already has the kettle boiling,' he replied.

He wasn't lying either. Across the Seven Seas there is no kitchen better stocked than on *Hecate* and no cook better equipped than Suzanne.

'Why is the sea so angry tonight?' I asked.

'It's always angry around here,' Matt said. 'It's because of the way the tidal currents flow between Portland Bill and the Shambles sandbank about three miles southeast of here ... they're permanently on a collision course. This is why even the most experienced sailors will get nervous when approaching the cliffs around here.'

He paused for a moment and pointed at the giant flashing light in the distance. 'That's why Portland Bill lighthouse was built.' Standing 41 m (135 ft) tall, the light flashes four times every 20 seconds, with a range of 25 nautical miles. It's acted as a waymark for ships navigating the English Channel since 1906.

With each flash of light, you could see the distinctive red and white tower. 'That's a good-looking lighthouse,' I said.

'Don't be fooled by the picturesque paintwork,' Matt warned. 'It's also a giant gravestone. I know of many ships that lay at the bottom of the ocean around there and I don't want you to join them.'

Those were Matt's final words to me as I suited up, tightened my goggles and entered the water that night. Immediately after jumping off the boat, I could feel the 'energy' in the ocean was different. It almost felt menacing and had all my senses heighted.

I wasn't the only one to notice either, Harriet was on watch and now standing on the deck of the boat, gripping the rigging so tightly you could visibly see how white her knuckles were turning. With every mile that passed, the waves tested the durability of the boat's bow and the rigging that held the two hulls of *Hecate* together.

But standing at the helm, Matt remained entirely stoic. His calm demeanour (cultivated over 40 years at sea) was infectious so I settled into a rhythm and began to glide through, over and under the waves. In fact, I was so calm I couldn't help but stop as we swam directly parallel to Portland Bill lighthouse to enjoy the view, much to Harriet's dismay.

'What are you doing?' Harriet yelled, her fingers still tightly wrapped around the rigging.

'Taking in the view and I need to visit the toilet,' I said smiling.

Harriet's knuckles were now white and her face was red. 'WHAT! You couldn't have picked a worst place to stop ... keep swimming!'

I could see why she was so angry, but swimming logic is very different to sailing logic. Travelling around Portland Bill in a boat could mean you capsize, tip over and sink. Travelling around Portland Bill in a wetsuit just means you capsize, tip over and begin swimming backstroke. But sensing this was no time for a debate (and also more scared of Harriet than I was Portland Bill) I swam for the next four hours as fast as my arms would take me. Determined to swim myself, the boat and crew to safety.

But this time it was my bladder that betrayed me. I badly needed to urinate and would normally visit the toilet on the boat. Not only because it was the gentlemanly thing to do, but also because the colour of my urine gave the best indicator of my hydration levels.[17]

DANGERS OF DEHYDRATION

A body's performance and hydration levels are inextricably linked. According to studies carried out at the Thermal & Mountain Medicine Division of the US Army Research Institute of Environmental Medicine, as well as the work published in the *Journal of Athletic Training*,[18] becoming dehydrated by just one per cent impacts performance.[19] And as dehydration increases, life-threatening impacts on the body become a real factor.

- 1 per cent dehydrated: reduced lung capacity and signs of thirst present.
- 5 per cent dehydrated: difficulty concentrating, increased heart rate and trouble breathing.
- 8–9 per cent dehydrated: dizziness, real difficulty breathing, confusion and increased weakness.
- 10 per cent dehydrated: involuntary muscle spasms, loss of balance and tongue swelling.
- 11 per cent dehydrated: delirium, risk of stroke, difficulty swallowing and death may occur.

But that night the toilet was well and truly closed. I knew we couldn't stop with waves crashing over the boat. I also knew the tide would run with me for six precious hours and that getting onto the boat to visit the toilet would mean valuable minutes of favourable swimming conditions would be lost. Valuable minutes I couldn't spare as we were racing to make it around Land's End by the end of the month.

My solution? That day, and every day beyond, I didn't hesitate (or feel any shame) when filling up my wetsuit with my own urine. But the problems occurred much later when, at the end of a day's swim, I had to hang it up to dry in my small, enclosed cabin onboard *Hecate*. I can hereby confirm that a urine-soaked, salt water-infused wetsuit is the world's worst air freshener.

I actually didn't mind the smell. I'd been living on (and in) the ocean for two weeks and had already bathed in my own sick around Dover, left layers of skin on bedsheets around Dungeness and lost parts of my tongue around the Isle of Wight. I had regressed into this sea-dwelling savage whose nose and sense of smell had been completely disabled by the constant salt water.

But Hester wasn't so accepting, and I can confirm the wrath of Portland Bill is nothing compared to the wrath of an angry girlfriend on finding out she has to sleep in a urine-scented cabin because her boyfriend said he'd swim around Great Britain.

'What is that smell, have you wet the bed?' she said on entering my cabin.

'No, of course not,' I replied, almost insulted that she would even ask.

'Much better. I didn't urinate *in* the bed … I urinated in my wetsuit hanging up *by* the bed,' I said smiling, trying my best to plead innocence.

'WHAT?! Ross that's disgusting. How's that much better?'

Thinking about it now I do see her point. It's probably not *much* better. But at the time I liked to think there was something chivalrous about it. After all, I did hang up the wetsuit on the side of the bed where I slept.

But the good news from this day on was that Hester's delicate and far more civilised nose became a good indicator of my hydration levels as follows:

- If she complained the cabin smelled really bad, it was likely I was dehydrated and my urine was more concentrated with a stronger ammonia scent than normal.
- If she didn't complain, it meant I was adequately hydrated (and would probably still have a girlfriend by the time I finished the swim).

Now, this is by no means an official or accurate measurement of your hydration status and I'm not sure the US Army Research Institute would approve. Equally, I'm not recommending you try it. But (surprisingly) after many more days at sea I still had a girlfriend, which meant I must have kept myself relatively well hydrated.

LESSON 3

- Studies show that **strength training** is one of the most effective conditioning protocols for injury prevention, and an effectively designed routine (especially during pre-season) can create a more robust and physically more resilient athlete.
- Sometimes the best athletes aren't the strongest, fastest or fittest, but they are **the best at suffering and enduring pain** (something the Kalenjin tribe have known for centuries).
- The ability to **'train pain'** is one of the most effective (yet most often overlooked) aspects of most athlete's conditioning.

LESSON 4 | TO WALK YOUR OWN PATH, WRITE YOUR OWN PLAN

LOCATION: Rame Head
DISTANCE COVERED: 280 miles
DAYS AT SEA: 24

Rame Head

It is 24 June and the sun is rising on the headland of Rame Head, Cornwall. It's a beautiful landscape of tidal creeks, sandy beaches and lush farmland that I can only view (not visit) from the boat. But these were the rules and I wrote them. For me, it only seemed right that if you intended to swim around Great Britain, you shouldn't step foot on land until the job was done. Maybe this was an old-fashioned and romantic ideal, but I just felt this swim should be done in a way befitting to the memory of Captain Webb and in a fashion that Sir Edmund Hillary and Tenzing Norgay would have appreciated.

Hotels, showers and home comforts didn't seem right.

But 24 days in and although urine-soaked and seasick, one of the worst things I've had to combat is the sheer boredom of swimming, alone, for 12 hours a day, *every* day. I was existing in a world of sensory deprivation with my sight impaired, hearing restricted, touch numbed by the cold and sense of smell almost non-existent. It was also the metronomic, mundane pace that I had to sustain that meant I almost yearned for another shipping lane to inject excitement into my days at sea. Since it wasn't all sunshine and dolphins, the reality was that 90 per cent of the time it was boring, dull and no longer a swim, but a war of attrition on the senses.

One thing that did help was new faces on the boat. This is because while Matt and I remained permanent features throughout the entire swim, the rest of the crew worked on a rota system so they could return to their lives back on land for a few weeks.

One of my favourite temporary crew members was Dom. Another university friend of Harriet's, he was a trained marine biologist and brilliant on a paddleboard. Day and night, mile after mile he would accompany me on the swim, often (skilfully) moving jellyfish out my way with his paddle.

And today there would be even more new faces. In understanding the pain I was going through, Matt informed me he'd received word over the radio that two special visitors would be joining us and they would be keeping me company during the swim.

This sounded great, I thought. Whoever it was would be so welcome, from open-water swimmers to a friendly fishing boat, or even the company of a kayaker would be incredibly appreciated if only for a few miles ... but what I got was even better.

My companions would be two giant 49-tonne patrol vessels from the Royal Navy. At 20 m (65 ft) long and 5.8 m (19 ft) wide, HMS *Charger* and HMS *Biter* had left the Royal Navy base back in Portsmouth over a hundred miles away and were travelling at 20 knots (23 mph) towards Falmouth on a training exercise. But while on route they heard from friends of mine at the Royal Marines that my morale was taking a bit of a battering and a visit might help raise my swimming spirits.

As a kid, I would play with toy boats in the bath. Now as an adult, I got to play with toy boats in the sea. Like two huge armoured tanks they appeared on the horizon and gradually slowed to a safe distance either side of me as I gazed up from the water. Dwarfed by their sheer size, with their enormous steel hulls shimmering in the sun, I could feel the sound of their engines rattle my bones and reverberate through the water around me.

'Good morning,' the commanding officer's voice came booming across the tannoy. 'HMS *Charger* here, and that is HMS *Biter*. Part of Her Majesty's Naval Service currently on a training mission deployment from Portsmouth to Falmouth.'

I panicked at how professional and polished his introduction was, and found myself replying in a less than deep and direct tone.

'Good morning, Ross Edgley here. Previously part of Grantham school boys swimming club and currently on a training mission deployment from Margate to ... Margate.'

Laughter then erupted from the deck of both boats. They asked if I needed anything to drink and we spoke about Dover, Dungeness and Portland Bill and I compared notes on our experiences of sailing across the English Channel.

This was a massive honour and one of the most memorable (and surreal) encounters at sea I would ever have. Sandwiched between two heavily armoured warships each equipped with an Oerlikon 20 mm cannon and three general-purpose machine guns, we talked sunrises, seasickness and I explained why I was smeared in Vaseline lubricant with rolls of duct tape and plasters around my neck.

Minutes later, it dawned on me I would likely never experience this ever again. It really was a once-in-a-lifetime experience. So, I did the only logical thing I could think of. I offered them a drag race.

'Where to?' the commanding officer asked, eagerly accepting the challenge.

'I can ask Dom to be the finish line on a paddleboard,' I said. 'Then we race from a standing start over 10 m, 20 m and 30 m, and winner takes home pride and bragging rights.'

'Ready when you are,' he said laughing.

Moments later and Dom was sitting on the paddleboard with a flag ready to officially start the drag race, and seconds later I would understand why they were laughing and so quick to accept the challenge. The ships may have weighed an almighty 49 tonnes each but they were also powered by two huge Rolls-Royce turbo engines meaning they could reach speeds of 27 knots (31 mph) with ease.

The crew from each boat then assembled on deck to peer over the side. Sandwiched between the two boats (and four engines, two either side) I knew if I didn't get a fast start I would be eating the waves created by the engines and be sent flying backwards.

'Ready?' Dom shouted, now sitting on his paddleboard 10 m away to signal the finish line. 'Three, two, one ... GO!' he screamed, waving his improvised starter flag.

Now the 'race' was maybe competitive over the first three metres or so, but beyond this I cannot claim it was even close. The water in front of me was churned up so much it was like swimming through white water rapids and I was sent hurtling back to Portsmouth.

The second race of 20 m wasn't any better, and the 30 metre race was outright embarrassing. But after being invited aboard HMS *Biter* to shake hands with the commanding officer and crew for a well-fought race, I will forever be grateful to the Royal Navy for what they did next. Presenting me with a specially made plaque, they said, 'You're our generation's Captain Webb and possess the same indomitable spirit that's become synonymous with great British explorers and adventurers.'

They added, 'Regardless of what anyone thinks, we know you will make it all the way around Britain and will join you for celebratory beers once you do.'

Trying my best not to cry in front of forty sea-hardened sailors, I took a minute to compose myself. After so many people doubted me, this seal of approval from a commanding officer of Her Majesty's Naval Service meant so much. We then spent the next half an hour or so bonding over our mutual love of Webb, who was a sailor himself before becoming the world's most famous swimmer almost two centuries ago.

CAPTAIN WEBB: SWIMMER EXTRAORDINAIRE

Captain Matthew Webb was told his planned 21-mile swim from Dover to Calais was impossible, and long before he entered the water on 25 August 1875 he was warned by everyone that he would fail. As a result, he received very little help in the beginning and had to write his own training programmes and pioneer his own nutritional preparation. But in 1873, that's what he decided to do after hearing about a failed attempt by J B Johnson on 24 August 1872 who was forced to give up after just 1 hour and 3 minutes.

Leaving his job as a ship's captain, Webb began training at the Lambeth Baths in London. Soon he moved on to the Thames (which is a feat in itself considering the water quality of the Victorian-era Thames) and when satisfied with his progress moved to Dover where (in June 1874) he swam from the Admiralty Pier to the North-East Varne Buoy, a distance of 11 statute miles.

Already having swum further than Johnson's attempted Channel crossing, Webb now sensed it was possible. He completed a number of training swims that got progressively longer, harder and colder, the most publicised of which was an 18-mile swim from Blackwall Pier to Gravesend Town Pier near London (in July). There followed a 19½-mile swim from Dover to Ramsgate (on 19 July) this time with support from locals where he was welcomed to the Flying Horse Inn by the landlord who believed in him.

On Tuesday 24 August 1875, after one failed attempt twelve days earlier, Webb was ready to try once more. Covering his muscular five foot eight inch frame with porpoise oil, he dived into the English Channel from the end of Admiralty Pier. Starting with the wind, tide and weather in his favour, he had three support vessels. One contained his brother and cousin who provided a plentiful supply of sandwiches washed down with ale and coffee.

After 21 hours and 45 minutes he had actually swum 39 miles (64 km) as he zigzagged his way across the channel while battling the tides, and at 10.40 a.m. on 25 August 1875 he reached land half a mile west of Calais.

I swam with goosebumps thinking of this story and wrote in my diary later that day:

> 'There is no blueprint when attempting the impossible.
> You must create your own.'

Which is exactly what I did. Months before arriving at Margate beach, I had begun to live like Captain Webb. I wrote my own plan and walked my own path and travelled between Loughborough University's School of Sport, Exercise and Health Science and the Royal Marine Commando Training Centre in Lympstone, Devon to try and understand *How to Create an Unbreakable Body.*

Did it work? Yes (so far).

We were now just a few days away from completing the first 350-mile swim in history down the length of the English Channel (143 years after Captain Webb heroically swam 21 miles across it). We could feel the tide of public perception turning, as more and more people thought our record-breaking swim around Great Britain might just be possible.

ONE RECORD DOWN ... MANY MORE TO GO

Land's End

LOCATION: Land's End
DISTANCE COVERED: 350 miles
DAYS AT SEA: 29

It's 11.00 a.m. on 29 June. We can finally see Land's End.

The most famous headland in Britain (also the most southwesterly point), it signals we've just completed the first 350-mile swim down the entire length of the English Channel. Looking up at the cliffs from the water, I can see tourists taking pictures by the iconic signpost that reads, 'New York, 3,147 miles' and points directly across the Atlantic Ocean. Erected in the 1950s, this now legendary Cornish icon attracts people from all over the world who arrive to have their picture taken underneath it.

But for a handful of athletes, this landmark is incredibly special for a different reason. For it's the starting point for those who run, walk and cycle the famous Land's End to John o' Groats route that covers 874 miles (1,407 km) across Great Britain.

Essentially, this is where many people's modern-day Okugakes starts.

But for me, my Okugake was far from over. This is why many tourists looked on in confusion as I quickly boarded the boat to initiate a giant, mid-swim sea hug. It began between me and Matt, but we were quickly joined by Suzanne and then engulfed by

Harriet, who emerged from the galley, and Taz, who climbed down the rigging.

No one spoke. Nothing needed to be said. That one brief group hug said it all. Throughout June this had become more than a swim for all of us. We were all now so personally invested in circumnavigating this island that we'd each forgotten about life back on land. We now all lived on our 16-metre (53-foot) long and 7-metre (23-foot) wide home that was *Hecate*.

Like a small, sea-dwelling family, each of us diligently fulfilled our roles as we passed every single beach, headland and lighthouse that had ever been formed or created on this rock we call Great Britain. Suzanne had cooked, created and cared for my monstrous calorie requirements that averaged 10,000 to 15,000 calories per day. Harriet, Peony and Taz had saved me numerous times from getting mowed down by cargo ships and sailing boats as they watched over me day and night, often just metres away in our small, motorised inflatable. Finally, Matt had expertly navigated and medically treated every single jellyfish-infested, chafed mile, rogue tide and busy shipping lane and led us as a team to where we were currently.

As a result, the sheer gratitude I felt that day was hard to put into words. But at that moment, there was no time to try. That's because within this family, I knew my role. Which is why I immediately jumped back in the water and continued to swim around Land's End and towards St Ives as the tide was still running in our favour and we had precious miles to make up.

As I resumed my swim, my phone (and the boat's radio) lit up like a Christmas tree with messages of support. It was at that very moment when everything changed. After more than 350 miles of swimming, we were finally heading north. It was a strange feeling, but the very fact we were now making progress in degrees latitude meant people began to believe this swim might just be possible and maybe (just maybe) we were crazy enough to do it. As a team, we even received emails from those journalists who had previously declined to cover the swim as they openly admitted they never thought we'd get this far.

As I continued to swim, I thought back to every cynic and critic. From George and his £100 bet with Barry, to the lab results that revealed my child-bearing, sumo-swimmer physique that was (supposedly) doomed to fail. But I was equally grateful to those who did think this was possible: from Mum and Dad, to the Mayor of Margate and to the crews of HMS *Biter* and HMS *Charger*.

Instead of posting reasons why I would stop and fail, people were now posting questions asking how I planned to continue and succeed, and the name 'Edgley' was gathering a niche level of notoriety back on land among the sports science community.

But the truth is, none of this surprised me. Reaching Land's End was the result of over a decade of research where I discovered that in order to create a more resilient and robust human, you must address four things:

- **The Body's Tolerability:** Regularly *manage* the body's ability to tolerate the stress and stimuli of training and/or competing.
- **The Body's Specificity:** Constantly *direct* the body's ability to tolerate stress and stimuli to a specific form of training and/or competition.
- **The Body's Durability:** Incrementally *increase* the body's ability to tolerate the stress and stimuli of training and/or competing.
- **The Body's Individuality:** Honestly *assess* the body's individual ability to tolerate the stress and stimuli of training and/or competing.

Once you understand these, you understand how to create a body that's resilient and robust enough to swim 1,780 miles around Great Britain without ever taking a day off, injured or ill. This all starts with *strategically* managing your body's tolerability, something I learned to do as I made my way around the Cornish coastline.

THE BODY'S TOLERABILITY

It's 11.20 a.m. on 30 June and following a 16.1-mile swim we can see St Ives. Considered the jewel in Cornwall's crown, this picturesque fishing harbour had seemed like a distant goal just a week ago, but Captain Matt had brilliantly timed (and tamed) the tides that surround Land's End with such precision that he'd managed to use the powerful currents to slingshot us around the Cornish coastline as we made our journey north. My job the entire time was simple:

- Keep afloat.
- Avoid hitting cargo ships with my face.
- Remain in the water swimming for as long as the tides were moving in our favour.

This wasn't an oversimplification either. In reality, it didn't matter if the tides changed at midday or midnight, as soon as they were moving in our direction I had to ensure I was in the water and making progress. Therefore, swimming technique became less and less important; instead it was my ability to get in the water and keep the body moving and functioning that was crucial.

How did I do this? I understood the body's tolerability and the need to constantly manage the body's ability to tolerate the stress and stimuli of swimming 12 hours per day, every day. This is based on the work of Hungarian–Canadian endocrinologist Hans Selye, who taught athletes to manage the amount of stress and stimuli their bodies are subjected to since we only have a certain amount of 'adaptive energy' for every day (or training session). If we subject our bodies to too much stress, we stop improving, plateau or break.

This is why after every swim I would perform an honest 'autopsy' on my body to see if I'd be physically ready to swim again during the next tide. Assessing overall wellness and fitness as well as the health of my limbs and ligaments, I would scan my body in its entirety to strategically manage stress and stimuli.

Today was no different. Pulling into the harbour, I jumped on the boat and climbed into the galley where I wrapped myself in a blanket and nestled myself into the corner so I was within grabbing distance of any (and every) food source from bananas to baguettes and protein bars.

As I did, I could see tourists making their way around the harbour through the boat's porthole. St Ives is renowned for its sandy beaches and arts scene and was recently named Britain's best coastal town. As a result, tourists come from far and wide to navigate the maze of narrow cobbled streets and visit the museums, art exhibitions and sculpture garden. But I had to forgo any sightseeing for two reasons:

- I vowed not to touch land until I had finished the swim.
- Walking around the cobbled streets would subject my body to more stress and stimuli than it could handle after a 20-mile swim that day, and would 'use up' valuable adaptive energy that should *only* be 'contributed' to helping me swim 1,780 miles.

So despite every picturesque harbour and charming fishing village we stopped in, I would deliberately lock myself in the galley with calories, cakes and protein shakes to 'manage stress and stimuli'.

If I didn't, I would be going against years of research. Back in the 1930s, Hans Selye found that stress is the key to adaptation. Something he discovered by gradually subjecting laboratory rats to an increased dose of poison until they began to develop a greater resistance to it. So much so, the rats remained unharmed when later subjected to lethal dosages of the same poison that had previously killed them.

He stated, 'By giving gradually increasing doses of various alarming stimuli, one may raise the resistance of animals ... rats pre-treated with a certain agent will resist such doses of this agent which would be fatal for not pre-treated controls'.

In his book, *The Stress of Life*, he concluded, 'Stress is the common denominator for all adaptive reactions of the body.' Years later, this inspired a new way of training athletes, as coaches considered training to the strategic application of stress (in the form of heavier weights, longer runs or faster swims) to bring about a desired adaptation (making them stronger, fitter or faster).

But there's a problem with that. Selye stated that each person has a given amount of energy available to handle stress and adaptation. Selye calls this 'adaptation energy' and in sport this is closely related to the body's plasticity, a term used when describing the trainability of an athlete.

> 'The loss of acquired adaptation during the stage of exhaustion is difficult to explain but as a working hypothesis, it was assumed that every organism possesses a certain limited amount of "adaptation energy" and once this is consumed, the performance of adaptive processes is no longer possible.'
>
> HANS SELYE, 1938

Plasticity, therefore, just means the athlete's ability to change and adapt. Now some athletes have greater adaptation energy (plasticity) than others, and we will talk about ways to improve this later, but for now, understand adaptation energy is finite and must be spent wisely. This is why I often say, 'Train as often as you need to, not as often as you can.' Since, once this limit is reached, further adaptation isn't possible. When training this means you plateau, but for me and my swim it means it would come to an abrupt halt.

Studies show that an increase in either frequency or intensity, in conjunction with insufficient recovery, may create havoc in the muscle tissue, upset the body's immunity and harass the delicate balance of the hormonal system.[20] Physiologists call this 'burnout' or chronic fatigue,[21] which can be defined as a condition where 'an athlete who was once energetic, competitive and resourceful becomes chronically exhausted, weak and debilitated. The illness causes curtailment of their competitive sport, professional career and social life for two or more years.'[22]

Now, worth noting is that science can help to an extent. Research published in the *Journal of Sports Medicine* suggests, 'A sports medicine provider could consider initial screening blood work for medical conditions to diagnose overtraining, with additional tests to assess the body's response to the training load,'[23] such as:

- Blood tests to monitor testosterone-to-cortisol ratio.[24]
- Urine tests to measure cortisol to cortisone ratio.[25]
- Variations in heart rate.[26]

The issue is we're at sea miles away from land, doctors and a laboratory. Sports science is a luxury I didn't have. Also, even if we were able to effectively monitor fatigue, it's obvious Mother Nature and the ocean doesn't care about chronic fatigue syndrome and will continue to change tides, waves and the weather regardless of what's happening within my own body.

So the best 'weapon' I had against chronic fatigue was an incredibly in-depth and intuitive understanding of my body's tolerability. This is quite possibly the single biggest reason I was able to continue swimming for 157 days, and for up to 12 hours per day. Not because of strength and stamina. But because I was good at strategically managing 'stress' from the comfort of the ship's galley (as I did that day in St Ives armed with a blanket, sandwiches, cakes and calories).

LESSON 4

- In 1875, Captain Matthew Webb became the first person to swim the English Channel, a feat many believed was impossible, which is why he had to write his own training programme. Remember: **There is no blueprint when attempting the impossible. You must create your own.**
- One key to Captain Webb's success was his **resilience**. To become a more robust and resilient athlete, your training must address FOUR things:
    - **The Body's Tolerability**: Regularly *manage* the body's ability to tolerate the stress and stimuli of training and/or competing.
    - **The Body's Specificity**: Constantly *direct* the body's ability to tolerate stress and stimuli to a specific form of training and/or competition.
    - **The Body's Durability**: Incrementally *increase* the body's ability to tolerate the stress and stimuli of training and/or competing.
    - **The Body's Individuality**: Honestly *assess* the body's individual ability to tolerate the stress and stimuli of training and/or competing.
- Together these all serve to increase **work capacity**: this is your body's ability to perform and positively tolerate training of a given intensity or duration.

LESSON 5 | MAKE THE BODY AN INSTRUMENT, NOT AN ORNAMENT

LOCATION: Trevaunance Cove
DISTANCE COVERED: 387 miles
DAYS AT SEA: 31

Trevaunance
Cove

It's 1.00 p.m. on 1 July and we are anchored near Trevaunance Cove, in St Agnes.

I was sat in my tiny toilet cabin putting on my wetsuit before the afternoon's swim, looking out the porthole at Cornwall's north coast. I love it here: every beach is equipped with a sand and shingle mix that looks even more vibrant in the midday sun. But perhaps more uniquely, this corner of Britain contains one of the best collection of rock pools and hidden caves I've ever seen. A reminder of its rich mining heritage, it's unveiled during low tide like an intricate mining mosaic.

Unfortunately, my enjoyment of all of this was cut short ... because I was stuck! Locked in a wrestling match with my own wetsuit that no longer fitted, it seemed my strangely shaped swimmer's body had become even more oddly proportioned after my first month at sea.

How? Because I had managed to constantly direct my body's ability to tolerate stress and stimuli to specifically swim for 12 hours per day, every day (the body's specificity).

THE BODY'S SPECIFICITY

This is also closely related to the SAID principle. Don't be fooled by this impressive sounding acronym. It stands for 'Specific Adaptation to Imposed Demands' and it just means your body adapts specifically to the demands you place on it and that you get really, really good at what you repeatedly practise.

Looking at myself in the bathroom mirror, it was clear what my body repeatedly practised as it was now custom-built for long-distance sea swimming, in that:

- My shoulders, arms and back had become thicker and fatter.
- My legs had shrunk and turned soft, losing any kind of muscle tone.
- My armoured rhino neck was becoming increasingly fortified.

What's more, studies in molecular biology show this rate of adaptation was accelerated in me because of the unique position I was in.

Based on research at the University of Illinois by Dr Robert Hickson and published in 1980, one study concluded that if you train for too many things at once (like strength *and* stamina) you 'dilute' the effectiveness of your training and won't improve optimally in one area. Hickson called it 'concurrent training' and put simply what he meant was 'if you're a jack of all trades, you will be master of none.'

Why? Because your body doesn't know whether to become stronger or more endured as the 'potency' of your training stimulus is lost. This is according to research from the Division of Molecular Physiology at Dundee University, which found that strength training and endurance training bring about very different adaptations within the body and combining both 'blocks each other's signalling' to adapt.

> 'During the last several decades many researchers have reported an interference effect on muscle strength development when strength and endurance were trained concurrently. The majority of these studies found that the magnitude of increase in maximum strength was higher in the group that performed only strength training compared with the concurrent training group, commonly referred to as the "interference phenomenon".'
>
> SPORTS MEDICINE[27]

But out here at sea, there was no 'interference phenomenon'. There were no conflicting forms of training that 'blocked each other's signalling' to adapt.

My life (and 'training') was very simple, I swam for 12 hours a day, every day, as I managed my body's ability to tolerate the stress and stimuli and avoided anything (like walking on the beach) that wouldn't help me swim around Britain.

Yes, I may have done some rehab, prehab and supplementary strength conditioning on my shoulder on the deck of the boat, but 95 per cent of stress, stimuli and my adaptation energy was managed and directed as illustrated in the pie chart below:

**Manage and Direct
Stress, Stimuli and 'Adaptation Energy'**

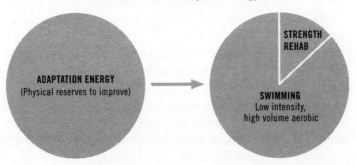

But wetsuits don't account for changes in body shape based on the SAID principle and 'potent' and clear 'cellular signals'. As a result, I found myself unpeeling the wetsuit from my body like Houdini in a straitjacket. I then went upstairs to find Matt in the galley. One thing I discovered was that when at sea, however strange the situation I found myself in, Captain Matt would find a solution.

'I've a problem,' I said.

'Neck? Tongue? Seasickness?' Matt replied.

'No, surprisingly they're all okay. It's my wetsuit. I seem to have put on quite a bit of sea bulk [fat and muscle] on my upper body, but lost muscle mass on my lower body and now none of my wetsuits fit. Any ideas?' I asked in desperation.

Matt paused to consider our options.

'How many wetsuits do we have aboard?' he asked as the cogs in his head started to turn.

'Maybe ten, if we include yours and Taz's,' I said.

'Okay, here's what we do. We cut the arms off my extra-large [XL] suit and the legs off Taz's large [L] suit. I can then use the body of your extra-extra-large [XXL] suit and we then piece it together on you like a sort of "Frankenstein wetsuit".'

This sounded crazy, but Matt's last invention of the sea scarf had worked brilliantly and saved us on the south coast of England. So maybe, just maybe, the Frankenstein wetsuit would save us on the west coast.

With all of us in agreement, we collected all the wetsuits we could find and then left them on the table with Matt and a pair of scissors. After an hour, his work was done and he called us into the galley to present his craftsmanship to us all.

As planned he had created a separate pair of extra-large (XL) wetsuit sleeves for the arms and a separate pair of large (L) wetsuit sleeves for the legs. But the pièce de résistance (and something I wasn't expecting) was the extra-extra-large (XXL) body suit that he now proudly held up to us all.

'WHAT IS THAT?' I asked laughing.

'It's a "waistcoat mankini" ... for the gentleman of the ocean,' he said

It looked like something you'd find in a fetish sex shop, but the theory was that by creating a thong for the lower half (wrapping around your crotch) it would stop the waistcoat from riding up. So, there was some method to Matt's madness.

Strangely, it also matched my sea scarf. I decided I was out of options and the waistcoat mankini was my only hope if I was to make progress up the north coast of Cornwall.

THE BODY'S DURABILITY

It was now 4.00 p.m. on 2 July, some 24 hours after Matt's new invention.

I was now a completely different swimmer to the one who completed the first 350-mile swim along the length of the English Channel. Not only did I look like a seaside, rubber-suited sex tourist in my new tailored wetsuit, but I had:

- Regularly *managed* my body's ability to tolerate the stress and stimuli of swimming 12 hours a day, every day (body's tolerability).
- Constantly *directed* my body's ability to tolerate stress and stimuli to swim 12 hours a day, every day (body's specificity).

As a result, I was now swimming with a newfound work capacity. What this means is I was able to perform and positively tolerate training of a given intensity or duration, free from injury, overtraining or illness. All because I had *incrementally* increased my body's ability to tolerate the stress and stimuli of swimming 12 hours a day, every day.

Now this sounds complicated, but (again) it's not. Basically, it just means my body now felt that swimming for 12 hours per day was normal and could happily tolerate covering more than 20 miles. The only issue we had on the boat was cooking, catering and fuelling this newfound work capacity, as we resorted to using an entire loaf of bread to make my sandwiches, and 1-kg tubs of peanut butter just became a 'snack'.

Of course, after 32 days at sea this had become completely normal for Suzanne and the team. But for two paddleboarders from Newquay, who'd decided to join us for that day's swim, it was a little odd to see Taz deliver two piping-hot Cornish pasties on a paddleboard to a man wearing a type of gimp suit mankini who then devoured them like a hungry elephant seal and continued swimming.

'Is that just a light snack?' one of them asked Taz jokingly.

'Yes,' Taz replied, but not joking.

'Oh,' he replied, 'If that's just a snack, what will he eat for dinner?'

'Probably more Cornish pasties.'

'You're still not joking, are you?' he asked, his smile fading.

'No,' Taz replied, shaking his head.

I should point out it wasn't always Cornish pasties, but my choice of swim snack would often be determined by which part of the coastline we were on since I loved to sample local delicacies. From the potato cakes of Wales to the deep-fried chocolate of east Scotland and the fish and chips of Grimsby, I would eat anything and everything to fuel my newfound work capacity.

But that day I set a new record of nine Cornish pasties in a single swim, all because I understood that in sport the best athletes are so often the hardest working with the highest work capacity. Take the Bulgarian Olympic Weightlifting team, for example. Few athletes raised the bar more in terms of work ethic than them. Their durability to train became world-renowned. For a period spanning 1968 to 2000, despite limited resources and poor economic conditions, this small country – with a population only slightly bigger than New York – produced a team of weightlifters under the tutelage of Ivan Abadjiev that achieved things previously thought to be impossible.

How? In short, the gruelling Bulgarian training system involved lifting close to your maximum weight, in a select number of exercises, every single day, 365 days of the year, for up to eight hours a day. All under the watchful eye of an expert coach who was constantly monitoring your recovery, your strengths, your weaknesses while continually making adjustments to your training. Sounds crazy? Well, 12 Olympic gold medallists and 57 world champions say otherwise.

It wasn't just the Bulgarian team who used this high-intensity, high-volume, no-rest-day system of training. In America, John Broz popularised the Bulgarian method when coaching one of his lifters by the name of Pat Mendes to squat 800 lb (360 kg), completely beltless, at only 20 years old.

The same can be found in endurance sports too. The Greater Boston Track Club of the 1970s and 80s was incredible. The mileage and duration of their training was unmatched. They loved running so much they didn't even stop to contemplate overtraining, rest days or the idea of fatigue. Bill Rodgers (four-time Boston Marathon Champion) said, 'We had fun with it. It wasn't a grind.' As a result, by the early 1980s the Greater Boston Track Club had half a dozen guys who could run a 2 hour 12 minute marathon time.

So, what was their key to their success? Worth noting is there is no set way to train for resilience and robustness. This is why the *Strength and Conditioning Journal* stated as far back as 1991, 'Is there a single, perfect workout? A workout with the best weight training, plyometric, flexibility and endurance exercises? A workout with the precise number of sets and repetitions? A workout that tells the athlete exactly how much weight to use? The answer is "No".'[28]

It's also why – after analysing thousands of studies from years of research – scientists from the Department of Sport, Health and Exercise Science at the University of Hull concluded there is no universally agreed consensus on the best way to train for endurance sports. 'There is insufficient direct scientific evidence to formulate training recommendations based on the limited research.'[29]

Basically, building physical resilience and the body's durability has no blueprint. But that's when we come to the theme known as the Habituation of Stress. This just means any stressor you're exposed to, whether it be psychological or physiological, provokes a stress response. However, the more times you're exposed to it, the less stressful it becomes. In simple terms this means that if your personal best squat is 200 kg, it's very likely that lifting this will be stressful to the body. But the Bulgarian training method believes if you lift this (or close to this) every day, your will learn to habituate the stress. So, a 200 kg squat will begin to feel normal and the same principle applies to running a daily marathon or swimming 20 miles per day.

Of course, I must mention this broke more champions than it made, and research published in the *British Journal of Sports Medicine* identified that variations in the DNA sequence of genes have an impact on an individual's vulnerability to sports injury.[30] But understand those athletes that did habituate the stress were like Hans Selye's indestructible laboratory rats who could eat poison for breakfast, lunch and dinner.

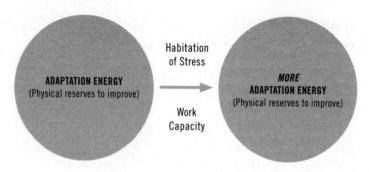

How? In short, work capacity. It's essentially the total amount of training you can perform (recover from) and adapt positively to, and having more of this means you have more adaptation energy and you increase the 'size of your circle'.

Too often this is overlooked. Too many coaches place too much emphasis on minimalism, specificity and recovery. We seem to forget that eventually you just have to do more work. It's that simple. People seem surprised when they plateau doing the same training routine, with the same repetition/set scheme for several months.

When this happens work, work and work some more.

Why? Because it increases the amount your body is used to recovering from. The whole point of increasing work capacity is for the stress of our training to ever so slightly outpace the rate of our recovery, until the rate of our recovery catches up to the stress of our training.

Once you've increased your work capacity and allowed recovery to catch up, you're in a position where you're able to tolerate much more volume – which means a greater training stimulus and an increased potential to become stronger, quicker and fitter.

Of course, I'm not entirely advocating the Bulgarian training model (again it broke more champions than it made) but I am saying there's a happy medium. Basically, don't be fooled. For all the tips, tricks and 'quick fixes' in the fitness industry, increasing your work capacity is the only way to constantly and continually improve.

Athletes can only ever claim they've reached the 'genetic ceiling' of their physical awesomeness when they no longer have the ability to increase their work capacity.

On that note, let's revisit the adaptation energy circle again, but I want to use an analogy I call your Training Tolerance Motorway.

- Imagine a road. Imagine the traffic travelling along that road is your training stress.
- Imagine the road itself is your work capacity (and adaptation energy).
- When there's little traffic (cars, lorries and buses) it means there's very little training stress. It's like a steady 2 km run or manageable 30-minute weights routine. You basically don't need a wide road (or a lot of adaptation energy). You will recover and adapt positively to the training.
- When there's lots of traffic (cars, lorries and buses) it means there's lots of training stress. It's like an intense 20 km run or a Bulgarian strength training session. You basically need a motorway (or a lot of adaptation energy) so you can recover and adapt positively to the training.

The important thing to remember is whatever your adaptation energy (size of your road) make sure it can cope with the level of stress (traffic) to ensure it's the ideal training volume and/or intensity and you're not overtraining or undertraining.

Low stress,
low work capacity,
low adaptation energy,
low recovery rate

IDEAL TRAINING

High stress,
low work capacity,
low adaptation energy,
low recovery rate

OVER TRAINING

Low stress,
high work capacity,
high adaptation energy,
high recovery rate

UNDER TRAINING

High stress,
high work capacity,
high adaptation energy,
high recovery rate

IDEAL TRAINING

So how do we increase work capacity and the body's durability?

History teaches us there's no set way. Considering our biological individuality, the right training programme will vary from person to person. But common methods employed by coaches serve to incrementally *increase* the body's ability to tolerate the stress and stimuli of training and/or competing. Here are four ways:

1. Include MORE Cardio

The easiest (and most effective) way to improve the body's durability (and work capacity) is to include additional cardio-based workouts around all your other training. This is why I would argue every athlete could (and maybe should) include swimming in their weekly routines. It's low impact, easy on the joints and isn't very taxing on the body's tolerability for stress and stimuli (therefore adaptation energy is kept intact). It also doesn't produce an 'interference phenomenon' and ensures you still send a clear, cellular signal to the body to adapt to all your other training goals.

2. Include MORE Sets

Another method that's just as easy to implement is to add sets to your workout routines. As an example, imagine you can do three sets of three repetitions with a 200 kg deadlift. What would then be easier? Trying to complete three sets of three repetitions with 210 kg or just adding another 200 kg deadlift for one repetition at the end? All coaches (and athletes) would agree the extra one repetition would be easier. This is because it's not that taxing on your body and isn't dramatically way above your established baseline.

Then the idea is once (and only once) that becomes comfortable, add two repetitions with 200 kg. Then three after that, then four and so on. Once you're able to do five to eight reps of three sets, your work capacity has improved which means you're ready to drop back down to three sets with more weight (and you can put 210 kg on the bar). Now it's less volume than you've grown accustomed to but with more weight.

3. Include MORE Repetitions

Just as simple is adding repetitions to your routines. Made famous by legendary Canadian strongman and weightlifter Doug Hepburn, you pick a weight you can do eight sets of one repetition with. Then slowly add an extra rep to each set until you can do eight sets of two repetitions. Then increase the weight and start over with one repetition.

4. Include 'Functional Finishers'

Some strength athletes don't want to add cardio conditioning to their routines in fear that it will tax the body's tolerability and the body's specificity too much and produce an interference phenomenon where they no longer send a clear, cellular signal to the body to adapt to strength. If this is the case, adding 'functional finishers' to the end of your workouts is a strength-based solution. These are quick, intense movement-specific exercises you can add to the end of your workouts:

- 5 × 10-metre rope pulls to condition the biceps and back.
- 5 × 20-metre sled sprints to condition the legs.
- 60-second intervals of battle ropes to condition the shoulders.
- 10 × 10-metre tyre flips to condition the back and lower body.

These exercises are inspired by the Russian training system known as General Physical Preparedness (GPP). This is a preparatory phase of training that is completely non-specific to a sport. Instead, it encourages lots of big, functional movements that use universal motor recruitment patterns to improve the body's durability (work capacity) while also providing balanced physical conditioning in endurance, strength, speed, flexibility and other basic factors of fitness.

According to the National Strength and Conditioning Association, 'The major emphasis of this period is establishing a base level of conditioning to *increase the athlete's tolerance for more intense training*. Conditioning activities begin at relatively low intensities and high volumes: long, slow distance running or swimming; low-intensity plyometrics; and high-repetition resistance training with light to moderate resistances.'[31]

The theory underlying this system is: if, as an athlete, you develop a well-rounded athletic base, your overall motor potential (ability to move) will correspondingly improve. Without it, coaches believe you will be forever training with a form of 'physiological hand-brake' on. They believe the direct relationship between the central nervous system (CNS) and physical training plays a paramount role in an athlete's adaptation to training. If as an athlete you are neuro-logically efficient, you will be able to develop (and specialise in a particular sport) later.

THE BODY'S INDIVIDUALITY

It was 11.00 p.m. on 3 July and we'd been at sea for over a month. During this time Captain Matt and the crew had seen me bruised, battered and bleeding but never witnessed me beaten. As a result, collectively we had come to the conclusion my body might have a genetic predisposition for durability. Thanks to my sport-fanatical family, it's likely I inherited some pretty good genetics. My dad was a tennis player, my mum was a sprinter, one grandad was in the military and my other grandad was a marathon runner. Putting it simply, I came from good stock.

Research has shown some people will be genetically more resilient than others. It's important to understand our genes control our biological systems such as muscle, cartilage and bone formation, muscle energy production, blood and tissue oxygenation. On the other hand, studies have identified variations in genes that have influence on factors such as vulnerability to injury and fitness components. For instance, an article published in the *Journal of Science and Medicine in Sport* revealed that mutations in a collagen called COL5A1 led to the structure that supports the tendon being more loosely connected, making the tendon less stable and perhaps more susceptible to injury.[32]

The science is incredibly complex and continually evolving, but to some degree we understood this as a team. In fact, the crew would often joke I was like a workhorse that needed to be 'flogged' if we were to continue to keep up the incredible pace needed to get around Great Britain before winter arrived.

Today's swim was no exception, and as the clock struck midnight it was time to go to work.

'Good morning,' Matt bellowed down into my cabin. He always sounded so cheerful no matter what time of day or night it was. 'We've great tides today, but you will likely take a battering from the wind and waves.'

This one statement perfectly summed up Matt: unconditionally supportive and encouraging, but equally incredibly honest and brutally realistic. He knew there was no time for sugar-coating instructions at sea, you only dealt in clear and precise facts.

Climbing up the ladder out of my cabin, I joined him on deck and peered bleary-eyed into the night sky. The light from the moon was kind on my drooping eyelids and the chill breeze served to gentle pry them open. Emerging from her cabin, Harriet was reporting for duty too.

'Feed Ross whatever he needs for a 10-mile swim and let's go,' Matt instructed Harriet.

Dutifully, Harriet made a gigantic bowl of porridge oats with chopped bananas, peanut butter and melted dark chocolate squares which went from the stove, to the bowl and directly into my stomach in a matter of minutes followed by an equally large cup of coffee. This I hoped would convince my brain that jumping into the sea in the middle of the night for a 10-mile swim was a good idea and that sleep, rest and the warmth of my bed was overrated.

But my brain (and body) wasn't convinced. Why? Because another thing to consider is *when* your body prefers to train. This sounds odd, but some people enjoy getting up at the crack of dawn and visiting the gym. Others can't think of anything worse and decide to tackle the weights room or swimming pool a little later in the day. But it's all related to your body's biological clock known as your circadian rhythm.[33] This is a cycle of physiological processes within the body that scientists discovered had a clear pattern from brainwave activity, hormone production, cell regeneration and other biological activities linked to this daily cycle.

Firstly, a study conducted at the W&M University's Department of Kinesiology & Health Sciences in Williamsburg, USA set out to discover the best time of the day for the optimum performance of your muscles.[34] Researchers took ten healthy, untrained men and made them perform a series of strength tests at 8.00 a.m., 12.00 p.m., 4.00 p.m. and 8.00 p.m. The results showed that muscle performance was greatest in the evening, but only during the exercises that involved faster movements. It's believed this is because the activation of fast-twitch muscle fibres (those required to lift heavy weights or run quickly) is easier when the body temperature is higher, which tends to be the case in the evening rather than in the morning.

Next, it's important to consider how your hormones alter during the day, more specifically testosterone levels (the muscle-building/ recovery hormone you want more of) and cortisol levels (the stress hormone you want less of). While experts all agree that resting testosterone levels are higher in the morning, a study published in the *Journal of Applied Physiology* showed that the rise in testosterone after exercise appears to be greater in the evening than it is in the morning.[35]

Another research study found that cortisol levels are also lower in the evening compared to the morning, and the cortisol response to exercise is lower in the early evening (7.00 p.m.) compared with the early morning (7.00 a.m.).[36] Put simply, this means the very best testosterone–cortisol ratio, where testosterone levels are highest relative to cortisol levels, is in the evening.

Lastly, despite all the studies, sports science concludes everyone's circadian rhythm (biological clock) is unique and everyone will peak at different times based on the tiny personal and individual fluctuations in hormone levels (like testosterone and cortisol), body temperature and cognitive functioning.[37] This explains why some people wake up fresh as a daisy in the morning, while others have to drag themselves out of bed to the nearest coffee machine.

In summary, it's important to listen to your body and decide for yourself whether you're an early bird or night owl. You are entirely and utterly unique: whatever your circadian rhythm, understand you must become your own best expert.

But regardless of the genetics you've been born with, research states, 'Training can be defined as the process by which genetic potential is realised. Although the specific details are currently unknown, the current scientific literature clearly indicates that both nurture and nature are involved in determining elite athletic performance. In conclusion, elite sporting performance is the result of the interaction between genetic and training factors.'[38]

What this means is you can *always* become a more resilient version of yourself. All you have to do is *Walk Your Own Path by Writing Your Own Plan* within a training programme

Five months before I stood on the beach at Margate, that's exactly what I did.

LESSON 5

- **Learn to make your body an instrument, not an ornament**. This closely related to the SAID principle, 'Specific Adaptation to Imposed Demands', which (put simply) means your body adapts specifically to the demands you place on it and that you get really, really good at what you repeatedly practise.

- Combining **work capacity** with **the SAID principle** has produced some of the greatest athletes in history, from the Bulgarian Olympic Weightlifting team to the Greater Boston Track Club of the 1970s and 80s.

- Any stressor you are exposed to provokes a stress response, but the more times you are exposed to it, the less stressful it becomes. Learn to **habituate the stress** in this way, and your personal best will become the norm.

- Non-specific-sport preparation training will **develop a well-rounded athletic base and improve your overall motor potential** (ability to move).

- Respect the **Body's Individuality**. You are entirely and utterly unique: whatever your circadian rhythm (biological clock), understand you must become your own best expert.

LESSON 6 | BUILD RESILIENCE BY 'GETTING WINTERED'

LOCATION: Lundy Island
DISTANCE COVERED: 475 miles
DAYS AT SEA: 36

Lundy Island

It is 8.00 a.m. on 6 July, and we are just off the island of Lundy in the Bristol Channel. Surrounded by clear Atlantic waters, the high and rugged cliffs on the western side of the island have been sculpted and shaped by the wind and waves, while the sheltered valleys of the eastern side are rich in wildflowers. It's an area that's been pioneering marine conservation for over 40 years.

From the deck of *Hecate*, I observed seals bathing in the shallow rock pools and leisurely feeding on the abundant supply of fish that populate the waters around here. Equipped with a wildlife book, I spotted peregrines, wrens and ravens and was told by Matt they are joined in the spring by breeding visitors (looking for a romantic holiday) that include skylarks, meadow pipits and pied wagtails.

But my favourite visitor on the island had to be the puffin. Arriving from April to late July during their breeding season, they are known as 'sea parrots' and the 'clowns of the coast' because of their brightly coloured bills, orange feet, waddling walk and less than graceful landings. At up to 30 cm tall, weighing 400 g and with a modest wingspan averaging 55 cm, they're not the best equipped to fly, yet will happily tumble and bumble their way around Lundy island. Watching them bounce off the land and water, I would often join Harriet and Peony on the side of the boat (between swims) to eat, rest and cheer on every tiny puffin that attempted to become airborne.

Unfortunately, my visit here could only be brief and my enjoyment had to be cut short. That's because once we left the shelter of Lundy island, I knew we would be faced with a 30-mile swim across the Bristol Channel, the stretch of water between south Wales and Somerset that boasts some of the strongest tides in the world.

In short, 'puffin playtime' was over. I left Harriet and Peony to continue supporting the flight plans of the puffins and joined Matt in the galley who was immersed in tidal maps, charts and weather forecasts.

'How bad is it?' I asked.

We had been at sea for 36 days up to this point. As I swam day and night for 475 miles, Matt had watched, navigated and been there for every single arm stroke, leg kick and breath of air. As a result, we had a unique understanding and never sugar-coated anything we said to each other. But even this reply was not what I was expecting.

'You're about to swim through a sea of shipwrecks.'

He continued, 'The strong tides have been used by sailors for centuries and made the towns of Cardiff, Barry and Penarth among the largest coal exporters in the world. But inevitably, with so much traffic flooding through here, there's been accidents and in 1948 there were 24 known shipwrecks on the seabed which included a tanker of over 10,000 tons that was sunk off Nash Point.'

Looking out the small porthole of the galley across the channel, I now sensed I was about to cross hallowed waters and this would be our most sombre swim to date.

How was my body's tolerability, durability and adaptation energy? Had my sea ulcers and wounds healed? Would my short sumo-swimmer frame withstand the waves, tides and forces of the Bristol Channel or would the ligaments and tendons in my shoulders be forced to surrender to the sea? Would my child-bearing hips and buoyant bum keep me afloat?

All these questions (and concerns) were running through my head as I sat there anticipating the miles that lay ahead. As they did, I began to think again about the legend of Captain Webb and how he trained for the channel crossing using the tides of the Thames and the piers of Blackwall and Gravesend as points of progression.

In many ways, he was 'Getting Wintered'. An idea central to Stoic Sports Science, this was inspired by Epictetus who advocated cold, hard and brutal preparation. He famously said, 'We must undergo a hard winter training and not rush into things for which we haven't prepared,' because so often wars were not fought in the winter in ancient Greece, therefore the time should be spent training and preparing for battles that could come in spring.

Drawing a direct comparison, Captain Webb's cross-Channel 'battle' was fought in the summer (25 August 1875). But you must understand, the outcome of that day was determined long before he set off from Admiralty Pier; it was determined the day he quit his job to swim mile after mile in Lambeth Baths and down the Thames as part of his training programme.

The same was true of the Great British Swim. After the idea was planted in my head in January 2018 during a visit to the Royal Marine Commando Training Centre in Devon, I had exactly five months to 'Get Wintered' and devise the following plan. I must stress I don't recommend this training programme to everyone. For most people, the sheer number of hours you have to commit to training makes it completely unrealistic. So instead, I advise you to read the following, take lessons and inspiration from it, and apply the principles to your own training.

MY 'GETTING WINTERED' PLAN

Firstly, my adaptation energy looked like this:

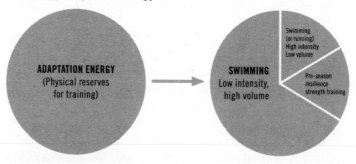

A week's workout would look like this:

	Monday	Tuesday	Wednesday
Morning	*Swim Training:* 5km swim Low intensity, aerobic, practise stroke technique	*Swim Training:* 10km swim Low intensity, aerobic, practise stroke technique	*Swim Training:* 10km swim Low intensity, aerobic, practise stroke technique
Afternoon	Strength Training General Physical Preparedness	—	Strength Training General Physical Preparedness
Evening	—	Interval Training High intensity, anaerobic training lungs	—

The theory behind all this being based on our well-known four principles:

The Body's Tolerability

- Each day the adaptation energy is first used on swimming-specific training.
- This is based on the SAID Principle (Specific Adaptation of Imposed Demands).
- Studies show that swimming technique, stroke rate and efficiency will play a key role in swimming performance.

The Body's Specificity

- Each workout has a clear cellular signal to adapt.
- The strength and stamina workouts are separate enough to avoid the training 'interference phenomenon' and to ensure they only complement each other.

Thursday	Friday	Saturday	Sunday
Swim Training: 10km swim Low intensity, aerobic, practise stroke technique	*Swim Training: 15km swim* Low intensity, aerobic, practise stroke technique	*Swim Training: 25km swim* Low intensity, aerobic, practise stroke technique	*Swim Training: 5km swim* Low intensity, aerobic, practise stroke technique
—	Strength Training General Physical Preparedness	—	Strength Training General Physical Preparedness
Interval Training High intensity, anaerobic training lungs	—	—	—

The Body's Durability

- Strength Training in General Physical Preparedness to incrementally increase work capacity.
- Holistically the entire programme looks to habituate stress as the volume and intensity of the training increases.

The Body's Individuality

- Train in harmony with your circadian rhythm and genetic resilience to injury.
- The entire programme is fluid, based on the body's individuality.

'WHALE-LIKE WORK CAPACITY'

It's 5.00 a.m. on 7 July somewhere in the Bristol Channel. I had been swimming for 21 hours (day and night and day) as the sun began to rise in the east. This made sighting off *Hecate* far easier as Matt kept a steady course towards the Pembrokeshire coast of Wales and I no longer had to rely on Harriet to shine a light from the bow of the boat to help me navigate in the darkness hours.

But despite the newly improved swimming conditions, I was struggling. Really struggling. Every ligament and tendon in my shoulder joint was sore and screaming for me to stop. The crew knew this, too. Now swimming at 3.5 knots (4 mph), my stroke rate had drastically slowed and my technique was now so clumsy and cumbersome it almost defied the laws of hydrodynamics. Even the length of my strokes had noticeably shrunk as the simple act of straightening my arm became hugely problematic.

My crew weren't the only ones to notice my struggles that day. A concerned 'lifeguard' was patrolling the waters that morning. But this was no ordinary lifeguard: she was over 5 m (16 ft) in length, must have weighed over 5,000 kg (5 tonnes) and had beautiful black and grey mottled skin with a white underbelly.

Yes, the lifeguard on duty that day was a giant, female minke whale. Although she had likely been tracking me through the night, she decided to make her presence known around 6.00 a.m. that morning by surfacing just a few metres away from me. Slowly emerging from the water, she expelled air from her blowhole in an eruption of stale carbon dioxide and then inhaled fresh oxygen into her giant lungs before diving below the surface.

'Should I stop or keep swimming?' I asked Matt.

This wasn't because I was scared or felt threatened. I knew I wasn't on the dinner menu of a minke since they have baleen plates (fine, comb-like filters) instead of teeth and only eat small fish like cod and herring. But I was always cautious not to interfere with the wildlife and was forever respectful that this was their swimming pool and I was just a guest.

'Keep swimming and maintain the same course,' Matt shouted from the boat.

Tired and riddled with fatigue, I now swam (and Matt sailed) with a deep sense of respect for my newly acquired five-tonne training partner as we made our way towards the Pembrokeshire coast. With every mile (and hour) that passed, she got closer and more confident and comfortable with me, this strange new sea mammal she'd found. Likely wondering what I was doing and where I was heading, she even began swimming some three metres directly underneath me for a few kilometres while blowing bubbles in my face.

'What's she doing?' I asked Matt as I stopped for a brief break of biscuits and energy drinks.

'Hmm, I think she's a mum,' he said as I looked at him a little confused. 'She clearly feels protective over you and maybe thinks you're an injured seal or something, because it's like she is guiding you to safety in the shallower waters.'

As Matt told me this, I had a new lease of life. Swimming through the pain and sleep deprivation, I didn't want to let my Minke Mother down and was determined to make it across the Bristol Channel so that she knew her newly adopted 'seal son' appreciated her watching over him.

As I did, I watched her as she effortlessly glided through the water, stoic and serene without a hint of fatigue on her face. North Atlantic minke can reach speeds of 38 km/h (24 mph) and migrate as far north as the edge of the Arctic Circle in the spring and as far south as the Equator to warmer waters in the autumn.

What's more, most whales never sleep, in the true sense of the word. Generally speaking, whales need to retain conscious brain activity in order to take a breath because they must be able to tell that their blowhole is at the surface. To get around this, they only sleep with one hemisphere of the brain at a time. This resting state is more like a very light nap and whales can still swim at the same time.

So whales truly embody this idea of 'getting wintered' and work capacity. No other species even comes close, which is why when swimming in the Bristol Channel that day I tried my best to emulate my Minke Mum. Sure, dolphins are fast and poetic to watch in the water. Many of my friends and training partners who are incredible, decorated Olympic swimmers resemble them when swimming. But I am not a dolphin (and nor did I want to be one). I wanted to be a short, stubby minke with 'whale-like work capacity' to get me around the coast of Great Britain.

Did it work? Did my body's tolerability, durability and tendons survive the Bristol Channel? Did I now possess a form of whale-like work capacity?

After swimming for 38 hours in total since leaving Lundy, we had arrived on the Pembrokeshire coast. So the answer was a definite 'yes'. The puffins were now a distant memory and we could see before us miles of magnificent, varied and crinkled coastline.

Sensing her work was now done, my Minke Mother then breached out of the water just metres from where I was swimming. Experts still don't know exactly why whales do this, but believe it may be a form of communicating. Communicating what exactly? Again, we don't know. But if you ask me, she was saying, 'Godspeed my strange, stubby son. You now have wintered whale-like work capacity and are ready for the Irish Sea.'

It wasn't just me who'd been 'wintered' in the Bristol Channel. This swim was a huge hurdle (and real test) for us as a team; we'd not only survived but we had thrived. Matt had pitted his seafaring wisdom, developed over more than forty years, against one of the biggest tides in the world and won. Harriet had fearlessly steered the rib (our rigid-hulled inflatable boat) through the night, shining a light to watch out for other boats and lobster pots. Then there was Suzanne. Not all heroes wear capes, some wear chef's aprons. We calculated she boiled, blended and baked over 30,000 calories within that one swim alone as she substituted bowls for cauldrons and spoons for ladles.

As a team, we had become wintered.

As an individual, I had developed whale-like work capacity.

LESSON 6

- A central tenet of Stoic Sports Science is to **Get Wintered.**
- It was Epictetus who famously said, 'We must undergo a hard winter training and not rush into things for which we haven't prepared.' This is because so often wars were not fought in the winter in ancient Greece; therefore the time should be spent training and preparing for the battles that might come in spring.
- Develop your own form of **whale-like work capacity** based on your body's tolerability, durability, specificity and individuality. Dolphins may be fast and poetic to watch but whales combine strength with endurance and a capacity to last the course.

LESSON 7 | FAST CAN BE FRAGILE AND SLOW CAN BE STRONG

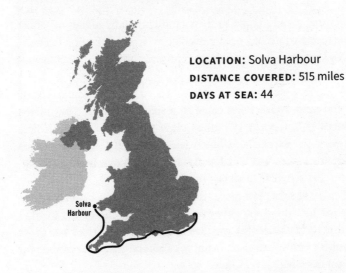

LOCATION: Solva Harbour
DISTANCE COVERED: 515 miles
DAYS AT SEA: 44

Solva Harbour

It's 5.00 a.m. on 14 July in St Bridges Bay, Wales. As a storm raged across the Irish Sea, we'd sought refuge in the small Welsh harbour of Solva, renowned for its quaint cafes, craft shops and galleries. Of course, I couldn't enjoy any of this, having vowed not to step foot on land until we reached the beaches of Margate again. But once the people of Pembrokeshire heard about the swim, they decided that if I couldn't visit Solva, Solva would visit me. By 6.00 a.m. a queue of locals had arrived alongside *Hecate* equipped with every form of Welsh potato cake ever invented.

Now I love any form of cake, but after arriving in Wales with muscles completely depleted of carbohydrates and a tongue still angry after being dragged across the Bristol Channel, I can honestly say these cakes will rank among my most memorable. They are Welsh comfort food at its finest as layers of sliced potatoes are baked together until sticky and golden. They basically tasted like a hug and smelt like happiness.

But with each visit to the boat came a new variant of this national dish, as every visitor brought a different kind of potato cake that was specific and unique to their family. Proudly telling me about their recipe which had been passed down from generation to generation, I sat on deck incredibly grateful and content for the company, carbs and calories.

An hour passed and it's very likely I set a new (accidental) record for the most Welsh cakes eaten in a single breakfast. How many? I honestly lost count (I'd guess close to thirty), but somewhere between the caramelised onion variant and the chocolate raisin alternative there was a call across the ship's radio from the coastguard that signalled breakfast time was now over.

I've never seen Matt move so fast as he popped up from his cabin and ran into the ship's galley with maps, tidal charts and weather reports tucked under his arm. Sensing something serious was about to happen, I finished the remaining cakes and thanked everyone for a breakfast I will never forget.

Opening the door to the galley, I had never seen Matt looking so pensive. With his various maps and charts sprawled across the table, he was double-checking and triple-checking his calculations with pen markings scribbled across the next section of our swim: the Irish Sea.

Ranked among the roughest seas in the world, this stretch of water separating Wales and Ireland is often described as treacherous, turbulent and violent, having claimed the lives of many sailors whose boats now lay on the ocean floor. Matt and I knew that once we left Solva harbour and the safety of the Welsh coast, we would have an incredibly nervous 200-mile swim all the way past Ireland

and on to Scotland. Which was why Matt was busy working out the best time for me to be in the water for this mammoth undertaking. He was cross-referencing everything from the weather, waves, tides and swells, since how these factors interacted would determine exactly how rough the 'swimming pool' would be that day.

Wind-generated waves are created by an imbalance of pressure and friction. Basically, waves are generated from energy transferred from the air to the water and (as current theories suggest) have their speed controlled by the relationship between wave length (the distance between two successive wave crests or troughs) and water depth. But despite this maths being pretty solid, waves remain fairly unpredictable.

Swells, on the other hand, can be a likened to the ripples made when a stone is dropped in water. Swells are collections of waves produced by storm winds raging hundreds of miles out to sea, rather than the product of local winds along beaches. They are formed by a combination of factors and provide the best conditions for surfers looking to catch a big wave. However, they're not so well loved by sailors (and swimmers) as large swells can capsize even big ships.

The final ingredient in this volatile oceanic cocktail is 'wind over tide', a term used to describe the wind and tide travelling in opposite directions which causes the waves to 'pile up' on each other. Ultimately, this causes dangerous sailing conditions capable of bullying boats, sailors and swimmers; hence the reason me, Matt and the entire crew had been looking out into the Irish Sea with trepidation.

But today we had been granted a gift. This came in the form of a five-day weather forecast of light winds, calm seas and incredibly benign conditions that was broadcast across the radio. Matt could barely believe what he was hearing.

'This never happens. I don't know how or why this has come about, but these could be the best conditions we've had in the last forty years in British waters.'

Closing books and folding maps he looked me directly in the eye. 'Get ready, we need to swim now,' he said.

Trepidation and anxiety had been replaced by adrenaline and sheer gratitude towards Mother Nature and/or Poseidon himself, as we hoped to sneak into Scottish waters before the ocean decided to change its mind.

As I put on my goggles, I knew Matt had done (and would continue to do) all he could to make sure I was swimming in the best weather conditions possible; while Suzanne, Harriet, Peony and Taz would continue to cross hell and high water with me day and night. And my own role within the team was clear: ensure the mind doesn't quit and the body doesn't break.

We left Wales that morning and I swam as hard as my arms, legs and lungs would allow me to, while never looking back. I thought again about how I was never meant to get this far. Conventional wisdom in sports science had advised me to stop strength training. Lose muscle mass. Obtain a body that more closely resembles a swimmer. Then try and swim around Great Britain in a few years.

Yet fuelled by Welsh potato cakes, I was proving conventional wisdom wrong. Inspired by my Minke Mum and wrapped in whale-like work capacity, my body would not break and my mind would not quit, and all because I knew *Fast Can Be Fragile and Slow Can Be Strong*.

FAST AND FRAGILE *v* SLOW AND STRONG

Worth (re-)stating is that in conventional sport, the results of the laboratory *were true*.

I am not a good endurance athlete in the traditional sense of the word, nor would I consider myself an elite swimmer when judged by Olympic standards. But swimming in 10-ft waves in storms out at sea is far from 'traditional' and 'conventional', so I was prepared to substitute speed and finesse for more strength and resilience.

To understand why, we first need to understand why in the sports laboratory that day I was told (based on sound research) my body was never built for endurance. So firstly, let's talk about endurance, weight and running.

The sports science student in me knows I will never be a fast, elite-level, long-distance runner in my current state. This is because (in reality) running is just a series of successive small jumps where research shows you can exert a load of as much as two to three times your bodyweight on a single leg as you come into contact with the ground.

Now it's worth noting that this is actually a reference to the maximum push-off value and varies depending on running speed. For example, a relatively slow pace of 150 m/min (5.5 mph) exerts a force of just over two times the runner's bodyweight, while a faster pace of 300 m/min (11 mph) increases this force to over three times the runner's bodyweight.

But for now, that's not important, just understand that power-to-weight ratio will have a profound impact on performance when running. All because weight and strength is crucial to the flexion and extension strength of the knee joint, as this prevents the athlete falling away from their centre of mass after landing and generates the leg drive required for running.

But it gets worse. For me (and heavier runners) research from the *European Journal of Applied Physiology and Occupational Physiology* showed as soon as you add weight, the heart, lungs and entire cardio-respiratory system must work harder. They examined the influence of carrying 10 kg, 20 kg and 30 kg of weight had on the body and measured oxygen uptake, heart rate and pulmonary ventilation. What they found was, 'Each kilogramme of extra weight increases oxygen uptake by 33.5 ml/min, heart rate by 1.1 beats/min and pulmonary ventilation by 0.6 l/min.'[39]

That's just one kilogramme of extra weight. This explains why when my chunky five foot eight, 98 kg frame tries to keep up with my

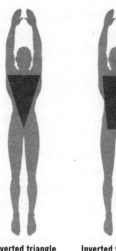  

Inverted triangle   Inverted trapezoid   Rectangle   Oval

Parameters	Inverted triangle shape	Inverted trapezoid shape	Rectangle shape	Oval shape
Height (cm)	182	182	182	182
Weight (kg)	64	68	72	79
Bust (cm)	102	104	106	108
Waist (cm)	70	73	77	85
Hips (cm)	85	87	89	96
Projected area (m^2)	0.109	0.113	0.122	0.131
Surface area (m^2)	1.894	1.929	1.999	2.053

five foot seven, 63 kg friends when running across mountain ranges, my legs and lungs 'complain' far more than theirs. Of course, swimming is not so strictly bound by the laws of gravity. But with such short, stubby arms and legs, it's obvious the laws of hydrodynamics (that govern how streamlined I am through the water) are not in my favour either.

Research conducted at the Department of Applied Mechanics and Engineering at Sun Yat-Sen University in China set out to analyse body shape and its impact on hydrodynamics and performance.[40] They started by saying, 'Swimming performance depends on lots of comprehensive factors such as propulsive forces, drag forces and power output.'[41] Swimming technique, stroke rate and efficiency also play a key role.[42]

But they go on to state, 'The analysis revealed that a swimmer's body shape has a noticeable effect on the hydrodynamic performance. This explains why a male swimmer with an inverted-triangle body shape has good hydrodynamic characteristics for competitive swimming.' Someone who has broad shoulders, a great height, long arms, a thin waist and a long torso will have:

- Powerful propulsion in the water.
- Favourable distribution of muscle mass.
- Reduced drag and advantageous hydrodynamic characteristics.

This final point is particularly important, because research published in the *Journal of Applied Biomechanics* found that, 'Resistive or drag forces encountered during free swimming greatly influence the swim performance of elite competitive swimmers. The benefits in understanding the factors which affect the drag encountered will enhance performance within the sport.'[43]

The diagram overleaf shows the total drag coefficient (resistance in the water) versus velocity (speed) for the different shaped swimmers and clearly shows that the swimmer with oval body shape gets the

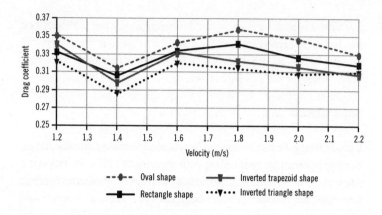

largest drag coefficient and the swimmer with the inverted triangle shape has the smallest.

But I would argue all of the above makes you fast and fragile. This is why research claims, 'Competitive swimmers are predisposed to musculoskeletal injuries of the upper limb, knee, and spine.'[44] Yet despite 157 days and 1,780 miles of swimming, my five foot eight frame that bulked up to over 100 kg on Welsh potato cakes and Cornish pasties, never got injured once.

How? I was not fast and fragile, I was strong and slow.

Yes, I understood that body shape influenced hydrodynamics and that technique and efficiency played a key role in swimming performance, but I also understood I couldn't afford to become injured and therefore resilience and durability were just as important. Strength training couldn't be ignored (as we discovered in an earlier chapter); according to the NSCA, 'When considering sports injury prevention strategies, the role of the strength and conditioning coach can extend beyond observing exercise technique and prescribing training to develop a *robust and resilient athlete*.'[45] In other words, speed is an advantage, but physical resilience is a necessity.

And the reason I was confident heading 200 miles up the Irish Sea was because, backed by thousands of studies in strength science, I had become 'wintered' with weight training back on land.

'WINTERED' WEIGHT TRAINING

A study in the *British Journal of Sports Medicine* emphatically states, 'Strength training reduced sports injuries.'[46] This is following research to determine which training protocol – strength training, stretching or proprioception (balance) conditioning – was most effective in reducing sports injuries.

After studying 26,610 participants with 3,464 injuries, what the study found was, 'Strength training reduced sports injuries to less than one in three and overuse injuries could be almost halved.' What's more, strength training performed better than both stretching or proprioception conditioning routines.

This study was not alone either; research around the world has found, 'Increasing strength training volume and intensity were associated with sports injury risk reduction'[47] in different sports[48] with athletes young[49] and old.[50]

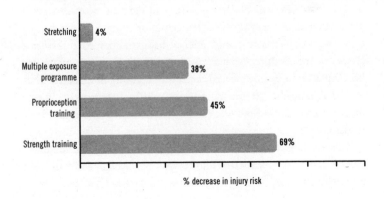

% decrease in injury risk

So, when should you do it? History teaches us heavy weight training and hard miles are best performed in pre-season training. This idea of managing and manipulating the schedule of your training has been used for hundreds of years and has become known as 'periodisation'. While today this concept takes many forms and it can get complicated, the idea is very simple.

From the early years of the ancient Olympics, athletes followed a very basic but logical method of training. Sometimes training for up to 10 months before the Olympics, they would prepare, compete, relax, recover and repeat.[51] This was periodisation in its most basic form as athletes followed training phases (now called preparatory, competitive and transition phases). All this was described by the Greek philosopher, Flavius Philostratus (170–245 BCE). His books on athletic training were pioneering at the time and shaped strength and conditioning as we know it today, but much of his work was destroyed by the passage of time.

Years later and the Russian professor Leonid Matveyev was the first to use the term periodisation to plan the phases of an athlete's training. Studying competitors from the 1952 and 1956 Olympics, he wanted to know why some achieved their personal bests while others didn't perform to their full potential. He then developed strategies for peaking at the right time and as a result the concept of periodisation which Flavius Philostratus first developed was brought into the era of the modern Olympic Games.

Does it work? History and science believes so.[52] This is why a study in the *British Journal of Sports Medicine* states, 'Regular participation in a multifaceted resistance training programme that begins during the pre-season and includes instruction on movement biomechanics may reduce the risk of sports-related injuries in athletes.'[53]

This study isn't alone in its findings either. Similar results have been found across all sports from rugby,[54] sprinting,[55] football[56] and baseball[57] as more and more coaches understand the benefits of

resilience and how, 'Maximising participation in pre-season training may protect athletes against in-season injury.'[58]

~

But what about me and the Great British swim? After 50 days and
670 miles at sea, had this concept of pre-season strength training
helped to keep my body from breaking? Yes, it seemed so. At 1.40
a.m. on 17 July, I stopped for a banana break to find Matt, Suzanne,
Harriet and Taz cheering from the boat underneath a full moon and
a star-sprinkled sky.

'What are we celebrating? I asked.

'You've just swum over a hundred miles in four days across the
Irish Sea,' Matt shouted as he threw a banana in my direction with
pinpoint accuracy.

'Also, that big rock in the distance is the Isle of Man which means
we're almost safely across.' I could sense both the relief and excitement in his voice.

I took a moment to enjoy one of the best tasting bananas I'd ever
had. Reflecting on the last one hundred miles, I realised it had only
been possible because as a team we had worked within:

- **The laws of the ocean:** Swam in strong tides with little wind
  and waves.
- **The laws of biology:** Swam within the body's tolerability and
  regularly managed my ability to tolerate the stress and stimuli in
  swimming 12 hours a day.
- **The laws of strength science:** Swam with months (and years)
  of strength and conditioning to create a 'robust and resilient
  athlete'.

In summary, my submarine skull, child-bearing hips and waistcoat mankini were never designed to be fast and fragile, they were

intended to be slow and strong, and as we continued towards Scotland my body refused to break.

LESSON 7

- To guard against injury, focus on developing yourself into a robust and resilient individual. So, while speed is an advantage, **physical resilience is a necessity**.
- Train according to the principles of a study that found: 'Strength training reduced sports injuries to less than 1/3 and overuse injuries could be almost halved.'
- Remember: **Fast Can Be Fragile and Slow Can Be Strong**.
- The concept of **periodisation** and training for many months (even years) before an event – in a cycle of prepare, compete, relax, recover and repeat – enables athletes to perform at their best when it really matters. From the early years of the ancient Olympics through to the modern Games, athletes who develop strategies for peaking at the right time give themselves the best chance of success.

LESSON 8 | STRENGTH IMPROVES STAMINA AND STAMINA IMPROVES STRENGTH

LOCATION: Isle of Man
DISTANCE COVERED: 715 miles
DAYS AT SEA: 50

It's 2.00 a.m. on 20 July as we approach the Isle of Man in the Irish Sea.

An island with a proud Celtic and Viking heritage, it's known for its rugged coastline, medieval castles and rural landscape and possesses a kind of medieval mystique and beauty that's almost timeless. You almost wouldn't be surprised to see King Arthur and the Knights of the Round Table enjoying ice cream on the shingle beaches, that's just how brilliantly the history of the island has been preserved.

Speaking to local fishermen on yesterday's swim they proudly told me tales of their homeland as I stopped by their boats for a brief banana break. It seemed everything on the island was wrapped in seafaring folklore, but my favourite story was about their beloved mountain peak known as Snaefell. According to local legend, from the summit which stands at 620 m (2,034 ft) you can see seven kingdoms: the Isle of Man, Scotland, England, Ireland, Wales, Heaven and Neptune (the sea). From the water that morning I felt privileged to be bearing witness to three of those kingdoms every time I turned my head to breathe.

But it wasn't just the scenery I was enjoying. You know the best thing about the coastline around Northern Ireland? The water tastes fresh, lush and organic. This may sound odd, but as I looked down at the bottom of the seabed for half the day (part of that in complete darkness) I basically existed in this strange world of sensory deprivation. My sight was impaired, hearing severely restricted, touch usually numbed by the cold and smell almost non-existent. Therefore, I took in my surroundings very differently to the rest of the team, mainly through my taste buds.

The time was 5.00 a.m. and I had been swimming since midnight. The sun had now risen and fully lit up the sea from a dark, deep blue into a vibrant turquoise colour. This was not only a pleasure to swim in, it also made spotting and dodging obstacles a lot easier. But those were the least of my concerns that morning as Matt stood at the side of the boat to deliver some bad news.

'The currents are pulling us in all directions,' he said.

I immediately knew why. The culprit was the Isle of Man which was serving as an obstruction in the middle of the Irish Sea and confusing the tides and currents that didn't know which 'kingdom' to flow into. As a result, I was being pushed, pulled and dragged around in the water.

'I know this is the last thing you want to hear after a 100-mile swim,' Matt said. 'But I need you to sprint so we can break into the North Channel (the strait between Northern Ireland and southwest Scotland) where the tides are strong again. If you do this, it will carry us to Scotland.'

This was completely counter-intuitive to any pacing strategy found in sports science (as you will discover later) and it also meant my body's tolerability, adaptation energy and overall physical reserves would be running dangerously low. But I knew he was right. Basically, Mother Nature (and Poseidon) didn't care about sports science and the fragility of my adaptation energy, which meant escaping the Isle of Man and getting into the Northern Channel (and Scotland) was going to be a fight, not a swim.

Fortunately, thanks to my strength training I was ready for the oncoming battle. There would also be the added bonus of a boost to my stamina, since research found that, 'Strength training can lead to enhanced long-term (longer than 30 minutes) and short-term (less than 15 minutes) endurance capacity both in highly trained individuals and top-level endurance athletes especially with the use of high-volume, heavy-resistance strength training protocols.'[59] Essentially, strength can improve stamina, something the world's most successful cyclists have understood for years.

STRENGTH IMPROVES STAMINA

By 2016, British cycling had dominated three successive Olympiads. Outside of the Olympics, Team Sky (based at the National Cycling Centre in Manchester) dominated the UCI World Tour and had the winning Tour de France rider in three out of the last four years. How? They understood strength improves stamina, and thanks to performance director Dave Brailsford included 'supplementary strength training' in their conditioning.

This was an idea backed up by a study in the *European Journal of Applied Physiology* which stated, 'Adding strength training to usual endurance training improved determinants of cycling performance as well as performance in well-trained cyclists.'[60] Now, of course each athlete's training would be complex, individualised and would include specific sessions to train mobility, power, speed, technique and more, but it would be fair to assume their adaptation energy pie chart could look like this:

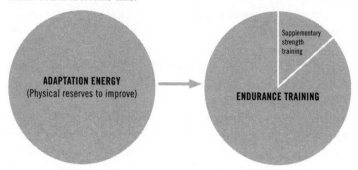

Note the words 'supplementary strength training'. This works in harmony with:

- **The body's tolerability,** since you are able to regularly manage the body's ability to tolerate the stress and stimuli of training.
- **The body's specificity,** since you are able to constantly direct the body's ability to tolerate stress and stimuli to your primary focus of training, with a small amount devoted to 'supplementary conditioning' which helps your primary focus.

Basically, each cyclist isn't looking to squat 300 kg or bicep curl 30 kg dumbbells, but they know how to use strength training to complement improved stamina. So we now understand that 'wintered' weight training can make you more robust and resilient to injury. But how exactly does strength training improve your stamina?

Firstly, sports science teaches us that there are two types of muscle fibres, Type I and Type II (Type II can also be further subdivided into Type IIa and Type IIb). Now, Type I muscle fibres (more commonly known as 'slow twitch') are great for endurance and needed to get through the Tour de France or London Marathon.

These are much more resistant to fatigue. Type II muscle fibres are more commonly known as 'fast twitch' and these are needed to power up the hills during a steep ascent (or break through tides, in my case) since they have a faster-contractile speed.

How do you build more of these for cycling? By strength training. A recent study concluded, 'Concurrent strength/endurance training in young elite competitive cyclists led to an improved 45-minute time-trial endurance capacity that was accompanied by an increased proportion of type IIA muscle fibre.'[61]

Next, if you move better you move further. As we discussed before, when it comes to swimming performance the Department of Applied Mechanics and Engineering at Sun Yat-Sen University in China found technique, stroke rate and efficiency will also play a key role[62] (the same is true of other sports too) and it seems strength training is a great tool to help this. This is why we find in the *Scandinavian Journal of Medicine & Science in Sport*, 'Adding heavy strength training improved cycling performance (by an) improved cycling economy (movement and efficiency).'[63]

Which is exactly why I decided to create a 'boat gym' aboard *Hecate* to perform some very basic, very simple, very short (in duration) 'supplementary strength training'. Since *Hecate* measured 16 m (53 ft) in length and 7 m (23 ft) in width, I actually had more than enough room on the deck to train. Plus, the ample rigging and ropes that held together the two parallel hulls meant I had lots of places to attach gymnastic rings, resistance bands and pull-up bars.

Finally, if I needed any additional weight I would often use Peony as a (willing) sandbag. Although she was so lean and light I'd often encourage her to have triple her dessert servings at lunch and dinner so she could offer more resistance during push-ups and overhead presses.

In the absence of a conventional gym it seemed logical to progressively 'bulk up' the crew to be used as dumbbells and barbells. But fishermen and coastguards around the Isle of Man would look on in sheer bewilderment as they saw me performing push-ups on the side of the boat with Peony balanced on my back eating a bowl of chocolate brownies and ice cream.

'Is everything okay, young man?' a group of elderly sailors asked in Port St Mary on the island's southwest coast where we briefly stopped so the crew could top up on supplies.

Now hanging from the rigging with one hand so I could remove a spoon of peanut butter from my mouth I replied, 'Oh yes, fine thank you. Yourselves?'

They nodded and looked at each other, trying to assess if I was sane, simple or stupid. Sensing their concern, I decided to explain myself and told them about the Great British Swim and my supplementary strength training.

They didn't look convinced. So (still hanging from the rigging) I said, 'So, this is called a dead hang and is a great example of supplementary strength training. The goal isn't to lift heavy or perform a number of sets, instead it serves to open up the acromion [bony articulation of the shoulder blade] and the head of the humerus [upper arm bone], potentially relieving any impingement of the rotator cuff tendons, strengthening the rotator cuff and increasing shoulder range of motion.'

Silence surrounded the boat as they considered their verdict. I tried to explain this was all based on the methodology of renowned orthopaedic surgeon John M. Kirsch. He claims that hanging from a bar for up to 30 seconds, three times per day, can fix up to 99 per cent of shoulder pain. Outlining this protocol in his book, *Shoulder Pain? The Solution and Prevention*, he believes the reason it works is because it brings back a long-lost form of shoulder prehab and rehab used by our evolutionary ancestors. Basically, we humans are considered part of the great ape family (orangutan, gorilla, chimpanzee and bonobo) and while all of the other great apes can still be found swinging from trees (known as brachiating), we stopped about 30,000 years ago. Fast forward to modern man and, despite sharing a similar shoulder structure, our joints aren't getting the exercise that nature intended and so they can weaken and become prone to injury.

'You're crazy, but you seem happy and harmless,' one of the sailors replied.

I laughed and they smiled (still clearly not sure what they were witnessing). 'God bless you,' they said. 'Wishing you safe passage on this swim of yours.' They tipped their caps and bid me farewell as I remained there hanging with the spoon in my mouth, now unable to tell them that while studies show that strength can improve stamina, it has also been found that stamina can improve strength too.

Yes, this is (again) contradictory to conventional sports science, but remember the scientists who claimed I was too big to be a swimmer? Well, they clearly had never met Eddie Hall. The largest human I've ever had the privilege of calling a training partner, Eddie was crowned the world's strongest man in 2017, his name forever cemented in strongman folklore when on 9 July 2016 he became the first person in history to deadlift over 500 kg (half a tonne).

But few people know he was also an elite, national-level swimmer in his youth, and although he now weighs 178 kg (28 stone) is still capable of swimming a 1 min 20 s split for 100 m intervals fuelled by 7,000 calories of cheesecake. Yes, this story is as strange as it is true, but I bore witness to the super-sized swimming spectacle that is Eddie when we trained together during one of my 'wintered' (interval) training sessions and the following was my eyewitness account.

STAMINA IMPROVES STRENGTH

Standing poolside my digestive system was struggling. Foolishly, three hours earlier Eddie and I had embarked on an impromptu eating competition that consisted of ten chicken wings, four servings of rice and chips, two chicken burgers and twelve portions of cheesecake and ice cream layered in honey ... each!

Needless to say, we were regretting our decision, but we were both too competitive (and stubborn) to back down. Now our stomachs were forced to face the consequences as we attempted 50 × 100 m sprints in the pool. I turned to Eddie, who was now basically sweating honey and adjusting his goggles.

'Do you think 7,000 calories of cheesecake and ice cream is performance enhancing?' I asked.

'No ... it was a terrible idea,' he replied as he refitted his goggles over his eyes. 'But I don't regret a single bite.'

I agreed and couldn't help but laugh, then instantly stopped as I felt my enlarged belly wrestling with the elastic waistband on my trunks.

Entering the pool cautiously, we both felt a sense of relief as the buoyancy of the water helped carry the burden that was our cheesecake-bloated bellies.

'Eddie,' I said, 'how well do you know the owners of the pool?'

'Why?' he replied concerned.

'Well, we were going to swim 5 km today in 100 m intervals, but I'm just wondering what pace we should set for the 100 m intervals and how long to rest in-between. Since I'm aware if we go off too fast, it could end badly and I'll end up being sick poolside.'

'Hmm ...' Eddie paused to consider his response. 'Put it like this mate, I know them well enough to be sick poolside, but not well enough to shit myself during interval sprints. Does that help?'

Strangely it kind of did. 'Okay, 1 minute 20 second intervals it is then,' I said setting my watch.

Hours, laps and intervals passed and I'm happy to report no accidents happened and no pool attendants or lifeguards needed to worry. In fact, we were actually swimming some good split times once the chicken and cheesecake had been fully digested.

Watching Eddie, it was incredible to see him swimming. He was so big, he didn't seem to travel through the water, instead it almost appeared that water got out of his way. Also, if I possessed 'whale-like work capacity' I would say that Eddie possessed, 'shark-like strength' since he completely defies what many thought was possible. The same way a Great White can grow up to 6 m (20 ft) in length and 2,000 kg (4,400 lb) in weight yet can travel at speeds of up to 40 km/h (25 mph), Eddie can maintain a 1 minute 20 second split for 5 km in 100 m intervals (on 7,000 calories of cheesecake) weighing 178 kg (28 stone).

How did he do this and yet still become the world's strongest man? It makes no sense based on conventional sports science. Strongman is a sport that contains some of the world's largest and strongest athletes and their sole goal is to train strength. This is their muscles' ability to generate force combined with coordinated neuromuscular activation (or put simply, how effective you are at generating force at the right times during lifts like the squat, bench or deadlift). Based on the 'interference phenomenon' we touched on earlier, it would make sense they avoid cardio training all together.

But speaking to Eddie, I noticed that wasn't the case. In fact, swimming conditioning had always been a part of his training. Even when he won the World's Strongest Man title in 2017 and set the world record for the 500 kg deadlift, he was doing some form of 'supplementary cardio' and while his training is complex, intricate and forever changing, it would be fair to assume Eddie's adaptation energy pie chart could look like this:

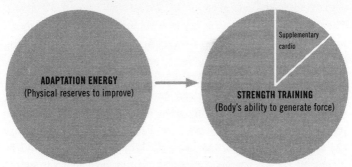

Eddie wasn't trying to set a 5 km personal best, but he knew how to use endurance training to complement his strength training. This is supported by research published by the Department of Health Sciences at Mid Sweden University in Ostersund that found that combining strength and stamina training actually elicited, 'Greater muscle hypertrophy than resistance exercise alone.' What this means is combining cardio with weight training could actually increase muscle size.[64]

To test this theory the Swedish took 10 healthy men between the ages of 25 and 30 and subjected them to five weeks of unilateral knee extensor exercises. One leg only strength trained and completed four sets of seven repetitions at 75–80 per cent of their one rep max. The other leg combined strength and stamina in completing the same strength routine but coupled with a 45-minute cycle during each session. Following five weeks, researchers analysed muscle biopsies and found:

- The vastus lateralis muscle (located on the outside of the leg) increased by 17 per cent in size in the cardio-trained leg compared to 9 per cent in the strength-trained leg.
- The quadriceps femoris muscle (found at the front of the leg) increased by 14 per cent in the cardio-trained leg compared to 8 per cent in the strength-trained leg.

They concluded, 'These results provide novel insight into human muscle adaptations and offer the very first genomic basis explaining how aerobic exercise may augment (improve), rather than compromise, muscle growth induced by resistance exercise.'[65]

So where did this strength and stamina sorcery come from? One reason could be that performing any form of cardiovascular training dramatically improves your capillary density. Capillaries are the small blood vessels that network through the muscles and by increasing their density you also increase your own ability to supply the working muscles with blood, oxygen and nutrients during training. This is one of the most overlooked aspects of strength training, as power athletes devote a lot of their adaptation energy on shifting iron and not a lot on caring for their capillaries. But research shows this could unlock strength potential you never knew you had.

For strength athletes it would mean faster recovery rates between sets and therefore an ability to increase the body's durability (work capacity). This is especially important for strength-training protocols like German Volume Training (GVT). This is often referred to as the 'ten sets method' since it involves completing 10 sets of 10 repetitions using a weight that's roughly 60 per cent of your one rep max (or a weight you could perform 20 repetitions with), all with only 60 to 90 seconds of rest in between sets.

Does it work? As a muscle-building training protocol, it's believed very few workouts are supported by as many experts as German Volume Training. Originating in the 1970s, it was made popular by Germany's weightlifting coach Rolf Feser who advocated its use to weightlifters who wanted to move up a weight class during off-season. Canadian weightlifter Jacques Demers, silver medallist in the Los Angeles Olympics, also famously used this training protocol and credited it for the renowned size of his thighs.

But it's easy to see how cardio and an improved capillary density can help you in those final sets. Even the strongest of athletes would struggle without any endurance capability and as a result would be unable to complete the workload recommended by GVT training to increase muscle mass. But for those like Eddie whose body's tolerability, individuality and durability can withstand 'high-volume, heavy-resistance strength training protocols'[66] it's clear how it can produce superhuman-endured strength athletes.

With all of this said (and chicken and cheesecake eaten) I took inspiration from the above and created the following 'wintered' weight training routine to build the 'whale-like work capacity' and sea-ready strength and speed that I'd need if I was to battle the rogue tides around the Isle of Man and make it into the North Channel. This is the exact *Great British Swim Training Plan*.

THE GREAT BRITISH SWIM TRAINING PLAN

SEA-READY STRENGTH AND SPEED: THEORY

Firstly, remember this is *supplementary* strength training.

My goal was *not* to lift Herculean weights and set a bench press personal best; the goal was to increase the body's durability (work capacity), improve physical resilience and use strength training to improve stamina. Therefore, for me it was crucial I always had enough adaptation energy to complete the workouts and that they complemented (and didn't hinder) my swimming training.

With that in mind I had to holistically consider the training programme in its entirety. No workout exists in isolation and each is interdependent: so, for example, Monday's 5 km swim will impact Wednesday's strength session in more ways than we will probably ever know. Each session basically operates in a complex system of interrelationships and the problem is too often sports science fails to acknowledge this. Training is studied in complete isolation and coaches compartmentalise energy systems that are never compartmentalised in nature. But not in this workout, since the body's tolerability, adaptation energy and overall physical reserves are at the heart of the entire programme and considered during every workout.

Next, understand this programme is a complete hybrid and combines many different training methods. While it is a form of Russian General Physical Preparedness (GPP), it also fuses power-lifting, strongman training, bodyweight conditioning and speed training from the old Soviet Union and is inspired by the work ethic of the Bulgarian training method.

The workouts themselves are then divided into these basic human movements from the sport of strongman which include:

1. PRESS: Movements include bench press, log press or military press.
2. PULL/HINGE: Movements include pull-ups, rows, deadlift and kettlebell swings.

3. SQUAT: Movements include back squat, front squat and lunges.
4. DRAG/THROW/FLIP: Movements include sled drags, medicine ball throws and tyre flips.

Mastering these will complement all other components of fitness since (according to the National Strength and Conditioning Association) big, functional movements that use universal motor recruitment patterns to develop neurological efficiency also increase an 'athlete's tolerance for more intense training.'[67] Essentially what we're saying is:

Speed is an advantage, but physical resilience is a necessity.

As for the specifics of the workouts themselves: Every routine contains four exercises that each have a specific focus and all complement each other to create a fast, strong, powerful and enduring athlete:

- EXERCISE 1: SPEED OF MOVEMENT.
- EXERCISE 2: STRENGTH OF MOVEMENT.
- EXERCISE 3: RANGE OF MOVEMENT.
- EXERCISE 4: CAPACITY OF MOVEMENT.

EXERCISE 1: SPEED OF MOVEMENT

Every workout starts with a fast yet controlled bodyweight exercise.

The is to build kinaesthetic awareness. Don't be put off by the technical name, this is just a complex way of saying, 'know where your body is in space,' and developing this ability helps you to better understand if the movements you're doing (like when swimming) feel right or wrong. Ultimately, mastering this kind of biological feedback and physiological intuition helps you make adjustments to move better and more efficiently when swimming through different wind, waves and weather.

The reason these movements are performed fast and controlled is because beginning your training with dynamic bodyweight movements has been shown to help complement your heavier strongman and powerlifting exercises by encouraging the muscle and joints to work cohesively, and also serves to get the central nervous system (and muscles) 'firing'. Known as Ballistic Training, this type of weightlifting is characterised by movements in which the athlete tries to apply the maximal force to the resistance with the goal of lifting, moving or projecting it as quickly as they can. If you consider every time you perform a conventional squat or bench press, your body naturally decelerates at the top of the movement. In fact, it's believed in a one-repetition maximum lift, as much as 24 per cent of the lift time is spent decelerating.[68] For a lift at 80 per cent of your one repetition, maximum deceleration can increase to as much as 52 per cent. Even if you perform them quickly ('speed reps') the speed decreases at the end of the concentric motion. It's a protective mechanism put in place by our joints that stops our shoulders from becoming detached from our bodies during a quick bench press. But ballistic training virtually eliminates this deceleration.

Consider a plyometric push-up where your aim is to throw yourself into the air and compare it to a bench press, and you'll see that same protective mechanism goes out the window. Instead, it means achieving maximal acceleration, optimal power, a fully firing nervous system and optimal activation of fast-twitch muscle fibres are all possible.

Does it work? Well, supporting this theory was a study published by the *Journal of Strength and Conditioning Research* which wanted to 'Investigate the additive effects of ballistic (speed) training to a traditional heavy resistance training program on upper body strength.' Seventeen athletes were selected and assigned to two groups. One group followed a traditional strength training protocol for eight weeks while the other combined traditional strength training and ballistic (fast) bodyweight training. This consisted of a conventional bench press coupled with plyometric push-ups where the athlete's hands leave the floor during the upward phase of the push-up (clapping mid-air is optional).

Following the eight weeks, the athlete's one-repetition maximum was measured on the bench press and results revealed that although both groups improved, the traditional strength training group increased by 7.1 per cent on average compared to 11.6 per cent for the ballistic-bodyweight training group. Scientists concluded the 'Inclusion of ballistic (bodyweight) exercises into a heavy resistance training program increased one-repetition maximum bench press and enhanced power.'[69]

This is why every workout begins with a fast, powerful and dynamic (ballistic) bodyweight movement such as plyometric push-ups, kettlebell swings and box jumps. You focus on *Speed of Movement* which primes the body for the heavier lifts to follow.

EXERCISE 2: STRENGTH OF MOVEMENT

Strength training is easy in theory, hard in practice. Strength (on its most basic level) can be defined as a muscle's ability to produce force, but this force can vary greatly throughout a particular lift and range of movement. To keep things simple, let's continue with a bench press example.

The force generated by the muscles to 'lockout' the final part of the bench press will be very different to the force needed to get out of 'the hole' at the bottom of the lift when the bar is closer to the chest. Basically, muscle force and tension varies throughout all movements. So, for you to become strong during a particular lift, it is:

Your muscle's ability to generate force combined with coordinated neuro-muscular activation.

Or put simply, how effective you are at generating force at the right times during the lift, which is exactly what we focus on during the second exercise in the Great British Swim Training Plan: adding more weight and resistance now the muscles, joints and central nervous system are 'fired up' from Exercise 1 where we focused on fast, explosive, ballistic *Speed of Movement*.

To understand why we add more weight, you have to understand the work of Sir Isaac Newton. An English mathematician and physicist, he is widely recognised as one of the most influential scientists of all time. He was also a former pupil at my school – The King's School Grantham – so I was very familiar with his *Laws of Motion* and is the reason why they had such an impact on the Great British Swim Training Plan.

Newton detailed that 'force' is calculated using the equation:

$$\text{Force} = \text{Mass} \times \text{Acceleration}$$

Therefore, it's clear to see that to generate more force we either need:

- More Acceleration: where you focus on fast, explosive *Speed of Movement*, or
- More Mass: where you focus on heavy, powerful *Strength of Movement*.

This is why every workout begins with a fast, powerful and dynamic (ballistic) bodyweight exercise that focuses on *Speed of Movement* since it primes the body for the heavier lifts. Then the focus shifts to *Strength of Movement* and generating more force by adding mass during exercises like the squat, bench and weighted pull-up.

EXERCISE 3: RANGE OF MOVEMENT

As we know from earlier, the *British Journal of Sports Medicine* emphatically states, 'Strength training reduced sports injuries.'[70]

How? Well, way back on the Isle of Wight when I was bruised and battered (but not quite beaten), my physio Jeff theorised this was because, 'the accumulation of strength over a period of time allows all of our body's structures to adapt and make us less prone to injury and more able to deal with the stresses and strains that we place upon it. Whether that be bones, muscles, joints, ligaments or tendons. All of these structures have the ability to adapt to the forces that are placed upon them.'

This is why within each workout (following *Speed of Movement* and *Strength of Movement*) the focus is on *Range of Movement* where we perform more complex, unilateral movements (meaning you only train one limb at a time) that require strength *and* coordination. The reason we do this is to engage the muscles of the core, an idea supported by research which sought to, 'Evaluate the effect of unstable and unilateral exercises on trunk muscle activation.' Using electromyography technology, they tested the activity of the muscles in the core and found, 'The most effective means for trunk strengthening should involve back or abdominal exercises with unstable bases.' They added, 'Furthermore, trunk strengthening can also occur when performing resistance exercises, if the exercises are performed unilaterally.'[71]

This is why every workout in our plan contains more complex, unilateral movements like single dumbbell flies, dumbbell Bulgarian split squats and single-arm rows. Since it's not enough to be fast and strong (*Speed of Movement* and *Strength of Movement*) you also have to train the *Range of Movement* too and condition the ligaments, tendons and joints.

EXERCISE 4: CAPACITY OF MOVEMENT

Every workout finishes on an exercise that focuses on Capacity of Movement. This is directly linked to work capacity and serves to incrementally improve the body's durability by adding functional finishers. (Again) these exercises are inspired by the Russian training system known as General Physical Preparedness (GPP).

This is why every workout ends with a 'low intensity, high-repetition resistance training with light to moderate resistances' (as per the teachings of the National Strength and Conditioning Association) to increase your 'tolerance for more intense training'. Essentially, focusing on *Capacity of Movement* to increase the body's durability (work capacity).

But arguably one of the most important workouts is the Drag/Throw/Flip routine which takes place after the longest (25 km) swim providing you have enough adaptation energy and your body's tolerability can cope with the volume (stress and stimuli) to recover. Based on the body's durability and body's individuality, you can reduce (or miss) this session if you honestly feel overtrained, but the reason this session is so good is because it provides all the benefits of strength training, with less muscle soreness (known as DOMS or Delayed Onset Muscle Soreness).

Research published by the NSCA found that by mixing up the types of muscle contractions during training you can build strength and improve the body's durability (work capacity) without the soreness.

To understand how, you must learn that a muscle contracts in three ways:

- **Isometric contractions:** This is where a muscle contracts but does not shorten, giving no movement. The Plank is a good example of an isometric contraction.
- **Concentric contractions:** This is where a muscle contracts and shortens in length. The upward movement of a dumbbell in a biceps curl is a good example.
- **Eccentric contractions:** This is where a muscle is in tension while it lengthens. A good example of this is when you land on two feet from a jump and bend your knees; you'll notice the

quadriceps are in tension to cushion the impact, but are lengthening.

Why is this important? Because research published by the NSCA stated, 'There is a significant amount of mechanical stress accrued during this (eccentric) part of the lift,' which, 'Has the potential to cause a significant amount of soreness, fatigue, and inflammation.'[72]

Put in simple terms, what this means is solely performing the concentric part of a lift and avoiding the eccentric phase means you could (in theory) avoid the 'fatigue, soreness and inflammation' usually associated with strength training in order to improve the body's durability (work capacity). Which is exactly why the Drag/Throw/Flip routine contains sled pushes, medicine ball slams and tyre flips since each movement reduces the emphasis on the eccentric part of the movement, therefore allowing the athlete to increase their tolerance for more intense training.

No eccentric phase. No soreness. No overtraining.

SEA-READY STRENGTH AND SPEED: THE PROGRAMME

	Monday	Tuesday	Wednesday
Morning	*Swim Training: 5km swim* Low intensity, aerobic, practise stroke technique	*Swim Training: 10km swim* Low intensity, aerobic, practise stroke technique	*Swim Training: 10km swim* Low intensity, aerobic, practise stroke technique
Afternoon	Strength Training Press-Based General Physical Preparedness	—	Strength Training Squat-Based General Physical Preparedness
Evening	—	Interval Training	—

SEA-READY STRENGTH AND SPEED: TRAINING NOTES

- The four workouts per week are biomechanically built around:
  - Press
  - Hinge/Pull
  - Squat
  - Drag/Throw/Flip
- Remember the purpose of this workout is 'supplementary strength training' to support the primary goal of becoming a more robust resilient swimmer.

As a result:

- Every strength workout is short to preserve adaptation energy (body's tolerability).
- Each exercise within every workout is composed of four principles that complement each other:

Thursday	Friday	Saturday	Sunday
Swim Training: *10km swim* Low intensity, aerobic, practise stroke technique	*Swim Training:* *15km swim* Low intensity, aerobic, practise stroke technique	*Swim Training:* *25km swim* Low intensity, aerobic, practise stroke technique	*Swim Training:* *5km swim* Low intensity, aerobic, practise stroke technique
—	Strength Training Hinge/Pull-Based General Physical Preparedness	—	Strength Training Drag/Throw/Flip-Based General Physical Preparedness
Interval Training	—	—	—

SPEED OF MOVEMENT

STRENGTH OF MOVEMENT

RANGE OF MOVEMENT

CAPACITY OF MOVEMENT

- Each workout serves to increase work capacity (body's durability).
- The entire programme can be modified if more recovery time is needed (body's individuality).
- The entire workout is designed to create a more robust and resilient human and complement your endurance training.

In more detail, a week's workout would look like this:

SEA-READY STRENGTH AND SPEED: WORKOUTS

STRENGTH SESSION 1 | MONDAY: PRESS

Plyometric Push-Ups

Reps: 5

Sets: 3

Rest: 120 seconds

% One-Rep Max: 87%

Focus: SPEED OF MOVEMENT | Fast and efficient movement patterns to get the joints and muscles working cohesively.

- Get in a press-up position. Hands shoulder-width apart and back straight. (If you can't manage full press-ups, do them on your knees)
- Lower your chest to the floor then push up explosively until your arms fully extend.
- Attempt to add claps into the movement while air-borne if possible.

Bench Press

Reps: 5

Sets: 3

Rest: 120 seconds

% One-Rep Max: 87%

Focus: SPEED OF MOVEMENT | Your body's ability to generate force.

- Lie on the bench with your eyes under the bar. Grab the bar with a medium grip-width (thumbs around the bar).
- Un-rack the bar by straightening your arms. Lower the bar to your mid-chest. Press the bar back up until your arms are straight.

Unilateral Dumbbell Press (Paused)

Reps: 20 (2 second pause)
Sets: 3
Rest: 60 seconds
% One-Rep Max: 60%

Focus: RANGE OF MOVEMENT | Tendon and Ligament Strength: Your tendons' and ligaments' ability to tolerate force coupled with quality range of motion.

- Lie flat on a bench holding two dumbbells above your sternum with straight arms and your palms facing away from you.
- Lower one dumbbell to the side of your chest. Pause, then press the dumbbell back to starting position. Repeat with the other dumbbell.

Bear Crawls

Reps: 10
Sets: 4
Rest: 60 seconds
% One-Rep Max: Load with hard but achievable weight

Focus: CAPACITY OF MOVEMENT | A General Physical Pre-paredness 'finisher' designed to improve the Body's Durability (work capacity).

- Get on the floor on all fours, with your hands directly under your shoulders and your knees under your hips.
- Bring your knees off the ground and travel forwards with only your feet and hands in contact with the floor.
- Keep your back flat at all times. Travel 10m forward, then reverse.

STRENGTH SESSION 2 | WEDNESDAY: SQUAT

Box Jumps (Depth Jump)
Reps: 5
Sets: 3
Rest: 120 seconds
% One-Rep Max: 87%

Focus: SPEED OF MOVEMENT |
Fast and efficient movement
patterns to get the joints and
muscles working cohesively.

- Stand with your feet shoulder-width apart, at a comfortable distance from the box.
- To initiate the movement, bend your knees and push your hips back while swinging your arms behind you.
- Push your feet off the floor explosively to jump onto the box.

Box (Seated) Back Squat
Reps: 5
Sets: 3
Rest: 120 seconds
% One-Rep Max: 87%

Focus: STRENGTH OF MOVEMENT |
Your body's ability to generate
force.

- With the barbell on your back, stand in front of the box/bench. lower yourself to the box/bench (as if you were sitting down).
- When your bum touches the box/bench, lift yourself back up by driving with the legs. A slight pause at the bottom means you have to recruit the big muscles in the lower body to push back up.

Dumbbell Bulgarian Split Squat (Paused)

Reps: 8 (2 second pause)
Sets: 3
Rest: 90 seconds
% One-Rep Max: 80%

Focus: RANGE OF MOVEMENT | Tendon and Ligament Strength: Your tendons' and ligaments' ability to tolerate force coupled with quality range of motion.

- Set up in a split stance position while grasping dumbbells by your side with a neutral grip. Position the back foot on a bench or circular pad to increase the range of motion.
- Descend by flexing the front knee and continue until the back knee touches the ground directly beneath the hip.
- Drive through the front foot and extend the knee as you return to the starting position. Repeat.

Sled Push

Reps: 20 metres
Sets: 3
Rest: 90 seconds
% One-Rep Max: 75%

Focus: CAPACITY OF MOVEMENT | General Physical Preparedness designed to improve the Body's Durability (work capacity).

- Load up the sled with weight; you'll soon know if you've loaded too much on, because you won't be able to move it.
- Adopt a low position against the sled pushing with straight or bent arms. As you move forwards make sure your core is braced and that you're driving through your forefoot. Remember that once the sled gets going it'll feel easier to move the weight.

STRENGTH SESSION 3 | FRIDAY: HINGE/PULL

Kettlebell Swings
Reps: 5
Sets: 3
Rest: 120 seconds
% One-Rep Max: 87%

Focus: SPEED OF MOVEMENT | Fast and efficient movement patterns to get the joints and muscles working cohesively.

- Start with the kettlebell on the floor slightly in front of you and between your feet, which should be shoulder-width apart.
- Bend slightly at the knees but hinge at the hips, grasp the kettlebell and pull it back between your legs to create momentum.
- Drive your hips forwards and straighten your back to send the kettlebell up to shoulder height. Let the bell return back between your legs and repeat the move.

Weighted Pull-Ups (Paused)
Reps: 5
Sets: 3
Rest: 120 seconds
% One-Rep Max: 87%

Focus: STRENGTH OF MOVEMENT | Your body's ability to generate force.

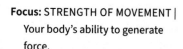

- Grip the bar with hands shoulder-width apart.
- Raise your feet off the floor and hang.
- Pull yourself up until your chin is over the bar and repeat.

Single Arm Rows (Paused)

Reps: 8 (2 second pause)
Sets: 3
Rest: 90 seconds
% One-Rep Max: 80%

Focus: RANGE OF MOVEMENT | Tendon and Ligament Strength: Your tendons' and ligaments' ability to tolerate force coupled with quality range of motion.

- Put your right leg on the bench and grab the far side with your right hand. Bend over so your upper body is parallel to the ground.
- Reach down and pick up the dumbbell in your left hand with a neutral grip (palm facing you), then hold it with your arm extended (back straight). Bring the dumbbell up to your chest. At the top of the movement, squeeze your shoulder and back muscles.
- Lower the dumbbell until your arm is fully extended again. Do all your reps on one arm before switching to the other side.

Farmers Walks

Reps: 30 metres
Sets: 3
Rest: 90 seconds
% One-Rep Max: 75%

Focus: CAPACITY OF MOVEMENT | A General Physical Preparedness 'finisher' designed to improve the Body's Durability (work capacity).

- Stand with 2 heavy dumbbells, kettlebells or farmer's bars in your hands. Ensure your core is tight, you're balanced and the weight is controlled.
- Walk at a controlled pace for the set distance.

159

STRENGTH SESSION 4 | SUNDAY: DRAG/THROW/FLIP

Sled Push

Reps: 20 metres
Sets: 3
Rest: 90 seconds
% One-Rep Max: 75%

Focus: CAPACITY OF MOVEMENT | General Physical Preparedness designed to improve the Body's Durability (work capacity).

- Load up the sled with weight; you'll soon know if you've loaded too much on, because you won't be able to move it.
- Adopt a low position against the sled pushing with straight or bent arms. As you move forwards make sure your core is braced and that you're driving through your forefoot with each step. Remember that once the sled gets going it'll feel easier to move the weight.

Medicine Ball Slams

Reps: 60 seconds
Sets: 4
Rest: 90 seconds
% One-Rep Max: 75%

Focus: CAPACITY OF MOVEMENT | General Physical Preparedness designed to improve the Body's Durability (work capacity).

- Stand with your knees slightly bent holding a medicine ball above your head with your arms extended.
- Bend forward at the waist and use your core muscles to slam the ball against the floor about a foot in front of you.
- Catch the ball on its way back up and repeat

Tyre Flips
Reps: 20 metres
Sets: 4
Rest: 90 seconds
% One-Rep Max: 75%

Focus: CAPACITY OF MOVEMENT | General Physical Preparedness designed to improve the Body's Durability (work capacity).

- Adopt a deep squat position, with hips low and pushed back, feet shoulder-width apart (ensure knees and feet are aligned).
- Place hands under the tyre as you press your chest against the tyre. Hips should be pushed back with your head up and shoulders wide to ensure you maintain a flat back and good posture as you drive powerfully through the legs and hips.
- As you do, generate enough momentum during the initial lift to allow you to get under the tyre, switching from an underhand pull position to a pushing/pressing position.
- Step forward and use your whole body to drive the tyre up and over. Focus on flipping and lifting in one smooth action, working quickly and with good technique.

So, did my 'wintered' weight training build sea-ready strength and speed? Yes, thankfully it did.

At 2 p.m. on 23 July, after battling the rogue tides of the Isle of Man, we officially (and finally) broke into the Northern Channel. We'd been at sea for 53 days and with no TV and limited knowledge of the outside world, we'd become totally in tune with every subtle and slight change in the ocean and our progress. Every fractional increase in speed was celebrated and every favourable weather report welcomed.

From the sea, you could *see* and *feel* the ocean's tides helping too. Visibly, the coastline passed by marginally faster and you could feel the stress and strain slightly alleviated from the tendons and ligaments in your shoulders.

Breathing a sigh of relief, I paused and looked back at the Irish Sea and the Isle of Man. For me, I didn't feel like celebrating since it didn't feel right. I hadn't conquered the Irish Sea, I had survived it. Thanks to 'wintered' weight training and sheer luck (as Mother Nature and Poseidon granted me safe passage) I was now on my way to Scotland with my body's tolerability for stress and stimuli (adaptation energy) intact and chronic fatigue still at bay.

LESSON 8

- **Strength training can improve your stamina**. If you concurrently train your **fast-twitch** and **slow-twitch** muscle fibres, your endurance performance will benefit.
- Strength training has been shown to improve movement and efficiency. And **if you move better, you move further and faster**.
- **Endurance training can improve your strength** by improving the efficiency of the cardiorespiratory system to deliver oxygen to the working muscles.
- An effective strength training plan involves:
  - **Speed of Movement** exercises (where the muscle and joints work cohesively together and get the central nervous system 'firing' ready for the heavier, subsequent lifts);
  - **Strength of Movement** exercises (focused on the muscle's ability to generate force combined with coordinated neuromuscular activation);
  - **Range of Movement** exercises (greater emphasis on co-ordination, controlled biomechanics and trunk muscle (core) activation during unilateral (single limb) movements); and
  - **Capacity of Movement** exercises (incrementally *increase* the body's ability to tolerate the stress and stimuli of training and/or competing (work capacity) without the soreness).

LESSON 9 | LEARN HOW TO CRUISE OR KILL

LOCATION: Mull of Kintyre
DISTANCE COVERED: 760 miles
DAYS AT SEA: 59

It is 2 p.m. on 29 July and we've arrived in the Mull of Kintyre. Like the gateway to the Inner Hebrides, everything now felt different as Scotland's coastline was among the most dramatic and dominant I'd seen in all 59 days at sea. But not in a bad way, in a great way as the rugged mountains and rolling glens were working in harmony with the ocean that day, offering some much-appreciated shelter from the wind and waves that could potentially plague our time here.

But when those same mountain ridges are 'at war' with the sea beneath, then it can produce dense clouds of sea mist that make navigation near impossible. Not just for ships either; the mist travels so high that it's caused many air crashes throughout aviation history.[73] For that reason the Mull of Kintyre (much like the Irish Sea and Bristol Channel) is feared and revered as a potential grave-yard for anything that attempts to cross it.

Fortunately for us, that day the Scottish waters were calm and kind. A wave of relief and excitement washed over the crew and the celebrations from the Northern Channel began to escalate from dancing on the deck (to commemorate the more favourable tides) to a full-blown party (to mark our arrival into Scotland).

Observing from the water, I watched as Suzanne commandeered the ship's air horn and began to sound its alarm in (surprising) harmony with Taz who was playing a ukulele that he'd found stowed away in the ship's galley for special occasions. Harriet, who'd emerged from her cabin, joined the festivities to dance on the roof of the galley and Matt sung at the top of his lungs every line of Sir Paul McCartney's 1977 hit song, 'Mull of Kintyre' with a deep bari-tone voice that echoed throughout the Hebrides.

Without doubt it was one of the strangest, most surreal and special moments of my life. As a team, we had always tried to temper any celebrations. From Land's End to the crossing of the Bristol Channel, we'd only allowed ourselves a brief moment to cele-brate, but Mull of Kintyre was an exception.

We were officially in Scotland! What's more, although the exact halfway point of our swim was hard to determine (due to the shape of Great Britain's coastline) for us we had always considered this to be it: the southwesternmost tip of the Kintyre Peninsula in south-west Scotland.

But the last 59 days and 760 miles had taken their toll and I was barely recognisable from the person who left Margate on 1 June. In many ways, my devolution into a primitive sea-bulked human was now complete, as was evident from the waistcoat mankini that was now getting a little tighter and snug when swimming.

But I didn't mind. The extra layer of fat was welcome insulation in waters that were noticeably colder now that we'd left the South Coast and the Irish Sea which receives some warmth from the Gulf Stream. Also, I knew the warmer days of summer were now behind us and we still had the entire coastline of Scotland to swim.

But Matt was worried and told me over dinner later that day why we should continue to swim with extra caution.

'I don't want to worry you, Ross,' he said.

I looked at him with unease, since I'd swum and sailed (day and night) with Matt for two months now and knew he would never voice a concern unless it was absolutely necessary.

'We received word over the radio that a pod of killer whales was seen off the west coast of Scotland. Basically, exactly along the route we're due to swim.'

'Do I need to worry?' I asked anxiously.

'Well, this is the thing. I've been speaking to marine biology experts and they say there's good and bad news for us.' He paused to consider which news to give first.

'The good news is there's never been a reported case of killer whales attacking humans in the wild. Since they're incredibly intelligent, know we're not on their "menu" and won't swap humans for seals because they know we're not very meaty.'

'Okay, that's good news. Right?' I said.

'Well, yes, but they also said the bad news is if they're going to attack anyone, it might be you. Since no human has ever spent this long in the seas around the coast of Britain before. What's worse, as the days go on you're looking more and more like a seal.'

Looking around the galley, I saw Suzanne, Harriet and Taz all nod. They had a point too. I now tipped the scales at over 100 kg which was 12 kg heavier than the lighter and leaner version of myself that left Margate.

'So, what do you propose I do?' I asked.

'Maybe leave pudding for tonight,' Harriet joked.

'Or maybe look less like a seal when swimming,' Matt suggested.

Both good suggestions, but I was more worried that the grey and black waistcoat mankini was a little too seal-like and began to wonder if we had any different coloured alternatives.

But joking aside, my body had been crafted by the sea and my body's tolerability (and adaptation energy) was being entirely spent on training my body to move better, faster and easier through the water within the realms of endurance sport.

As a result, I did swim like a seal.

My newly acquired physique had only two speeds: cruise or kill. Much like the grey seals of Lundy, it meant I would swim at a slow and steady pace (cruise), expending only as much energy as I needed to until the time came when I might have to sprint across a shipping lane to avoid a head-on collision with a cargo ship (kill). By doing this I was able to continue providing enough oxygen (and energy) to my body to continue operating at different intensities and speeds at different durations.

But this idea of cruise or kill is closely related to the tried and tested 80/20 polarised training method that's been used by endurance athletes for centuries.

CRUISE OR KILL: 80/20 POLARISED TRAINING

The 80/20 polarised training method is simple. You spend 80 per cent of your time training *aerobically* at a low intensity and slow pace, then spend 20 per cent of your time training *anaerobically* at a high intensity and fast pace.

Aerobic is defined as 'occurring in the presence of oxygen' which means your body uses oxygen to create the molecular energy of the muscles needed to power all movements within the body. This energy is in the form of a chemical known as adenosine triphosphate (ATP). Producing energy this way is slow but comes in great supply, and it's this energy system we use during a well-paced marathon, a 5 km swim or 30 km bike ride. Within the Great British Swim Training Plan this is the energy system I train first thing, every morning, with a slow and steady swim ranging from 5 km to 25 km.

Anaerobic energy, on the other hand, can be created without oxygen and instead breaks down carbohydrates from blood glucose or glucose stored in muscle to produce the molecular energy of the muscles needed to power all movements within the body (ATP again). Producing energy in this way is far faster but is limited and in short supply, and it's this energy system we use during a 400 m race, strongman training or an explosive 1,000 m row. Within the Great British Swim Training Plan, this is the energy system I train twice a week, in the evenings, with interval sprints ranging from 20 x 100 m sprints to (occasionally) a Zatopek-inspired 100 x 400 m sprints (this is brutal and I wouldn't recommend this to 99 per cent of people).

Essentially, the difference between aerobic and anaerobic exercise is *oxygen*. The reason you separate your low-intensity aerobic training from your high-intensity anaerobic training is to ensure each session has a specific focus to provide a 'clear cellular signal' of what you want your body to adapt to (basically the body's specificity, where you are constantly directing the body's ability to tolerate stress and stimuli to a specific form of training and/or competition).

80% Slow-paced and Low Intensity Training	20% Fast-paced and High Intensity Training
You swim, cycle or run at an intensity and pace that means your body *can* provide enough oxygen and energy to the working muscles for long durations. This improves Aerobic Fitness.	You swim, cycle or run at an intensity and pace that means your body *cannot* provide enough oxygen and energy to the working muscles for long durations. This improves Anaerobic Fitness.

80% Slow-paced and Low Intensity Training	20% Fast-paced and High Intensity Training
The emphasis is on training: Technique and movement efficiency The heart, lungs and body's ability to use oxygen to produce energy.	The emphasis is on training: Pain tolerance and getting comfortable being uncomfortable The muscles' ability to produce energy without oxygen.

When these separate workouts are fused together in a well-designed programme, each training session (jointly) improves your body's ability to operate at higher intensities at different durations and to provide enough oxygen and/or energy to continue whatever the pace and intensity of the hike, run, cycle or swim.

ENERGY EXPLAINED

Worth noting is that all energy systems are constantly working at the same time. However, the predominant energy system used to resupply adenosine triphosphate (the molecular energy of the muscles) depends on the intensity and duration of the activity. To see how this looks in a graph, see overleaf.

Again, it's important to note that in reality the energy systems never work in isolation and are all working at different percentages at different times. For example, when jogging, the body will still be using a small proportion of the anaerobic system and when sprinting the aerobic system will also be used (albeit in small amounts). Basically, the use of each energy system will be constantly changing.

How do you know which energy system you're predominantly using (aerobic or anaerobic)? Putting advanced techniques aside, one of the easiest ways is to see if you can run and talk comfortably at the same time.

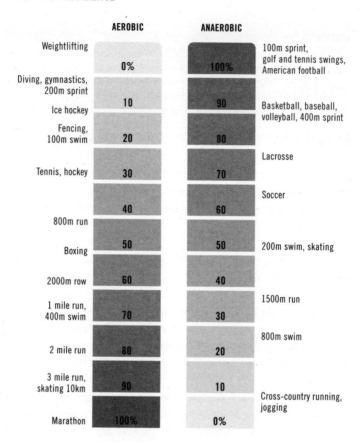

	AEROBIC	ANAEROBIC	
Weightlifting	0%	100%	100m sprint, golf and tennis swings, American football
Diving, gymnastics, 200m sprint	10	90	
Ice hockey			Basketball, baseball, volleyball, 400m sprint
Fencing, 100m swim	20	80	
			Lacrosse
Tennis, hockey	30	70	
	40	60	Soccer
800m run			
Boxing	50	50	200m swim, skating
2000m row	60	40	
1 mile run, 400m swim	70	30	1500m run
2 mile run	80	20	800m swim
3 mile run, skating 10km	90	10	
Marathon	100%	0%	Cross-country running, jogging

- **If you can speak in complete sentences** you're running at an aerobic pace, which is sustainable for a long time. This is the speed at which you 'cruise'.
- **If you cannot speak in complete sentences** you're probably running at an anaerobic pace, which is not sustainable for a long time. This is the speed at which you 'kill'.

The point where you cross over is known as your anaerobic threshold. This is when your body must switch from your aerobic energy system to your anaerobic energy system. Studies show the fitter you are (more efficient your cardiorespiratory system), the longer you can fuel your body with the aerobic system before the anaerobic system needs to take over.

LEARN TO CRUISE: 80 PER CENT SLOW (AEROBIC)

In any endurance-based sport, movement efficiency is key. It doesn't matter if you're running, swimming or cycling, the more efficiently you move the less prone to injury you become and the faster and further you're able to travel.

The reason is that all movements have what's known as a kinetic chain. Dr Arthur Steindler, one of the early pioneers of this theory, defines a kinetic chain as, 'A combination of several successively arranged joints constituting a complex motor unit,' or put simply, how all your joints work together during certain movements.

This efficiency of movement is especially true of swimmers, for whom researchers noted, 'The average competitive swimmer swims approximately 60,000 to 80,000 m per week. With a typical count of 8 to 10 strokes per 25 m lap, each shoulder performs 30,000 rotations each week. This places tremendous stress on the shoulder girdle musculature and glenohumeral joint and is why shoulder pain is the most frequent musculoskeletal complaint among competitive swimmers.'[74] This is why spending 80 per cent of your endurance training drilling an efficient kinetic chain of movement patterns is so important and is why I started every day by spending my body's tolerability (and adaptation energy) on this.

So how do we develop good technique? The answer is practise, practise and practise some more. There's no substitute for hard-fought miles and 'getting wintered'. Too often we're told tips, tricks and shortcuts may help us run a better marathon time or swim a faster 10 km, but the reality is there's no substitute for hard work.

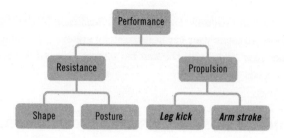

This is the only way you become an expert in biomechanics, hydro-dynamics and the laws of movement that govern your sport.

For swimming, this is brilliantly described by the *Journal of Swimming Research* which found, 'When considering what variables might affect performance, reference to a model (above) is useful. Resistance and propulsion, together with physiological capacity of the swimmer, are the key determinants of performance.'

Now my own shape in the form of my submarine skull, buoyant duck bum and sumo-swimmer stature had already been identified as not having 'good hydrodynamic characteristics for competitive swimming' because of the increased drag caused.

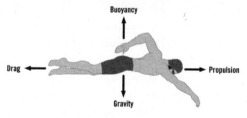

But something else to consider is posture. Now most studies on hydrodynamics are limited to objects of regular, symmetrical and unchanging shape. In contrast, the human body is not regular, and constantly changes shape during swimming. So, even an athlete with the perfect swimmer's body will produce irregular shapes that cause drag, whether that's due to the pull and recovery action of the arm or turning to breathe. Therefore, the overall aim is to maintain a shape that minimises resistance while still positioning the body and its limbs to generate propulsion in an energetically efficient manner. This requires trade-offs to optimise the combination of resistance and propulsion to maximise speed at a sustainable energetic cost. This is why a basic understanding of Newton's laws of motion helps since they pervade all human movements and cannot be ignored when describing or analysing competitive swimming techniques. Take his first law for example:

Newton's First Law. A body remains at rest, or continues to move in a straight line at constant velocity, unless acted upon by a net external force.

In swimming, there are forces that accelerate a swimmer, for example the propulsive forces generated by the power-phase in arm strokes, and forces that negatively accelerate a swimmer, for example, resistances and counter-productive movements.

What is a desirable conclusion from this interpretation of Newton's First Law is that propulsive forces should be magnified and applied continuously and that resistive forces should be minimised. That would result in a high level of 'propelling efficiency' (represented in the image below) and we do this by refining our technique so we're better able to 'cruise and kill'.

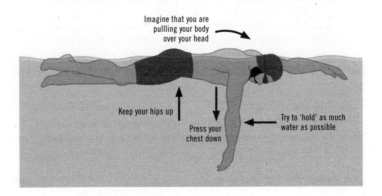

Imagine that you are pulling your body over your head

Keep your hips up

Press your chest down

Try to 'hold' as much water as possible

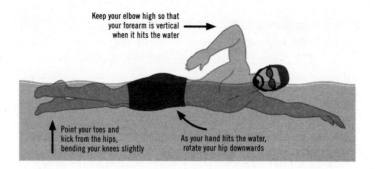

Keep your elbow high so that your forearm is vertical when it hits the water →

Point your toes and kick from the hips, bending your knees slightly

As your hand hits the water, rotate your hip downwards

BODY POSITION	BREATHING
• Aim to keep your body position as flat as you can to be streamlined in the water with a slight slope down to the hips to keep the leg kick underwater. • Try to keep your stomach flat and level to support your lower back. • With eyes looking forward and down, your head should be in line with the body and the water level should come between your eyebrows and hairline. • Try to keep your head and spine as still and relaxed as possible. Instead, rotate your hips and shoulders to generate momentum through the water. Your head should only join the rotation when you want to breathe. • Your shoulder should come out of the water as your arm exits, while the other arm begins the propulsive phase under the water.	• Try to keep your head turn as smooth as possible when you breathe. Your neck should remain smooth with your head and spine joining the rotation of the shoulders. • One side of the face should remain in the water and you may want to stretch your mouth to one side to keep it clear. • Try not to lift your head too much out of the water – the more your head raises, the more your feet and legs will sink in the water. • After a sharp inhale, turn your face quickly and smoothly back into the water in time with the rotation of your shoulders. • Exhalation takes place in the water when the head is back to a neutral position and can be gradual or explosive. • The regularity of breathing is not set in stone – it is better to simply inhale when necessary. A standard technique is to breathe every three strokes, thus

BODY POSITION *Cont.*	BREATHING *Cont.*
• The hips should not rotate as much as the shoulders.	alternating the side which the head turns and maintaining balance through the stroke.

ARM STROKE	LEG KICK
• Keep your elbow slightly bent as you reach your hand in front of your body to enter the water. • Entry should be between the centre line of the head and the shoulder line and the hand should be directed with the palm facing down and out so the thumb first enters the water first. • Don't start pulling back as soon as your hand is in the water – you should give yourself room to reach forward under the water before you start to bring your hand back to the body. • The power-phase comes from the pull just above the head and to the hip.	• Studies show your leg kick (during front crawl) only accounts for 10–20%[75] of your overall propulsion and its main role is actually to keep the body in a streamlined position and thereby reduce drag.[76] • Your legs should be close together with ankles relaxed and in a continuous motion. • There's no need to take large down and upbeats (kicks of leg) – a steady, small motion is fine. While the most pressure should be on your feet, remember to move your whole legs. • Try to keep your legs as straight as possible. There should be a slight knee bend between the end of the upbeat and beginning of the downbeat but generally the straighter your legs, the more efficient and powerful the kick. • The more kicks per cycle, the more energy you will use. Sprint swimmers will typically use six or eight kicks for a cycle but someone swimming longer distance should use fewer, more pronounced kicks.

INDIVIDUAL VARIATION

Finally, a quick word of caution on technique. It's important you find a technique that works for your individual physiology, as sports scientists warn about trying to replicate movement images displayed by successful athletes.[77] Research printed in the *Scientific Principles for Swimming Techniques* states that, 'When one considers the differences in lever lengths, the origins and insertions of muscles, the shape of fluid flow about the body, and the actual mindset that controls the application to swimming techniques, it quickly becomes obvious that no two swimmers should expect to look completely alike when swimming any competitive swimming stroke.'[78]

It's also why scientists wrote, 'It must be recognized that asymmetry is not necessarily associated with a decrease in performance.' Asymmetries are where body parts (and movement) are not equal, in balance or symmetrical. For example, an early study of breaststroke swimmers revealed that technique asymmetry is very common and does not necessarily reduce performance.[79]

LEARN TO KILL: 20 PER CENT FAST (ANAEROBIC)

Sprint. Rest. Repeat. Quite possibly the simplest training method you will ever undertake. Known as high-intensity interval training, it can be used in any sport and in any activity from cycling and sprinting to swimming and running, but it involves repeating a series of fast-paced and slow-paced running intervals to improve the body's ability to move, train and work at a high pace when you're not able to provide enough oxygen to the working muscles (relying on anaerobic energy production).[80]

For swimming, interval training can be as simple as sprinting 25 m front crawl as fast as you can and then swim slow breaststroke back, allowing your heart rate to drop. Sprint and repeat as many times as you can (aiming for at least 10 sprints). For Olympic-standard swimmers the principle of sprint, rest and repeat is exactly the same, but instead athletes might perform 20 x 100 m sprints holding a 1 min 25 s pace, with 30 seconds rest between sets.

Why is this such a good training method? Because studies show this type of training improves both aerobic *and* anaerobic fitness. Researchers from the School of Human Movement Studies, University of Queensland (Australia) wanted to test the 'Effects of moderate-intensity endurance and high-intensity intermittent training on aerobic fitness and anaerobic fitness.' Contrary to popular belief, they found that 'Moderate-intensity aerobic training that improves aerobic fitness does not change anaerobic capacity and that adequate high-intensity intermittent training may improve both anaerobic and aerobic energy supplying systems significantly.'[81]

But the power of high-intensity training doesn't stop there. Scientists also believe such training methods not only expand the capabilities of the muscles and heart but also recalibrate the brain's horizons and perception to pain. This is based on research which found that high-intensity training does not change your pain sensitivity (the point at which you acknowledge pain), but can increase pain tolerance (how long you're willing to endure pain).[82]

One man who understood this better than anyone was Emil Zatopek. A pioneer of high-intensity training, during the mid-1950s he was famously performing up to one hundred fast 400 m laps (with 150 m jogs in between) in a single training session. Fred Wilt, an American runner, wrote in his book *How They Train* (1959), 'Nobody had realised it was humanly possible to train this hard.' As a result, Zatopek's regime became legendary. He trained in the forests, running through deep snow in heavy army boots, and adopting a lolloping gait to avoid getting stuck in snowdrifts. Sometimes he trained carrying his wife on his back or ran on the spot in his bath on a pile of wet clothes.

Basically, he trained like a madman because he understood training not only expands the capabilities of the muscles and heart but also recalibrates the brain's perception to pain.

Suitably inspired by Zatopek I would sometimes perform a special kind of high-intensity interval training where I would swim and sprint 100 x 400 m sprints. The session would amount to 40 km in total, would take an entire day (and lots of food) and I wouldn't recommend it to anyone. But every painful sprint was a homage to the great man who famously said, 'When you can't keep going ... go faster'. Also, every painful sprint embodied Stoic Sports Science and improved my 'capacity and mental clarity to apply proven principles of sports science and psychology, under conditions of extreme exhaustion, stress and adversity'.

CRUISING THROUGH SCOTLAND

It was 8.00 a.m. on 4 August, a day after my battle within the Corryvreckan. With wounds still raw, it would have been easy for me to get downhearted, but today I couldn't help but swim with a smile. It was my dad's birthday and he decided to spend it among the Inner Hebrides aboard a boat with my mum, my girlfriend and her family as his feral son slowly made his way around the Isle of Mull, the fourth-largest island in Scotland.

Quite content, he looked out from the boat as I continued to swim at a snail's pace, utterly happy to take in the views of castles, cliffs and hopefully catch a glimpse of the incredibly rare white-tailed sea eagles that were native to these parts of Scotland.

In the water, I was anxious to pick up the pace and every few minutes would check the tracker on my watch. This is because I knew that the harbour of Tobermory was just over 30 miles away. Built in the eighteenth century, it's renowned for being the most beautiful harbour in all of Scotland which is why I wanted to reach it on today's swim so that everyone could go on land (apart from me, of course) and celebrate my dad's birthday among the whisky distillery, cafes and quirky shops.

But working out the time, distance, tides and swimming speed, it was clear I wasn't going to make it. So, feeling slightly defeated and deflated, I stopped and turned to my dad from the water.

'Sorry, Dad,' I shouted. He looked down from the boat's deck with a cup of tea and slice of birthday cake,

'What for?' he asked.

'I'm aware I'm swimming quite slow because of fatigue, the Isle of Mull is quite large and Tobermory is miles away. So I won't be able to provide the most "dynamic" tour of Scotland for your birthday ...'

My dad smiled and shook his head. He had been a tennis coach for years and an athlete for many more before that, so he knew the importance of pacing and 'cruising' (especially following the impossible pace of the day before when I had to outswim the Hag Goddess). He also knew I had bigger things to worry about than the opening times of the whisky distillery on Tobermory.

'I'm having a brilliant birthday,' he said as he sipped his tea. 'So, can we agree that you focus on this swim of yours and I'll focus on this cake of mine?'

He continued smiling, but was also quite serious. You see, my dad has always been diplomatic and had a way with words, but this was his way of saying 'shut up and swim' and stop worrying about other people.

He was right and for five miles that's what I did. Continuing to breathe to my right to sight off the boat, I could see my mum had emerged from the galley to join my dad on deck. She was wearing two jumpers and a red coat with the hood pulled over her head and toggles pulled tight as the wind (and waves) had begun to pick up. She could barely move because she was wrapped up so tightly, but at least she looked cosy and content. A few more miles in and Matt sensed a storm was coming.

'It might be best for you to go inside!' he shouted to my mum and dad.

I could see this didn't quite compute and my mum replied, 'Oh, thank you, but we're fine. As long as our son is out there, we will be here watching over him.'

Mum then gripped the rigging tightly to stop herself from falling overboard, while my dad heroically shielded his final slice of birthday cake from the rain that was now practically falling horizontally from the sky as the storm took hold.

As the winds raged and waves crashed into the boat (and my shoulders) all I could see was a tiny, tanned, curly-haired lady and a stocky, silver-bearded man standing at the bow of the boat. Both refusing to budge for a Scottish storm and determined to watch over their son and celebrate a birthday irrespective of the conditions Mother Nature and Poseidon threw at them.

So that day it was easy for me to 'cruise'. Although I was engulfed by waves, I swam with an immense sense of gratitude, making progress up the Scottish coastline knowing there was my parents, girlfriend and birthday cake waiting for me at the end of this swim.

By 1.00 p.m. the tide began to turn and rush in the opposite direction to which we were travelling. Having covered 12 miles, Matt and I decided that it had been a great start to the day and we would resume the swim in six hours' time when the tides would be in our favour once again.

Climbing onto the boat, I hugged my dad and apologised again.

'What for now?' Dad asked, still with his arms wrapped around me.

'Because it's your birthday, we're hugging and my wetsuit is soaked with seawater and urine.'

Dad was unfazed. 'Fondly or not, I will always remember this birthday,' he said laughing as we remained there in a father and son embrace on the stormy seas off the Scottish Hebrides, and although we didn't make it to Tobermory that day, we were content ... and cruising.

LESSON 9

- There is no universally agreed consensus on the best way to train for endurance. But one method that's proved highly successful over the years is the **80/20 polarised training** approach.
- The basic premise is:
  - You spend 80 per cent of your time training *aerobically* at a low intensity and slow pace (at **'cruise' speed**) with an emphasis on technique and the heart, lungs and body's ability to produce energy with oxygen.
  - You spend the other 20 per cent of your time training *anaerobically* at a high intensity and fast pace (at **'kill' speed**) with an emphasis on pain tolerance and the muscles' ability to produce energy without oxygen.
- When these separate workouts are fused together in a well-designed programme, each training session (jointly) improves your body's ability to operate at higher intensities at different durations and to provide enough oxygen and/or energy to continue whatever the pace and intensity of the hike, run, cycle or swim.
- During your slow, low-intensity training, it's important to **find a technique that works for your individual physiology**, rather than trying to replicate movements by successful athletes.

LESSON 10 | LEARN TO LIMIT LIMITATIONS

The Hebrides

LOCATION: The Hebrides
DISTANCE COVERED: 930 miles
DAYS AT SEA: 79

Between 29 July and 18 August, I lived among the Hebrides. An archipelago comprising hundreds of islands off the northwest coast of Scotland, it's divided into the Inner and Outer Hebrides groups and is filled with rugged mountain ranges, wildlife and more jelly-fish than I can count. Amid its sparsely populated fishing villages and remote Gaelic-speaking communities, I'd spent the past 20 days immersed and engulfed in its bleak beauty.

During that time, we set the record for the world's longest stage swim, entered (and escaped) the clutches of the Corryvreckan, cele-brated my dad's birthday in a storm (with tea and cake) and passed under the 1.5 mile-long Skye Bridge that connects the island of Skye to the village of Kyle of Lochalsh on the mainland.

As a result, I wasn't just physically reshaped, but mentally reformed too. My brain no longer computed time, but instead worked in tides. My spare time was spent studying shipping charts and quizzing Matt's wave and weather wisdom. Finally, I had become an accidental, reluctant but inevitable expert in giant jelly-fish stings to the human face.

I say 'inevitable' because the islands of the Hebrides act almost like a funnel, which serves to guide Scotland's population of jellyfish into a kind of gauntlet that I was forced to run every day and night. Of course, the day swims weren't so bad, since with a bit of visibility you could spot the creatures in your peripheral vision and so give them a wide berth. But at night you had to enter the water knowing you were going to be stung probably up to a dozen times and would spend the rest of the night picking tentacles out of your face with a tweezer while generously applying a vinegar ointment to soothe the pain.

How bad and how big were the stings? Well, the Scottish waters contain many different kinds of jellyfish, but my arch nemesis was the lion's mane jellyfish and the waters throughout the Hebrides were rife with them. Also called the giant jellyfish, they are the largest species of their kind known to man. The biggest recorded specimen was found washed up on the shore of Massachusetts Bay in 1870 and had a bell with a diameter of 2.3 m (7 ft 6 in) and tentacles 37 m (120 ft) long. They use their tentacles to sting, capture, pull in and eat prey such as fish, sea creatures and smaller jellyfish.

Thankfully I am none of the above, but as I swam at night I knew our paths would inevitably (and painfully) be doomed to cross. That's because lion's mane jellyfish remain mostly very near the surface and (like me) work with the ocean currents to travel great distances.

In other words, we were effectively sharing a swimming lane. What's worse is marine biologists off the coast told us they are most often spotted during the late summer and autumn, when they have grown to a large size. This meant our swimming lane would be crowded.

Finally, medical journals state there's a significant difference between touching a few tentacles with fingertips at a beach, and getting straight-up motorboated by one in the face. Experts warn that when stung by an entire jellyfish – including the inner tentacles, of which there can be over a thousand in number – a visit to the hospital is recommended because 'deep water severe stings can cause panic followed by drowning'.

But the worst thing about jellyfish is their behaviour is devoid of logic since they don't have a brain or central nervous system. Instead, they're equipped with a very basic set of nerves at the base of their tentacles which detect touch, temperature, salinity and (of course) my face.

My personal record was 22 stings straight to the face in a single night. Emerging from the water on that occasion, I could barely speak since I had been stung so many times in and around my mouth that my lips were numb. What's worse is I even got a tentacle directly in my left ear and now it felt like it was on fire from inside and out.

'Are you okay?' Matt shouted in my unstung (good) right ear.

'No. I got a wet willy from a jellyfish,' I said.

Trying not to laugh, Matt passed me some vinegar and bowl of warm water. Soaking a towel in the bowl, I then pressed it against my face to numb the pain.

Sitting there in silence, I was considering my options. It seemed the Scottish waters were lacking in basic rules. It's the wild, wild west of Britain and is entirely lawless, which makes combating an enemy that cannot think with any sort of logic virtually impossible.

'Okay, this sounds crazy,' Matt added before long. 'But while you were swimming we had an idea.'

I looked at him with my face smelling of vinegar and decorated with tentacles and assured him I was open to any and every suggestion that might help in the war against the lion's mane.

'We thought—,' he said, clearly apprehensive to tell me his plan.

'Yes?' I encouraged him to go on.

'—hmm ... that a well-fitted, rubber gimp mask might work?'

This was no joke. Yet as weird as it sounded, I did kind of see his logic. A gimp mask would fit around my face tightly enough to shield me from the jellyfish with a hole just big enough for my mouth to allow me to breathe. It was crazy, and with my waistcoat mankini it was bordering on perverted, but out here as I swam the jellyfish gauntlet, I didn't know what other options I had.

Matt continued, 'Our issue is there are not many shops in the Hebrides selling latex gimp masks and many of the online stores we rang won't deliver up here.' He sounded genuinely disappointed at the lack of support from Scottish sex shops in the highlands.

'But we did find a neoprene skull cap on board,' he said, handing it to me.

Like an ordinary swim cap, only larger, it covered more of the back of the head and neck and had a chin strap to keep it more secure. Matt then said we could turn it around (essentially wearing it the wrong way and backwards) and cut out holes from the fabric for my eyes, nose and mouth.

'That really could work,' I said laughing, but equally keen to try it.

Later that day I joined Matt in the galley with a pair of scissors and the neoprene skull cap, and we got to work. After an hour of careful tailoring around my nose, eyes and mouth, I emerged ready to swim the next tide looking like a low-budget masked superhero.

Standing on deck wearing my black sea scarf, greyish-black waistcoat mankini and now a black gimp mask, I looked like a cross between Cat Woman, Black Panther and Aquaman. But whether I liked it or not, this was now the uniform of the lesser known superhero, Rhino Neck.

Did it work? Amazingly, yes, as later that day I ploughed through the jellyfish armies of the Hebrides with lion's mane bouncing off my newly shielded face. Mile after mile passed and not only did I become accustomed to my new attire, I came to like it.

Matt really could invent anything from anything.

But from this day onwards, this is how we spent every day as a team. We would continually try to limit these limitations and research restrictions with the sole goal to swim as fast as possible, for as long as possible, with as few obstacles, issues and problems as possible.

RESEARCH RESTRICTIONS

Being mentally and physically tough is not enough to be truly resilient. You also have to be strategically strong and study your suffering. Based on the teachings of the psychobiological model of fatigue, 'Fatigue is a central brain perception, which is based on the sum of the sensory feedback from a variety of organs to the brain, and which is expressed physically as the alteration in pacing strategy (running, swimming or cycling speed) caused by a reduction in the muscle mass activated by the motor cortex in the brain.' This is according to Tim Noakes, a world-renowned authority on endurance performance in sport (and the scientist behind the central governor theory that we discussed earlier).

Put more simply, it's sensory feedback from the legs, lungs and heart that triggers our brain to slow us down and prevents us from reaching complete exhaustion and hurting ourselves. Research from the *British Journal of Sports Medicine* also states this feedback varies depending on the specific exercise, sport or adventure. 'The mechanisms of fatigue vary depending on the specific *exercise stressor* ... and fatigue varies with the type of exercise.'[83]

This is why it's not enough to be mentally and physically tough with a superhuman ability to tolerate pain and fatigue. You also need to be strategically strong to identify this sensory feedback and manage it before your body and brain shut down. As further studies from the *British Journal of Sports Medicine* found, 'Fatigue is the result of the complex interaction of physiological systems and the brain … all changes within the body act as *different signallers* which modulate control processes in the brain telling us to stop or slow down.'[84]

Therefore, the key to be strategically strong and resilient is managing the various exercise stressors so that they don't trigger signallers to tell the brain to stop or slow down. This is the only way to keep the brain happy while at the same time pushing as hard as is physically possible in your chosen sport. In keeping with our jellyfish example, this means being resilient is not about enduring the pain of a tentacle sting, it's about being wise and experienced enough to know how to avoid it.

How do we do this? You must limit limitations by researching restrictions. This is something we've known for years, since, although the ancient stoics weren't aware of the psychobiological model of fatigue, Marcus Aurelius was aware of our perception to pain and the need to limit limitations. He said, 'Whenever you suffer pain, keep in mind that it's nothing to be ashamed of and that it can't degrade your guiding intelligence, nor keep it from acting rationally and for the common good. And in most cases, you should be helped by the saying of Epicurus, that pain is never unbearable or unending, so you can remember these limits and not add to them in your imagination. Remember too that many common annoyances are pain in disguise, such as sleepiness, fever and loss of appetite.'

With this said, with each mile swum through the Hebrides came new reasons to quit as I encountered more and more stressors. Detailing each in my diary, I began researching each restriction which included (but was not limited to) the following:

- Pain
- Pacing
- Fear
- Food and Fuel
- Stress
- Sleep

LESSON 10

- Based on the teachings of the psychobiological model of fatigue, **fatigue is a central brain perception**, based on the sum of the sensory feedback from the legs, lungs and heart which triggers our brain to slow us down and prevents us from reaching complete exhaustion and hurting ourselves.
- This feedback varies depending on the specific exercise, sport or adventure. It was found that: 'The mechanisms of fatigue vary depending on the specific exercise stressor … and fatigue varies with the type of exercise.'
- This is why it's not enough to be mentally and physically tough with a superhuman ability to tolerate pain and fatigue. You also need to be strategically strong to identify this sensory feedback (resulting from that specific activity) and manage it before your body and brain shut down.
- How? **Limit limitations by researching restrictions**.

LESSON 11 | THE TWO WAYS TO PROCESS PAIN

Not all pain is bad, as it alerts us to danger.

Take running the jellyfish gauntlet, for example. When swimming at night I couldn't see anything when my face was under the water, so I had to rely on my perception of pain to show me the route that was the least densely populated with jellyfish.

If I swam on a particular path for an hour, received a slap-battering from jellyfish tentacles and my face was on fire, I would know that was a bad route to take and it was likely many more stings lay ahead. So I would change my plan of attack through the Hebrides. But if I swam for an hour sting-free, I would likely stay on that particular route.

The same is true of refining your technique too. Let's take running as a different example, since pain can alert you to dangerous forces. This helps you avoid bad movement patterns that may result in injury to the ligaments, tendons and muscle tissue and is why long-distance runners have inadvertently become leading experts in pain management.

Scientists claim that, 'Marathon runners have a reduced experience of pain compared with non-runners,'[85] while another study suggests, 'Low pain perception may predispose a person to become a long-distance runner.'[86] To put it simply, few sports involve such liberal doses of self-inflicted pain as marathon running.

Research published in *Pain: The Journal of the International Association for the Study of Pain* set out to analyse how ultra-marathon runners manage such hardship.[87] They studied 204 participants during 155-mile multistage run events across the desert and had the athletes provide data over five consecutive days on pain severity, pain interference, exertion and coping. What did they find?

- Participants reported spending about 30 per cent of their racing time thinking about pain.
- Their average pain levels were about 4 on a scale of 0–10.
- Successful athletes were more likely to use adaptive coping responses to pain.
- Unsuccessful athletes were more likely to use maladaptive coping responses to pain.

This last point was the most interesting. The term 'maladaptive' is defined as *not adjusting adequately or appropriately to the environment or situation*. Therefore, maladaptive coping strategies are associated with catastrophising pain. This is the tendency to describe an uncomfortable experience or sensation in more exaggerated terms than the average person. Athletes say things like, 'I cannot go on' or 'the pain is unbearable' and generally complain to themselves and others as a way of coping.

Somewhat unsurprisingly, science shows this is a bad idea. In fact, within this study it was shown that this coping mechanism increased pain sensitivity and reduced pain tolerance,[88] and meant runners spent more time dwelling on its impact on performance. This is why we didn't allow maladaptive coping strategies, and language associated with it, on the boat.

I wasn't tired from swimming 930 miles ... I was incredibly well practised and 'warmed up'.

I wasn't stung by jellyfish ... the jellyfish hugged my face.

I wasn't wearing a waistcoat mankini and gimp mask ... I was wearing an advanced form of sea swimming technology.

As a team, we were using an adaptive coping strategy for everything and anything. It didn't matter if we were tired, injured or ill, we would always accept the environment and our situation and ease our suffering by choosing a better mindset[89] that helped us manage the various 'exercise stressors' so that they don't trigger 'signallers' to tell the brain to 'stop or slow down.'

Even outside of sport, researchers studying patients with chronic pain conditions found adaptive coping strategies help 'to restore a sense of self-control over pain (and thus congruence with the situation).'[90]

One strategy that had always worked for me was humour.[91] For over ten years I had tried to smile, laugh and joke my way around marathons and long-distance swims, and the following story explains why.

SMILE WHEN YOU'RE SORE

It's 17 April 2008 and I am naked in the Amazon jungle. Sitting cross-legged on a fallen tree, the potent, psychedelic jungle drug known as ayahuasca[92] courses through my veins and I try to decide if the family of ants now circling my (ever nervous) genitalia are a real threat or just an hallucination. Deciding it was best not to find out, I cup my gentlemanly parts and move them back from the edge of the tree stump out of harm's way.

In most cultures, this would be considered odd. But this is deep in the Brazilian rainforest, my hosts are the Jaminawa tribe and they aren't 'most cultures'. A highly respected community of herbal spiritualists, they're said to have an understanding of fruits, flowers and plant-based drugs that's often beyond the comprehension of modern nutritional science.

To them this wasn't odd ... to them this was Tuesday. Performing the same ritual their ancestors had performed for hundreds of years to communicate with celestial supernatural forces (or the spirits of the jungle), there wasn't much they hadn't seen. Which is why out of the 24 Jaminawa men also in attendance and on their own spiritual journey, not one battered an eyelid or raised an eyebrow when I projectile-vomited my dinner across our campfire in twin steams that sprayed from my mouth and nose.

Apparently, it was perfectly normal. Apparently, this was known as the 'purge' and part of the healing process. So there I was, naked, intoxicated and embracing the exorcist-like convulsions starting in the depths of my bowels and reverberating through my body as the words of Henry David Thoreau played on repeat in my head:

'Not until we are lost do we begin to understand ourselves.'

An hour passed and my stomach was now empty. This meant my digestive system was granted a moment's peace before more ayahuasca was poured. Not entirely confident I was ready for round two, I did what any polite, travelling Englishman would do. I nodded when offered a second serving of psychedelic potion and thanked my hosts for their hospitality.

Needless to say, I would instantly regret being so English. As the cup touched my lips it was immediately obvious this was a stronger batch. Within minutes my tongue was entirely numb and I'd lost all sensation in my mouth which meant I no longer possessed the power of speech.

Now unable to voice my concern to everyone around our sick-soaked campfire, I had to sit there helpless as the trees overhead began to spin, the floor beneath my feet began to move and more ants circled my ever-nervous testicles.

I was in trouble.

What's worse is my senses began to wrestle with each other. I was hearing smells and seeing sounds and could no longer decide what was real and what was a figment of my ayahuasca-infused imagination. Dazed and confused, I looked up at the trees that towered above. Swaying in the wind their branches began to menacingly gesture in my direction as if they were angry with me. Also, the ruffling leaves began to sound like a thunderstorm forming directly over my head.

I wanted it to stop.

Thinking about those 'exercise stressors', I was overheating, hungry, dehydrated and my heart was beating impossibly fast for someone sitting around a campfire barely moving. The entire time this was happening, I looked across and noticed Tiago and Gabe (two of the younger tribe members) had found a bright blue Macaw feather and were taking it in turns to lick it and 'taste the colours'. Gesturing to me to try, I accepted in the hope it would make the jungle stop spinning.

It didn't. All I could taste was parrot bum.

Noticing I wasn't a fan of the feathered food like my Jaminawa brothers, Carlito – the most senior and respected elder in the entire tribe – came to my rescue. He was small with dark, tanned, leather-like skin. Wearing a smile and this intricate body paint, he was basically a miniature, naked, tattooed jungle genius and came complete with a small bag made of leaves that he wore on his shoulder.

Placing his wrinkled bum cheeks on the tree stump in front of mine, he cupped my face in the palm of his hands and inspected my dilated pupils and swollen tongue. Sensing my discomfort and inability to cope with the stifling heat and humidity, he then paused before deciding on the best remedy for my spiritual psychedelic journey.

Without saying a word, he placed his hand under his armpit, grabbed a handful of sweat from his fully-functioning Amazonian sweat glands and wiped it on my face to cool me down. He then reached into his bag and pulled out a handful of mint leaves for me to chew on.

To my surprise it worked. My senses were no longer wrestling with each other, but rather playing in the playground that was my minty mouth. Also, the previously angry winds had now turned into a light breeze which meant the trees no longer ominously gestured in my direction, but rather danced and played as the breeze cooled my now sweat-soaked forehead.

Life was good again, as the mint had helped me 'to restore a sense of self-control over pain (and thus congruence with the situation).'[93]

Hours passed, my stomach settled and I was then told the second part of the ceremony would begin. Unbeknown to me at the time, ayahuasca only forms the purging part of the ceremony. For the next phase, we would be tattooed in a semi-permanent paint and asked to climb a giant tree covered in gigantic fire ants.

The Jaminawa believe that after the ayahuasca you must pay a ceremonial penance of pain for your past wrongdoings. To this day, I'm not sure what 'wrongdoings' I had to repent for, but decided I wanted to leave the Amazon jungle with a squeaky-clean conscience so visited the Shamans who were doing the tattooing.

Joining the back of the queue, I stood with my friend Nick. He and I had travelled together to over eight countries in eight months and had the battle scars to prove it. Battered and bruised from herding bulls in Ecuador and bitten by sharks in the Bahamas, no matter how painful or uncomfortable the situation was, we always used humour as an adaptive coping strategy, often at each other's expense.

This is why months before when reindeer herding during the Siberian winter, Nick agreed to hold the reins of my small herd while I went behind a tree to relieve myself. I thought he was being kind, but it turns out Nick knew that reindeer consider urine-soaked snow a delicacy ... almost like a flavoured snow cone.

Waiting until my pants were down, he then released the reins and laughed hysterically as five large reindeer came running towards me. Still peeing, I then tried running away in 3 ft deep snow with my trousers around my ankles while vowing that one day I would get my retribution.

Well, unbeknown to Nick, today was that day at the Shaman tattoo parlour.

He was summoned first. Watching on, I saw five Shamans in total draw these incredible and intricate designs all over his body. The body paint was a thick, black resin made from the fruit of the Genipapo tree. Obviously, it was an honour to witness this (having only previously read about the ceremonies and rituals) but I also sensed I might never get this opportunity again.

As Nick stood there with his arms out and eyes shut, entirely engrossed in the ceremony, I silently crept up behind him and quietly gestured to the chief tattooist asking if I could try. Handed a paintbrush, I then proceeded to draw a giant penis on Nick's back.

The Jaminawa immediately saw what it was and burst out laughing. Sensing what I'd just drawn, Nick turned around.

'It's a penis, isn't it?'

I nodded and told him I'd have my revenge.

'Well played, sir,' he said, and with that we were even.

Now, was it immature? Yes. Was it funny? Yes (even the Jaminawa appreciated my artwork). Lastly, did it help? Absolutely. Bearing in mind that minutes later, Nick and I were both climbing trees covered in fire ants in a ceremonial penance of pain for past wrongdoings.

The task proved difficult at first, since the trunk of the tree was so thick (almost a metre in circumference) and it had very few branches or footholds to grip. As a result, I had to grip the trunk in a bear-hug motion and inch my way up slowly, which was painful as I lost layers of skin from the tree bark. In the meantime, my body became engulfed in ants that were now biting with such ferocity to show I wasn't welcome.

After another three metres or so the ants sensed I wasn't slowing so began attacking my face and neck, turning my cheeks a bright red colour. This is because the venom of fire ants is mainly composed of oily alkaloids mixed with a small amount of toxic proteins which creates a painful burning sensation that's swiftly followed by a rash.

But do you know what made this whole penance of pain easier? Humour and the giant phallic masterpiece painted on Nick's back.

Now I don't make a habit of embarking on Shamanic rituals and nor do I claim to fully understand them, but I do know that on that day this strange form of 'comedic-psycho-spiritual' mastery of discomfort worked,[94] and as I turned to Carlito he too was giggling and seemed to approve.

This probably explains why ever since my time in the Amazon, humour has always been my default adaptive coping mechanism for pain.

But it's not always possible to 'swim with a smile' and sometimes there would be a second coping strategy that I would employ ... but cautiously and only in extreme circumstances. A powerful animal-istic mechanism used by injured animals, it's a concept which scientists call 'stress-induced analgesia' and is something I learned from a great explorer, adventurer and one of Britain's most celebrated soldiers, Ant Middleton.

STRESS-INDUCED ANALGESIA

The date was 23 May 2018 and a week before we were due to begin the Great British Swim.

The boat was now packed. My body was prepped and well trained. Finally, the tides and times had been calculated with military precision. Therefore, when considering the framework of Stoic Sports Science, I already had:

- A Strong Body
- A Strategic Plan

But I knew the stoic mind needed some refining. I wanted to pre-empt how to limit limitations before I was confronted with fatigue, pain and discomfort and my body's innate, inbuilt self-preservation mechanism (psychobiological model of fatigue) and desire to slow down or stop (to maintain safe homeostasis).

Fortunately, I had Ant Middleton to call on for help. One of Britain's new breed of explorers, he was a great training partner, a brilliant mentor in the military mindset, but above all else he was an even better friend. But the reason his advice would be so valuable is because he had just returned from a mountaineering expedition to Everest.

But he didn't just summit Everest, he survived it. Caught in one of the worst reported storms of the year – which claimed the lives of even the most experienced Sherpas – Ant spent an unprecedented 21 hours with no sleep, food, water or oxygen in the 'death zone'. This was after the crossing at the Hillary Step became impassable and mountaineers froze (literally and figuratively) to the edge of the cliff face.

He told me, 'It was a cocktail of disasters you couldn't prepare for. There was a queue of around 10 other climbers ahead of me, waiting to descend, when an unforeseen storm with 70 mph winds and a total white-out hit us, people were getting blown off the mountain and you could hear others panicking and screaming, "Get off the mountain, you're going to die."'

The 'death zone' is a term used to describe the area at high altitude where there is not enough available oxygen for humans to breathe. This is usually above 8,000 m (26,247 ft) and since the Hillary Step sits at 8,790 m (28,839-ft) above sea level, it's not surprising this part of Everest has claimed the lives of over 200 climbers. Whether this is through direct causes (loss of vital functions) or indirect (reduced cognitive functioning leading to accidents), the human body simply cannot survive for extended periods of time here, and without supplementary oxygen the result is a deterioration of bodily functions, loss of consciousness and, ultimately, death.

At 8,790 m above sea level, Ant was painfully aware of this and was snow-blind in one eye trying to navigate his way down. Worth noting is that Ant is part of a rare breed of British soldier. Serving with the Special Boat Service (SBS), the Royal Marines and 9 Parachute Squadron Royal Engineers (RE), he achieved the holy trinity of the UK's Elite Forces training (P Company, Commando Course, UK Special Forces). Fortunately for him, many of the skills he used that day would have been so well-drilled and so deeply engrained that they were almost automatic.

One thing he credits for his survival was his animalistic way of coping with pain. 'I ran out of oxygen eventually. For a brief moment, I definitely considered throwing myself off the mountain to die, rather than perishing slowly without air, but I pulled myself together. I told myself, "Ant, get a grip and practise what you preach. You're the only person who can rescue you." You go into fight-or-flight mode and fortunately, I chose the former.'

Basically, at that moment in time Ant was describing an extreme version of the psychobiological model of fatigue. Sensory feedback from the legs, lungs, heart and every other part of his body was signalling to the brain to shut down all systems as the 'exercise stressors' went into meltdown.[95]

But instead of shutting down, he invoked a kind of 'stress-induced analgesia.'[96] More commonly associated with injured animals who (during stressful situations) are able to function without feeling pain, this explains why an injured lion will fight to the death even when bitten, injured and surrounded by a pack of hyenas, since the adrenal glands powerfully pump hormones into his bloodstream to sharpen the senses, focus the mind and numb the body to any sense of pain.

'We conclude that the functional advantage of a reduction of pain during stressful situations is significant because it allows the animal to react in threatening and perhaps critical situations as if there were no pain. Once the pain system is inhibited, other systems modulate and mediate adaptive responses that expedite the survival of the animal.'[97] So according to this journal article from the American Physiological Society, Ant essentially battled the psychobiological model of fatigue and won.

Sadly, others did not that day.

What he told me the following week (one week before my swim) had a sobering effect on me. He said, 'Some people just ran out of oxygen and one of the people that I went past was a Sherpa. I saw that he had no oxygen and then, just by his reaction, telling me that he wanted to go to sleep, that he didn't want to move, I knew that he had gone way past that stage of trying to save himself and he had gone into that stage of his body shutting down.'

He added, 'There was no way we were going to drag him off the mountain because obviously we're suffering ourselves. When I tried to pull him down, he shrugged my arm off, told me that he was "sleeping". He then curled up in a ball and I knew that was it for him.'

Ant then looked me dead in the eyes. Knowing me well, he knew that smiling was my default coping mechanism, but he taught me (and warned me) to add another method to my arsenal since he was aware I was about to embark on 1,780 miles of hell and high water.

'It will be less about swimming and more about surviving,' he warned.

His final words were to use this powerful, primitive mechanism of stress-induced analgesia sparingly, since when you understand the science of invoking your fight-or-flight mode, you understand it comes at a cost that entirely alters your biochemistry. Emerging from my Scottish Hebrides adventure, I would come to understand what that cost was.

LESSON 11

- Studies suggests low pain perception may predispose a person to become good at long-distance events.
- **Adaptive coping strategies** (adjusting to the environment or situation) can help to restore a sense of self-control over pain.
- **Humour** can be a default adaptive coping mechanism for pain.
- Another powerful and primitive form of pain suppression is **stress-induced analgesia**. Much as an injured lion will fight to the death when surrounded by a pack of hyenas, we humans have this in-built self-preservation mechanism where the adrenal glands pump hormones into the bloodstream to sharpen the senses, focus the mind and numb the body to any sense of pain.

LESSON 12 | COMBAT FEAR WITH 'FERAL FEAR THEORY'

The Summer Isles

LOCATION: The Summer Isles
DISTANCE COVERED: 960 miles
DAYS AT SEA: 81

It is 21 August and we've arrived in the Summer Isles. Consisting of about 20 islands, rocks and islets (islands that are so small they serve no real purpose), it's a place that can only be described as a rough, jagged and wild oasis that's tucked away within one of the untouched corners of western Scotland. Human sightings are rare in these parts as many of the islands have remained uninhabited since the eighteenth century when Tanera Mor, the largest island, proudly stood as the centre of a thriving herring fishing industry.

But today the fishing empires are a distant memory. Instead, the archipelago is the battleground for the most epic game of 'hide and seek' between man, storm and sea. A brooding storm has arrived from Iceland and its 40 mph Arctic winds are smashing into the cliffs with such force that the sea mist is sandblasting the granite stone, which means we're unable to stay (and sleep) at sea between swims.

As a result, we're having to swim. Record the point where we stop. Rush to safety and seek refuge among the summer isles. Wait until the storm has abated. Then return to our waypoint to start the next swim from exactly the same spot.

This 'game' had been going on for the past 48 hours, but as the storm continued to rage we were running out of places to hide as the huge Atlantic swells meant anchoring had progressed from tricky to outright impossible. Therefore, with no logical harbours among the abandoned islands, rocks and caves, every mile swam was precious progress, since as a crew we knew we wouldn't be allowed to rest or relax until we made it around the most northwesterly point in mainland Britain known as Cape Wrath that was now 40 (storm-riddled) miles away from our location.

During every sunset and sunrise, I swam. Sleep deprived, tormented by the storm and removed from civilisation, my head began to go to some pretty weird places. Maybe it was the salt water or maybe it was the 81 days of sensory deprivation, but with every ripple of the water and shadowy shape on the sea's surface I began to develop a sense I wasn't alone in the Summer Isles.

Someone (or something) was sharing my 'swimming lane' with me.

By 8.00 p.m. my suspicion had turned to unease. As the mist descended and the sun set, we could see (and smell) a rotting corpse on the nearby island of Glas-leac Beag; possibly a sheep, but more likely a seal, we couldn't be sure, since it had decayed beyond recognition.

Continuing to swim into the night, I began to think of the Jaminawa and how the great Shaman elders had relied on the guidance, wisdom and symbolism of spirit animals for thousands of years.

Scotland was of course thousands of miles away from the Amazon jungle, but out here in the wild waters west of Britain I began to think symbolism might be all I had and concluded a decaying seal/sheep corpse might not be a good sign.

But stopping was never an option and progress was always paramount. So, with every breath and every stroke I continued to look for something else that could provide some form of comfort. A pod of dolphins would be great and a majestic sea eagle would be brilliant, but in desperation I would even take a lone sea otter right now.

Moments later, Scotland delivered something I wasn't expecting, in the form of a 5 m (17 ft) long basking shark. The second-largest living species in the water (after the whale shark) he was a greyish-brown colour with mottled skin and had decided to pay me a visit to see what this strange human was doing swimming in a storm, as he floated along the surface dining out on plankton with its gigantic mouth, conical snout and hundreds of teeth. Fortunately for me, Englishmen were not on the menu of this particular species of shark.

Hours passed as he watched me and I watched him. We floated north and spent the evening together as one of the strangest pairings Scotland had ever seen. The entire time we shared a weird, unspoken understanding that we were both just grateful for the company, since I imagine this corner of the Highlands can often get quite lonely even for a 5 m basking shark.

Maybe, just maybe, he too didn't like the thought of being stuck out here on his own in a storm. I knew I wasn't. So together (under the protection of Captain Matt and the crew) we navigated our way around headlands, rocks and islands.

Now your head can play tricks on you after almost three months of swimming at sea, but I began to think me and my new friend weren't too different. In fact, I wasn't too different from all the wildlife in Scotland, from the osprey circling in the sky to the highland cow grazing on the moors. Our brains process fear, danger and stress in very similar ways. For that reason, in the Summer Isles I developed what I call 'feral fear theory' which is our primitive form of programming fear.

'FERAL FEAR THEORY'

We humans still process fear in a very animalistic, primitive way. Yes, we now understand this far better than our cavemen ancestors. Yet our brains are still wired to cope with fear in exactly the same way as our forefathers who relied on their inbuilt fight-or-flight response to escape an angry sabre-toothed tiger.

But today there aren't many angry sabre-toothed tigers. So the challenge that faces us modern humans is ensuring we can elicit fight or flight depending on the situation we face. Basically, we need to exercise some control over our animalistic brains. To understand how to do this, we must understand the concept of 'feral fear theory' which is composed of:

- Fight-or-Flight Response
- Habituation of Stress
- Stress-Inoculation Training
- Stress-Induced Analgesia

Essentially, this was my operating system to manage fear.

FIGHT OR FLIGHT/SINK OR SWIM

The term 'fight or flight' was first used by used by the American physiologist Walter Cannon (the same genius who pioneered our understanding of homeostasis). It's also known as hyperarousal, or

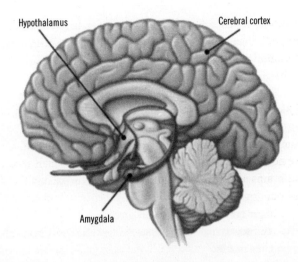

the acute stress response, and is a physiological reaction that occurs when there's a threat to our survival. Cannon's theory stated way back in 1915 that during any stressful situation a cocktail of stress hormones is released into the body to bring about well-orchestrated physiological changes that for years have ensured our survival.

These physiological changes range from our hearts beating faster to our muscles becoming flooded with hormones that prime us for either fight or flight (or in my case sink or swim).Ultimately, we are physiologically prepped and ready for danger.

This all begins in the brain (see above) that manages a carefully orchestrated (near-instantaneous) sequence of hormonal changes that works like this:

- Our eyes and ears send information to the amygdala. This is an area of the brain that contributes to emotional processing that we're in trouble.
- The amygdala then decides if we're in real danger.

- If we are, it sends a distress signal to the hypothalamus. This is the area of the brain which functions like a command centre that prepares the body through the nervous system for fight or flight.
- It does this by sending a signal to the adrenal glands.
- These glands respond by pumping the hormone epinephrine (also known as adrenaline) into the bloodstream. As epinephrine circulates through the body, it brings on a number of physiological changes:
  - The heart beats faster than normal.
  - It pushes blood to the muscles, heart and other vital organs.
  - Pulse rate and blood pressure go up.
  - The person undergoing these changes also starts to breathe more rapidly.
  - Small airways in the lungs open wide to take in more oxygen.
  - Extra oxygen is sent to the brain, increasing alertness.
  - Sight, hearing and other senses become sharper.
  - Blood sugar (glucose) floods into the bloodstream to supply energy to the body.

All of these changes happen so quickly that people aren't aware of them. In fact, the wiring is so efficient that the amygdala and hypothalamus start this cascade even before the brain's visual centres have had a chance to fully process what is happening. That's why people are able to jump out of the path of an oncoming car even before they think about what they are doing.

As the initial surge of epinephrine subsides, the hypothalamus activates the second component of the stress response system, known as the HPA axis. This network consists of the hypothalamus, the pituitary gland and the adrenal glands. The HPA axis relies on a series of hormonal signals to keep the sympathetic nervous system – the 'gas pedal' – pressed down. If the brain continues to perceive something as dangerous, adrenal glands are prompted to release cortisol. The body therefore stays revved up and on high alert, and only when the threat passes will cortisol levels start to fall.

All of these physiological and hormonal responses are therefore needed and are partly the reason we have survived as a species. But science teaches us we can also overreact to stressors that are not life-threatening and that don't require this carefully orchestrated (near-instantaneous) sequence of hormonal changes.

For example, while sitting at your desk being stressed about work, it's unlikely you would need the sequence of hormonal changes described above in the same way your ancestor running from a mountain lion did.

This can then result in a suppressed immune system,[98] depression,[99] poor sleep and recovery,[100] and has been linked to a whole other list of diseases.[101] Which is exactly why we modern humans must keep our fight-or-flight response in check.

This was particularly important for me during my swim. I simply couldn't afford to send my fight-or-flight response into overdrive every time I came across a stressful situation, since in reality the entire swim was stressful. That is why I had to learn the Habituation of Stress.

HABITUATION OF STRESS

We first came across this in Lesson 5. Habituation is a psychological learning process where there is a decrease in response to a stimulus after being repeatedly exposed to it. It sounds complicated, but it's not. It means any stressor you're exposed to (whether it be psychological or physiological) provokes a stress response. However, the more times you're exposed to it the less stressful it becomes.

It was first described in a landmark paper by R F Thompson and W A Spencer in 1966 entitled, 'Habituation: A model phenomenon for the study of neuronal substrates of behaviour'[102] but has since been expanded upon to find habituation causes a variety of responses in the body and mind that can influence behaviour.

One of these responses is related to our fight-or-flight response and the release of hormones, since it has been known that, 'The magnitude of hypothalamic–pituitary–adrenal (HPA) activation occurring in response to a stressor declines with repeated exposure to that same stressor.'[103] This explains why scientists found karate fighters with three years of experience had a greater control over their stress hormone release compared to untrained subjects. Researchers found, 'Long-term karate practice is associated with a significant modulation of stress hormones.'[104]

Worth noting is these are only preliminary results and while some studies show most people's stress response decreases the more times they're exposed to something psychologically stressful, for some, it does not change or even increases. This is largely based on your *subjective* evaluation of the situation, sport or adventure and the level of stress.[105]

> 'The latest studies indicate that the neuroendocrine response to competition depends more on subjective factors related to the cognitive evaluation of the situation.'
> NEUROSCIENCE & BIOBEHAVIOURAL REVIEWS (2005)

Let's take skydiving as an example. Research published in *Frontiers in Human Neuroscience* stated that, 'It is uncertain whether stress reactivity habituates to this stressor given that skydiving remains a risky, life-threatening challenge with every jump despite experience.'[106] But it went on to say, 'Results suggest that experience may modulate the coordination of emotional response with cortisol reactivity to skydiving,' and, 'Alters the individual's engagement of the hypothalamic–pituitary–adrenal axis.'

Just like the experienced karate practitioners mentioned before, this partly explains why I felt perfectly at home swimming in a storm in the Summer Isles with a giant basking shark for company. I wasn't brave or courageous, I was simply habituated to this specific form of stress. Partly, because I'd been living at sea for over 87 days, and most recently swimming against Arctic winds in Scotland and through constantly changing tides. But also, because controlling your fight-or-flight response is a necessity when diving with sharks who are very aware when you're stressed and your heart is beating faster and breathing is elevated.

STRESS-INOCULATION TRAINING

It's 20 May 2008 off the coast of the Bahamas. I am a trainee shark wrangler and currently have over a hundred of them circling me as I float on the ocean bed watching my mentor feed, study and inspect each one. His name was Jeremiah Sullivan and, fortunately for me, he was one of the world's leading shark experts.

Holding a bait box full of fish, Jeremiah was feeding them one by one and attracting most of the attention as some of the sharks jostled for position in an attempt to jump the dinner queue. Standing a few metres away, I had a job that was much simpler: watch and observe while remembering my training to control my fight-or-flight response. Otherwise the sharks would be very aware I was stressed, as their super-sensitive electro-sensory organs would pick up that my heart was beating faster and that I didn't belong at their dinner table with them.

After another 15 minutes, dinner time was over. Jeremiah was out of food; the sharks were happy and my training had worked. Again, was this because I was so brave that my heartbeat barely registered with the sharks? No, it was because I was able to regulate my stress response through 'stress-inoculation training'.

A training method used to enhance performance under stress, it's commonly used in physically and psychologically intense roles like firefighting and law enforcement where failure can have tragic consequences. It's become increasingly popular in recent years, especially within the military, as it's far more cost effective to create better soldiers than it is to create better equipment.[107] Equally, the most high-tech equipment in the world is only ever as good as the person using it.[108] Hence, why modern-day stress-inoculation training has been neatly categorised into three stages:

Phase 1: Conceptual Education

In the first phase, athletes are taught the types of skills needed to optimise performance under stress. This can include control of your fight-or-flight response, energy/arousal control[109] and confidence building relating to that specific activity. This is why long before I joined the sharks for dinner, Jeremiah took me to shallow water and taught me how to dive wearing protective chainmail, how to breath in an armoured face mask and also a kind of water jiu-jitsu needed to wrestle with sharks.

Phase 2: Skills Acquisition and Consolidation

In the second phase, the skills are drilled and practised more. The goal is to make the movements automatic, quick and accurate. So much so, a person should be able to do them automatically, quickly, accurately, and perhaps even while paying attention to something else. Since they don't have to consciously think, they can just do them intuitively.[110] Jeremiah was the perfect example of this. Watching him dive, I saw that every movement was made up of an integrated, subconscious sequence that processed faster than conscious thought.[111] In comparison, I needed reminding and prompting to control my breathing and buoyancy and the sea life were very aware that I was a trainee still far from graduating.

Phase 3: Application and Follow-Through

The final phase requires all of the above with more stress, complexity, intensity and volume. During this stage, it is important to retain all the skills you've learnt (especially managing the stress response). Obviously, Jeremiah didn't want to throw me in at the deep end, and adding sharks was a big jump between phases 2 and 3. That's why the day before my maiden voyage with sharks, he arranged a special kind of dive.

He told me we were exploring a shipwreck and tasked me with remembering a specific code that would unlock a safe located somewhere on board. My job was to remember the code, retrieve what was inside and return to the surface. Or at least that's what I thought.

Little did I know this was *not* the test.

After finding the safe I knelt down and began unlocking the padlock. Carefully turning the dial to match the digits I had memorised, I was so intent on remembering the code that I failed to acknowledge Jeremiah and two of his friends were hiding inside the shipwreck and about to jump out at me and replicate a shark attack.

As I entered the final number, they sprung their attack. Now 40 m below the surface, my mask was ripped from my face so I was semi-blind. Then my regulator was pulled from my mouth so I was without an air supply. Next, my tank was spun upside down and I was (literally) kicked and punched to further hurt and disorientate. At one point, I think someone even bit my leg.

But amid the punching and biting I remembered my training. I calmly looked for my secondary mask and regulator and turned my tank the right way around. Now with the ability to see, I was able to defend myself marginally better from the peppering of punches still being thrown my way. After another 40 seconds, the onslaught stopped and my training was complete.

Years later and in many ways the entire Great British Swim was a form of stress-inoculation training that enabled me to moderate my fight-or-flight response by habituating stress, which meant I kept my immune system intact and was able to sleep and recover sufficiently.

But no amount of stress-inoculation training could prepare me for what was next.

LESSON 12

- As humans we still tend to process fear in a very animalistic, primitive way. We need to manage our internal operating system by understanding the concept of **feral fear**.
- During any stressful situation **a cocktail of stress hormones is released into the body** to bring about well-orchestrated physiological changes, from our hearts beating faster to our muscles becoming flooded with hormones, that prime us for either **fight or flight** and help ensure our survival.
- You can regulate your response to stress through **stress-inoculation training**. Commonly used in firefighting and law enforcement professions, this multi-phase programming involves skills acquisition and consolidation, energy control and confidence building, and stress-testing in real-time situations.

LESSON 13 | LEARN THE POWER OF A HIGHER PURPOSE

Cape Wrath

LOCATION: Cape Wrath
DISTANCE COVERED: 1,010 miles
DAYS AT SEA: 83

It's 23 August and we have Cape Wrath in our sights. After 83 days and 1,000 miles, we were finally approaching the most northwesterly point of mainland Great Britain. But it had taken its toll. Swimming in what can only be described as majestic bleakness, we hadn't seen a human in days and as I turned to breathe all I could see were the mountain peaks that plunged into the sea below and desolate highlands decorated with a few lonely sheep.

But with every arm stroke my goal was clear: to swiftly sneak around Cape Wrath. I say 'swiftly sneak' because not only does Cape Wrath represent the most northwesterly point of our journey, it also represents where:

- The Atlantic Ocean and the North Sea powerfully collide to create some of the world's most dangerous sailing (and swimming) conditions.
- The Ministry of Defence (ever since 1933) use it for naval gunfire practice and for army artillery and mortar range firing.

What's worse, the coastguard would later tell me it's the only place in the Northern Hemisphere where NATO forces combine land, air and sea capabilities in assault mode for training manoeuvres, deploying bombs of up to 1,000 lb (450 kg), and where winds as high as 140 mph (230 km/h) have been recorded at Cape Wrath lighthouse.

Although exhausted, you can understand why me, Matt and the entire team were desperate to make it around and over the top of Scotland. But navigation wasn't just hard, it was outright dangerous.

Swimming between the Outer Hebrides and mainland Scotland, there is nowhere to hide from the winds and waves, and all I could see was infinite sea and sky. Matt would spend hours in the boat's galley researching tidal charts and coastal maps, and I would swim for hours in the sea hoping they were right.

Our only issue was that all advice from the North of Scotland sailing authorities related to sailing boats. Because no one had ever swum around Great Britain before, there was no best practice when passing Cape Wrath in a pair of goggles. This is why one manual reads, 'The dangerous seas, violent waves and strong tidal races around Cape Wrath should be avoided by small craft at all costs.'

Reading the warning, Matt and I weren't sure if I qualified as a 'small craft'.

Another sailing manual states, 'A good engine is needed since there are many places where swell from the Atlantic or North Sea can contribute to dangerous sea conditions, or penetrate to some of the anchorages.'

(Again) I'd been swimming for 83 days, so at this point Matt and I weren't sure if I had a 'good engine' anymore. But one thing we knew for sure, we'd come too far to quit now. Some way and somehow, we would swim around Cape Wrath.

Swimming with the words of Ant Middleton (and the lessons of Everest) playing on repeat in my head, I was fuelled by a kind of 'feral fortitude'. I was trying my best to override the exercise stressors, which were signalling me to stop or slow down, by managing my very basic primitive needs of food, water, warmth, rest and safety.

Essentially, psychologists would say I was at the very bottom of my human needs. This is based on the pioneering work of Abraham Maslow, an American psychologist who created a theory of psychological health predicated on fulfilling innate human needs in priority, culminating in self-actualisation (fulfilling one's potential). It became known as Maslow's Hierarchy of Needs and it looks like this:

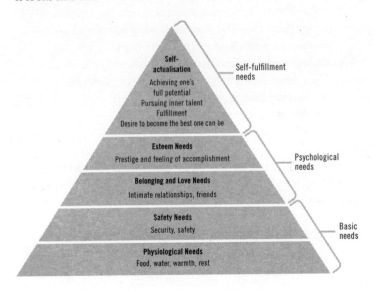

Human needs are depicted as five hierarchical levels within a pyramid, covering from base to apex:

- **Physiological needs.** These are biological requirements for human survival. Examples include oxygen, food, water, shelter, clothing, warmth and sleep, and if these needs are not satisfied the human body cannot function optimally. Maslow considered physiological needs the most important as all the other needs become secondary until these needs are met.
- **Safety needs.** For me this meant protection from the wind, waves, tides and cold, but in the broader sense this can mean security in the form of law, order and freedom from fear.
- **Belongingness and Love needs.** Only after physiological and safety needs have been fulfilled, the third level of human needs is social and involves feelings of belongingness. The need for interpersonal relationships motivates behaviour. Examples include friendship, intimacy, trust and acceptance, receiving and giving affection and love. Essentially, being part of a group whether that is family, friends, crew or a team.
- **Esteem needs.** Maslow classified these into two categories:
  - Esteem for oneself (dignity, achievement, mastery, independence).
  - The desire for reputation or respect from others (e.g., status, prestige).

Maslow indicated that the need for respect or reputation is most important for children and adolescents and precedes real self-esteem or dignity.

- **Self-Actualisation needs.** Realising personal potential, self-fulfilment and seeking personal growth. A desire 'to become everything one is capable of becoming'.

Right now, I was only concerned with my *physiological needs*, because for the past 83 days and 1,000 miles I had been functioning at the very bottom of Maslow's hierarchy. Battling hypothermia and full-blown fatigue, I was only able to operate at the base of the pyramid.

But one phone call was about to change all that.

BAD WEATHER AND BAD NEWS

I'm often asked, 'What was the hardest part of the swim?' Certainly, the tentacle-tickling incident in the Corryvreckan was no picnic. Equally, dodging giant French cargo ships when seasick in Dover was not something I wanted to repeat. But the worst part of the entire swim (up until this moment) was at 3.00 p.m. on 23 August and took place within the four walls of my cabin aboard the boat.

After a big 15-mile swim we had put ourselves within touching distance of Cape Wrath which was now only five miles away. Sitting on the horizon almost daring us to swim around it, the tide had changed so Matt and I decided to drop anchor. Rest. Eat. Then launch a swimming assault in six hours when the tide was running in our favour again.

Our theory was that if we timed it right, we could break through the strong tides where the Atlantic and the North Sea converge. Then we would 'ride' the compressed currents that come rushing through the Outer Hebrides as they become squeezed and funnelled into the Pentland Firth (along the top of Scotland) where tidal flows reach 12 knots between Duncansby Head and South Ronaldsay. If this worked, I would be shot across the top of Scotland like a slingshot. If it failed, I would be spat back out and heading across the Atlantic to America.

The Scottish coastline wasn't going to make it easy for us either. Although the powerful tides were in our favour, the winds were not, hence a 'wind over tide' situation (wind travelling in the opposite direction to the tide which we first encountered when we entered the Irish Sea), creating dangerous conditions for 'small craft' like me.

But that day, piled-up waves were the least of my concerns. This is because while looking through my cabin's porthole at Cape Wrath, I got a phone call from my older brother, Scott. He told me he was at the hospital with my mum, after dad had been rushed in for treatment.

'Sorry I had to be the one to tell you this,' he said. Immediately, I feared the worst.

'It's Dad. He's been sick since you started the swim, but he didn't want to tell you because he didn't want you worrying about him.'

'What do you mean sick?' I asked.

Scott then paused for what may have only been a split second, but which felt like an eternity.

'He's got an aggressive form of cancer,' he said.

His words evoked a visceral reaction deep in my stomach. Feeling physically sick, I then instantly substituted despair for anger and an immediate need for answers and solutions. As I hurled questions down the phone, Scott did his best to calm me down.

In that moment, storms and dangerous currents no longer mattered. Physically I was fine and the remaining mileage actually seemed doable. But news of my dad's health felt like I'd been punched in the stomach and run over by that French cargo ship. This is why my first thought was to cancel the swim and return to land so I could be with him and the family.

I wasn't thinking clearly. I had forgotten everything I had learned about stoicism and being mentally tough and was now purely thinking through emotionally charged reflexive reactions rather than logic.

Fortunately, my dad wasn't. The most stoically strong man I've ever known, for over 32 years he'd been my compass of common sense and now (miles away from home) it was no different. Dad knew exactly how I'd react and so from his hospital bed he'd told Scott to remind me that I vowed not to step foot on land until I had circumnavigated Britain. Thinking logically and rationally, he then also reminded Scott his immunotherapy treatment didn't start for another few weeks, so even if I did arrive on land there wasn't anything I could do to help.

'You know he's right,' said Scott after relaying Dad's instructions.

I sat in silence, unable to speak and feeling utterly helpless. With the phone pressed against my ear, minutes passed as the waves crashed into the side of the boat as a constant reminder that I was miles away from home. Scott then handed the phone to Mum, hoping she'd be able to make me see sense.

'Dad has asked if you can make him a promise,' she said.

'Of course,' was my immediate reply.

'You have to promise you will come home ... but *only* via the beach at Margate once you've finished what you started. Promise?'

As a dutiful son, I promised.

In that moment I realised what my dad was doing (and saying). He selflessly wanted me to ascend Maslow's Hierarchy of Needs since he knew finishing the swim would mean I'd begin operating within my 'self-fulfilment needs' (becoming the most I could be and achieving my full potential).

This of course didn't make the news any easier to accept, but from his hospital bed, in the face of sheer adversity, he still wanted me to realise the Power of Seeking a Higher Purpose.

I thanked Scott for being there for Dad when I couldn't be, and told my mum I loved her very much and would be home as fast as the waves, tides and my own limbs would allow. I then sat in my cabin staring at Cape Wrath in the distance.

Suddenly, there was a knock on my cabin door. It was Matt who'd come to check I was okay to swim again in a few hours. Unable to keep any secrets from him or the team, I told him the bad news and the promise I'd made, and then continued peering out of the port-hole.

Taking a seat on the bottom step of the ladder, Matt paused to consider his response carefully. This is because after 83 days and over 1,000 miles he had witnessed me go through almost every human emotion possible, but he also knew this one was very different. After a few more moments, he broke the silence in a way only he knew how.

'Cape Wrath has been a pivotal point of nautical navigation throughout history. In fact, even the name "Cape Wrath" comes from the Norse word *hvarf*, meaning "turning point", as this was the point that Viking warships used to turn east for home.'

I smiled, I knew exactly what he was saying.

'The tide changes in five hours,' Matt continued, now standing up from the ladder's step. 'I know the North of Scotland sailing authority states dangerous seas, violent waves and strong tidal races should be avoided by small craft, but you're not a 'small craft'. You're a Viking warship making your way home to fulfil a promise made to your dad.'

I nodded. Cape Wrath now had new meaning for me.

Fuelled by a deep-rooted determination to get home, I no longer saw 10 ft waves crashing into the famous lighthouse that's stood there since 1828 as limitations or restrictions. Instead, I saw a giant signpost (and Viking 'turning point') signalling the way home.

From that day on, I understood the *Power of a Higher Purpose* and began swimming according to the top of Maslow's Hierarchy of Needs.

LESSON 13

- Medical science shows us that **psychological health** is predicated on fulfilling innate human needs in priority, known as **Maslow's Hierarchy of Needs**.
- From most to least important, these needs are:
- **physiological** (need for food, water, oxygen, sleep, for example);
    - o **safety** (security in the form of law, order and freedom from fear);
    - o **belongingness and love** (friendship, intimacy, trust and acceptance, receiving and giving affection);
    - o **esteem** (for dignity, achievement, status); and
    - o **self-actualisation** (realising personal potential, self-fulfilment).
- Understanding the **Power of a Higher Purpose** can help you overcome restrictions or limitations and bring a new meaning to your challenge.

LESSON 14 | ACCEPT THE UNCONTROLLABLES

John o'Groats

LOCATION: John o' Groats
DISTANCE COVERED: 1,100 miles
DAYS AT SEA: 90

It's 1.30 p.m. on 29 August and we've arrived at John o' Groats. Known for being Britain's most northeasterly point, this was a MONUMENTAL moment in the swim and the media knew it too. Within minutes of passing this tiny Highland village my phone (and the boat's radio) practically blew up with requests from journalists who'd been tracking our progress since we passed England's most southeasterly point over 60 days before.

The journey from Land's End to John o' Groats (known as LEJOG) is a sacred and famous one here in Britain, with cyclists, runners and walkers attempting the 874 mile (1,407 km) route like a modern version of an Okugake. Worth noting is the record to cycle this route is 41 hours, 4 minutes and 22 seconds, and the record to run is 9 days, 2 hours and 27 minutes.

But swimming by sea I can confirm it takes a little longer ... 61 days to be exact. Which in comparison seemed painfully slow, but we were later told we had accidentally more than halved the previous LEJOG swimming record of 135 days. I say 'accidentally' since, while this record was nice, I was never trying to break it. Instead, the relentless pace we'd set as a team was necessary in a bid to make it around the top of Scotland before winter arrived and Icelandic storms threatened to bring a halt to the swim.

So, today I'm able to muster a (semi) smile. Not a full smile, since news of my dad's health still haunts me during every mile of every swim, but a partial grin (through gritted teeth) because at least John o' Groats represents another Viking 'turning point' towards home. A significant one too, since every stroke from this day forward would take me south, which meant every degree of declining latitude brought me closer to Margate beach.

Sitting in the galley that night, I calculated that Margate (and therefore the family) was now 770 miles away. Based on this maths, I was prepared to swim day and night as fast as my lungs, limbs and ligaments would propel me in order for me to be home in a month or so.

Unfortunately, I knew it wasn't as simple as that. After 1,100 miles and 90 days at sea, I also knew I couldn't control the ocean. The tides, waves and winds out at sea were entirely out of my hands, which meant so was my finish line. Which is why despite being in hurry, the north of Scotland decided to teach me an important lesson: *Accept the Uncontrollables and Control the Controllables.*

In other words, events may not be under our control, however our attributions and interpretations to them are. To quote Epictetus again, 'The chief task in life is simply this: to identify and separate matters so that I can say clearly to myself which are externals not under my control, and which have to do with the choices I actually control. Where then do I look for good and evil? Not to uncontrolla-ble externals, but within myself to the choices that are my own.'

Nowhere was this truer than the Pentland Firth. The narrow strait of water which separates the Orkney islands from mainland Scotland contains some of the most powerful tides in the world. In fact, stories of their sheer strength can be traced back to Norse sagas, texts of the Roman empire and are woven into the very fabric of Scottish folklore. But the stories aren't quite as daunting as the statistics. For as the tidal currents flow between the Atlantic Ocean and the North Sea, the water gets squeezed and compressed between the islands and produces ferocious currents that can reach speeds of 16 knots (18.5 mph). To put this into perspective:

- Humans can swim at around 3 knots (3.5 mph).
- A dolphin's cruising speed is around 6–7 knots (7–8 mph).
- Dolphins have been clocked at speeds as high as 15 knots (17 mph).

So, to try and swim against the currents would be foolish and poten-tially fatal. But if we got our timings right, I would be swimming with the currents at the speed of a dolphin.

Fortunately, Matt is a nautical genius and wizard of the ocean and we timed it perfectly. Working with the tides, I actually trav-elled faster than a dolphin ... without actually trying. Reaching 14 knots (16 mph) and setting a new Great British Swim record, I must have looked so odd to the coastguards watching on, since my lazy and leisurely stroke rate didn't correspond to the impossible pace.

But what 90 days at sea had taught me was that if ever there was a time to 'cruise' now would be that time. Fusing the laws of the ocean with proven sports science theories, I was the fastest *and* laziest swimmer in Great Britain that day.

But joking aside, I was picking my fights carefully. When it came to setting a pace, I 'cruised' and only 'killed' when I needed to. It could have been so easy to get carried away, but after months at sea

I had matured since Margate and knew a conservative speed was needed if I was to:

- Continue swimming around Great Britain in pursuit of a bigger record, a higher purpose ('self-fulfilment needs' as per Maslow's Hierarchy of Needs).
- Manage exercise stressors and work within the laws of the psychobiological model of fatigue (central governor).

Also, as a team we were very aware that the Scottish waters were being kind today. Moments later we were poking our heads 'around the corner' of John o' Groats looking at the waves and weather, with our ears pressed against the radio and eyes glued to tidal maps to see what conditions Scotland would give us as we attempted to cross the Moray Firth.

This was our biggest test to date. The Moray Firth is a giant, triangular inlet on the northeast coast of Scotland and is the country's largest firth with over 500 miles (800 km) of coastline. But with autumn now upon us, and winter fast approaching, we couldn't afford the time to 'hug' the coastline and seek shelter from the cliffs. Instead, we knew we would be forced to swim 63 miles (over 100 km) straight across the bay.

Matt continued to listen closely to the weather report with his eyes fixated on tidal charts. As he cross-referenced and processed all the information we had available to us, I hadn't seen him this pensive since the Bristol Channel or the Irish Sea. As we waited for our weather window to attempt the crossing, I was eager to know what lay ahead.

'How's it looking?' I asked, visibly biting my fingernails (a habit I thought I'd stopped as a kid, but had since picked up during my time in Scotland).

'I won't lie, it's going to be like swimming in a washing machine .... in the dark,' he said. I appreciated his honesty, but dreaded the news.

After almost three months at sea, I was aware that the biggest uncontrollable is the sea itself, and if Mother Nature and Poseidon decided to turn on the wave machine and make the 'swimming pool' rough that day, as a mere mortal there was very little I could do about it.

'Get some rest,' Matt said. 'As soon as we have our weather window we'll make a sprint for it.'

So, for the next 24 hours that's what I did. Sleeping, resting and reading, I researched how best to *Accept the Uncontrollables,* with help from the ancient stoics and Thomas Edison (one of the world's greatest inventors), and this is what I learned.

THE UNCONTROLLABLES: THE SEA

Throughout the swim I encountered many uncontrollables. From rogue tides, unpredictable waves and weather, bad family news, unpredictable seals, wild whales and untamed sharks. But it was Marcus Aurelius who said, 'When you are stressed by an external thing, it's not the thing itself that troubles you, but only your judgement of it. And you can wipe this out at a moment's notice.'

He was absolutely right.

When I first heard news of my dad's illness, I was purely thinking through emotionally charged reflexive reactions rather than logic. The entire situation was being made worst by my judgement of it and it was only because my dad was thinking so rationally that I was able to continue the swim.

Another concept used to cope with uncontrollable events is known as *amor fati* which is Latin for 'love of fate'. The exact term can be traced back to the nineteenth-century German philosopher Friedrich Nietzsche who describes it as, 'My formula for greatness in a human being is amor fati: that one wants nothing to be different, not forward, not backward, not in all eternity. Not merely bear what is necessary, still less conceal it ... but love it.'

Basically, do not wish for reality to be any different, rather accept and even love whatever happens. Something Epictetus agreed with over two millennia earlier when he said, 'Seek not for events to happen as you wish but rather wish for events to happen as they do and your life will go smoothly.'

Stoics later came to call this the 'art of acquiescence'. This is the act of accepting rather than fighting every little thing as stoics tried to cultivate acceptance to whatever happened to them. 'If this is the will of Nature then so be it.' Most events happen without you having a say in the matter. You can either enjoy and love whatever happens, or you get dragged along anyway.

This is why Seneca said, 'Fate leads the willing, and drags along the reluctant.'

As a metaphor, imagine a dog leashed to a moving cart. The wise man is like a dog leashed to a moving cart, running joyfully alongside and smoothly keeping pace with it, whereas a foolish man is like a dog that grumblingly struggles against the leash but finds himself dragged alongside the cart anyway. The moving cart stands for your life and everything that happens. The dog stands for us. Either we enjoy the ride and make the best of our life's journey, or we fight against everything that happens and get dragged along anyway.

Which dog has the better life?

Both dogs are in the same situation, one just enjoys it much more because he doesn't fight against what he can't beat – fate. Nobody wants to get dragged along, so there is really just one option: make the best of the journey the cart driver chooses for you.

My favourite story of amor fati involves the great Thomas Edison. An expert in accepting *The Uncontrollables*, what happened on 9 December 1914 demonstrates why he's widely regarded as one of the greatest inventors the world has ever known. At 5.15 p.m. a huge fire was triggered by highly combustible nitrate film and destroyed over half the buildings in Edison's West Orange Laboratory. By 9.30 p.m. powerful explosions from stores of volatile chemicals inside the buildings rocketed flames 100 ft aloft, causing secondary fires as far away as five blocks. Damages reached seven million dollars, with only two million covered by insurance, according to the *New York Times* article. It's hard to imagine the sheer level of devastation caused and many employees scurried about to secure precious artefacts from Edison's famous office, trying to save his life's work and legacy.

But it's what happened next that, for me, makes Edison a stoic genius. According to a 1961 *Reader's Digest* article by Edison's son Charles, Edison calmly walked over to him as he watched the fire destroy his dad's work. In a childlike voice, Edison told his 24-year-old son, 'Go get your mother and all her friends. They'll never see a fire like this again.' When Charles objected, Edison said, 'It's all right. We've just got rid of a lot of rubbish.'

Later, at the scene of the blaze, Edison was quoted in the *New York Times* as saying, 'Although I am over 67 years old, I'll start all over again tomorrow.' He told the reporter that he was exhausted from remaining at the scene until the chaos was under control, but he stuck to his word and immediately began rebuilding the next morning without firing any of his employees.

But do you know what's even more amazing? Amid the disaster Edison noticed how the firefighters were hampered by the loss of power and light. He puzzled over the problem and came up with the battery-driven light source idea and design. At age 67, Edison's pace of work and inventions had slowed, but they could hardly be described as declining years. Within six months, Edison was demonstrating his latest invention in a nearby park, attracting curious onlookers who wondered where the bright light was coming from. He subsequently rebuilt his empire, and in 1915, Edison Industries chalked up US$10 million in revenue.

In summary (and to quote Seneca), 'Floods will rob us of one thing, fire of another. These are conditions of our existence which we cannot change. What we can do is adopt a noble spirit, such a spirit as befits a good person, so that we may bear up bravely under all that fortune sends us and bring our wills into tune with nature's.'

Which is exactly what I did. Knowing I couldn't control the sea, I decided I would try my best to 'spar' or 'dance' with it, and I wrote the following words in my diary before we started our swim across the Moray Firth:

> When ocean swimming you have to learn to fight or dance with Mother Nature. But understand she is completely unpredictable: some days you might need your dancing shoes and other days you might have to wear your boxing gloves.

On 1 September, we got our weather window and began our crossing. Leaving the harbour, I packed both my 'boxing gloves' and 'dancing shoes' for whatever uncontrollables lay ahead.

THE TAMING/TIMING OF THE TIDES

LOCATION: Moray Firth
DISTANCE COVERED: 1,125 miles
DAYS AT SEA: 100

It's sometime in September and somewhere across the Moray Firth. We were engulfed in darkness after leaving land, light and the safety of Wick fishing port behind us days ago, and now every arm stroke since had sent us further and further into the dark abyss that was the Moray Firth. With no headlands, lighthouses or visible targets to aim for, this was the strangest swim I'd ever done as I'd never experienced such a bleak, barren and beautiful form of black.

It even played with your senses (in a good way), for after hours of swimming you almost became incapable of knowing if your head was under the water or not, since the stars in the night sky looked the same as the phosphorescent organisms (in the form of algae) suspended in the water. It was what I imagined swimming in a black hole would feel like as you floated through sea and space.

Days passed and this was my life in the Moray Firth. With no harbours to visit or fishing boats for company, I completely lost track of time. Hours, days and weeks have no meaning here. If the (wild) west coast of Scotland was lawless, the east coast was its timeless counterpart.

The only sign of night turning to day was the fleeting glimpse of the sun trying to pierce the unending gloom. But after so long at sea, I would often ignore my watch and the overhead conditions, and instead listen to the tides.

CELEBRATING 100 DAYS AT SEA

The Moray Firth was such a wide and expansive stretch of open water that you felt you were so far from land and wouldn't (and couldn't) see or hear anything, but today was different. I had settled into a steady rhythm and was breathing bilaterally, when I noticed out the corner of my eye that from the boat deck Harriet seemed preoccupied. I immediately sensed that something was up. For months now I had sighted off our boat to keep a steady course;

I knew every detail of its structure and if anything on the boat changed, I would know about it. So if a cabin door was left open, if the towels were hung out to dry but a peg was missing, if the hull had acquired new barnacles ... I would notice.

So, when Harriet's head was tilted to the sky (and not at the sea) I noticed. Moments later, I stopped swimming, looked up and was startled to see two aircraft flying in unison and performing an acrobatic 'dance' in the sky, twisting and turning as they expelled what looked like a special kind of smoke in the shape of ... a heart.

At first, I panicked. Had I forgotten Valentine's day? Had Matt arranged this for Suzanne to celebrate a special anniversary (which again I'd forgotten)? But looking at Matt from the water, I could see he was as clueless as me, so I breathed a sigh of relief. With pinpoint accuracy, the aircraft then continued to write something else in the sky. As they did I turned to Harriet and asked her what was going on.

'It's for you,' she said.

'But it's not my birthday for another month?' I replied, panic and hesitation in my voice. I knew I'd been in the Moray Firth a long time but was pretty sure it was the start of September and my birthday wasn't until 13 October. Had I really been lost in here that long?

'No, no. They are celebrating our 100 days at sea,' she said smiling.

A wave of relief surged through my weary body. To be completely honest I really appreciated the gesture. The private air show and skywriting is something I will never forget, truly a once-in-a-lifetime experience. But I did always wonder whether it only served to remind me just how long I'd been swimming. One hundred days seemed an eternity. I'm not sure I wanted to think about it at the time, never mind have it written in giant letters across the sky. Again, I must stress I didn't want to appear ungrateful, it was incredible to see. But when I turned to Matt, I was only thinking of one thing.

'This is amazing,' I said, 'but do you know what would have been better?'

'Go on?'

'Bread,' I replied.

Matt smiled. He understood exactly what I was saying.

'I'm being serious ... brown, white, granary or plain,' I said. 'We're down to our last loaf and while smoke signals and skywriting is awesome, I would have preferred it if they'd stopped off at the bakery beforehand.'

Matt nodded (still smiling), since, although this was a great idea in theory, it was too far up Maslow's Hierarchy of Needs for us to truly appreciate it at that moment. A personal and private air show to celebrate 100 days at sea is definitely what Maslow would class as an esteem need (the desire for reputation, status, prestige and a feeling of achievement). But all I wanted was bread, which Maslow would deem a physiological need, and my family which Maslow would consider a belongingness and love need.

Both of which were way down the Hierarchy of Needs.

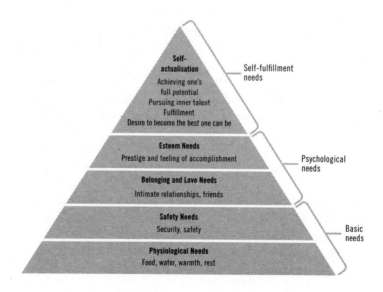

As the smoke cleared and the planes departed, silence fell upon the Moray Firth once more. Still incredibly appreciative of what we just saw (even though it was bread-less) I continued to swim on, fuelled by a fervent desire to get home and see my dad.

LESSON 14

- When you are stressed by an external force, it's not the force itself that troubles you, but only your judgement of it. Once you understand this, you can learn to **Accept the Uncontrollables** and practise the **Art of Acquiescence** to achieve your goal.
- You might have to learn to **fight or dance** when tackling an external force. But that force might be totally unpredictable: some days you might need your dancing shoes, whereas on others you might have to wear your boxing gloves. For things you cannot change, **adopt a noble spirit, bear up bravely, and tune in to nature's will**.

LESSON 15 | CONTROL THE CONTROLLABLES

LOCATION: Aberdeen
DISTANCE COVERED: 1,215 miles
DAYS AT SEA: 103

At 7 a.m. on 11 September, my brother Scott rang me as I was preparing for the day's swim past Aberdeen harbour. Waking from a nap, I immediately sensed something was wrong, so cleared my blurred vision and answered the phone.

'Sorry to be the one to tell you, it's Dad.'

I instantly felt sick (again). This was without doubt the worst pain I had experienced on the entire swim and I knew I would rather face any of the numerous hardships on my journey than listen to the news of this phone call.

'The scan revealed it's stage 4 melanoma. It's terminal,' Scott said. 'Doctors are doing everything they can, but any treatment they give him will be palliative care meaning it can't be cured and he can only be medicated to help provide some relief from the symptoms and pain.'

Ever stoic and strong, Dad told Scott to remind me of my promise.

'Remember what he said ... come home but only once you finish what you started.'

Immediately I hung up the phone, checked the tide times, put on my goggles and leapt off the boat and into the water. Without saying a word Matt (sensing what was wrong) quickly turned the motor on and began tracking alongside me.

Needless to say, I wasn't thinking straight at all.

Swimming like a man possessed down the east coast, my coping mechanism was to swim hard. Then whenever I started to feel upset and dwell on the worst possible outcomes, I would swim harder. Basically, progress was the best remedy and hard-fought miles were the best medicine.

The problem was both Matt and I knew this wasn't sustainable (physically and mentally). I'd been swimming for over 100 days and covered over 1,200 miles which meant the fatigue I was experiencing was my body breaking down. I was losing parts of my skin from chronic salt water exposure at a faster rate, and my ligaments, tendons and muscles were now struggling to keep me afloat as waves of 6 ft or more crashed over me. But with every stroke and every mile, my mind urged the arms to keep moving.

Moments later, we were approaching Aberdeen harbour. On any other day and under any other circumstances I would have approached with caution. It's one of the busiest commercial shipping lanes in the world and annually handles around 8,000 vessel arrivals and 5 million tonnes of cargo. Not to mention the 200 ft tankers travelling out of the port daily.

But that morning I was swimming like an injured animal in a pure state of stress-induced analgesia and would have happily swum headfirst through boats, ships and anything that got in my way. At this point, I want to stress that I'm not saying this to make myself sound heroic or fearless, since it was stupid, certainly not stoic and almost served as a sense of false bravado to convince myself it was helping our progress in some way.

In short, and with retrospect, I was an idiot and can now acknowledge it. Fortunately, at the time, I had Matt who was always thinking clearly and always looking out for me. I was able to outsource common sense to him as I continued to swim with my head down.

As we radioed ahead, the Port Authority kindly granted us a short window of 30 minutes to cross the shipping lanes, after which a huge cargo ship from Norway would be coming our way.

But that day I didn't even need 30 minutes. Swimming at almost 5 mph on pure adrenaline, my amygdala and hypothalamus had sent a cocktail of hormones coursing through my veins, which (as we know from Feral Fear Theory) inhibited my perception to pain and sent my body and brain into hyperarousal.

This was of course completely counter-intuitive, contradicts the cruise/kill pacing strategy discussed before (that's backed by thousands of studies) and goes against almost every long-distance swimming guide ever written. But as I gasped for air, I completely ignored my exercise stressors and signallers, along with the logical and rational sports science part of my brain, and made it across.

But there were no celebrations. Aberdeen is an incredible city, but it wasn't Margate and therefore wasn't the finish line I wanted. So, without even pausing we continued to work with the powerful tides and ate up the east coast, taking out over 10-mile chunks of the journey with every swim.

We arrived in Arbroath harbour at 7 a.m. on the morning of 14 September. As the sun rose, our swim ended for that morning so I boarded the boat, hung my wetsuit up on the deck and ate breakfast with Matt in the galley.

'You're a very different animal to the one that swam across the shipping lane in Dover,' Matt said, taking a sip of his tea and a bite of his crumpet.

'Thank you,' I said, taking a bite of mine too.

'Oh ... I'm not sure it's a *good* thing,' he replied. 'You cannot continue to swim like this, taking out your anger on the sea. You know this. You cannot sustain this pace and it's a shoulder injury waiting to happen.'

He was of course right, but I wasn't listening. I continued to swim down the east coast like a madman, no longer gliding through the waves but punching my way through them. This continued for a week, until once again Mother Nature and Poseidon (with the help of a storm) decided to intervene and teach me my most painful lesson to date.

A STORM CALLED 'ALI'

LOCATION: Dunbar
DISTANCE COVERED: 1,350 miles
DAYS AT SEA: 110

It's midnight on 18 September, in Dunbar harbour. After enjoying progress (and therefore some form of 'inner peace') my coping mechanism, of swimming so fast that the fatigue numbs any negative emotion, was still working. But as I crossed the Firth of Forth, this came to an abrupt halt as the weather closed in.

A warning was broadcast across the radio notifying all vessels in the vicinity of a huge storm that was sweeping in from the Atlantic. Named Storm Ali, it was the first of the 2018/19 winter season. How bad was it? Well, certain areas such as Cairngorm Summit in the Scottish Highlands (only 100 miles from us) had recorded maximum winds of 105 mph and the Tay Road Bridge (even closer, just 25 miles away) endured winds of 102 mph.

Shouting from the helm of *Hecate*, Matt was in emergency mode.

'ROSS, WE CANNOT STAY OUT HERE!'

'COME ABOARD ... WE NEED TO FIND SHELTER AND SAFETY FAST!'

I will never forget the look on Matt's face. It wasn't a look of fear, it was a look of a dad, husband and captain entirely committed to protecting his family (and me). Matt had been sailing for over 40 years and had skippered boats all over the world, from across the Pacific, Indian and Atlantic oceans, so he knew the metrics reported over the radio of Storm Ali would translate into damage and death.

He wasn't wrong. Over the next 48 hours, Storm Ali caused extensive power outages and travel disruption in Northern Ireland and Scotland, including the closure of exposed bridges. There was also damage to buildings and vehicles alongside many fallen trees across the northwest of the UK. Finally, we were informed two people had sadly lost their lives as a result of the storm.

At 1.00 a.m. we (along with many other boats) arrived into Dunbar harbour seeking refuge. Room was kindly made for us by the harbour master who was working through the night to ensure everyone was safe. But despite the incredible hospitality, there was a sombre mood among the sailors who had a profound, collective understanding of the severity of what happens when storms strike these parts.

Sitting in my cabin aboard the boat, I realised it was no longer going to be a place to sleep as Dunbar felt the full force of the storm that raged outside its walls. At just 4 ft wide and 7 ft long and housed in the hull of the boat, my bedroom was like a prison cell where I would spend the next four days battling my own thoughts, fears and frustrations.

As I turned to stoic philosophy for answers, the words of Marcus Aurelius, Epictetus and Admiral James Stockdale came to my rescue. After days of reading (and sleepless nights), this is what I learned.

THE CONTROLLABLES: THE MIND

Our emotions are categorised as 'Controllables'. This is why Marcus Aurelius famously once said, 'You have power over your mind – *not outside events*. Realize this, and you will find strength.' This is closely related to the ancient stoic idea of 'The Inner Citadel'. A citadel was the fortified area of a town or city, at its core and usually built on higher ground (such as Ancient Sparta), which the Greeks used as a stronghold and place of safety during times of war. Hence, the idea that your 'Inner Citadel' is what protects your soul.

> 'Things cannot touch the Soul.' 'They have no access to the Soul.' 'They cannot produce our judgments.' 'They are outside of us.' 'They themselves know nothing, and by themselves they affirm nothing.'
> MARCUS AURELIUS, MEDITATIONS IV, 3, 10; V, 19; VI, 52; IX, 15

The stoics believed we might become physically vulnerable and are often at the mercy of outside events that are outside of our control (the Uncontrollables), but that our inner domain (the Controllables) cannot be conquered without our consent.

Yet history teaches us that impenetrable fortresses can still be breached, if betrayed from the inside. The citizens inside the walls (if they fall prey to fear and greed) can open the gates and let the enemy in. This is what many of us do when we lose our nerve and make emotionally reflexive decisions based on fear.

Epictetus said, 'No, it is events that give rise to fear – when another has power over them or can prevent them, that person becomes able to inspire fear. How is the fortress destroyed? Not by iron or fire, but by judgments ... here is where we must begin, and it is from this front that we must seize the fortress and throw out the tyrants.' This quote later inspired one of the greatest stories of resilience from the legend of Admiral James Stockdale.

A keen student of stoicism, Stockdale survived over seven years of imprisonment when, as an American fighting the Vietcong, his plane was shot down in 1965 over Vietnam. On being held captive he told himself he was 'entering the world of Epictetus' and even after years of torture refused to offer any intelligence to his captors. As a result, he earned the US Congressional Medal of Honour. But how was he able to maintain such resilience in the face of over-whelming and (seemingly) never-ending hardship?

In an interview with Stockdale, business guru and author James C Collins named it the 'Stockdale Paradox'. Referring to his coping strategy during his period in the Vietnamese POW camp, Stockdale said, 'I never lost faith in the end of the story, I never doubted not only that I would get out, but also that I would prevail in the end and turn the experience into the defining event of my life, which, in retrospect, I would not trade.'

When Collins asked who didn't make it out of Vietnam, Stockdale replied, 'Oh, that's easy, the optimists. Oh, they were the ones who said, "We're going to be out by Christmas." And Christmas would come, and Christmas would go. Then they'd say, "We're going to be out by Easter." And Easter would come, and Easter would go. And then Thanksgiving, and then it would be Christmas again. And they died of a broken heart.'

Stockdale then added, 'This is a very important lesson. You must never confuse faith that you will prevail in the end – which you can never afford to lose – with the discipline to confront the most brutal facts of your current reality, whatever they might be.'

So this philosophy of duality is the Stockdale Paradox.

Stockdale had faith in his dream of returning home again but didn't allow himself to tie his hope to an external circumstance over which he had zero control. Instead, he turned inward and focused on keeping his mind free and resilient even if his body was trapped in a cell. This is how he kept his head above water and his spirit strong for the better part of a decade.

What Stockdale possessed was not quite optimism, but a profound sense that he would ultimately realise his dream, whether that time was near or far off. Other POWs in Vietnam may have been optimists; Stockdale was firm in his hopeful equanimity. He quenched his desires and focused exclusively on the Controllables (his emotions) rather than the Uncontrollables (his situation).

This is exactly what I learned to do. At 11.47 p.m. on 22 September, we were ready to resume our swim after the wind and waves of Storm Ali had passed. Swimming through the night, I would do this equipped with a newfound (and upgraded) understanding of Stoic Sports Science (Controlling the Controllables) which had been forged around (and by) the storms and seas of Scotland.

SWIMMING IN THE STOCKDALE PARADOX

LOCATION: Berwick-upon-Tweed
DISTANCE COVERED: 1,480 miles
DAYS AT SEA: 116

Berwick-upon-Tweed

It is 24 September and we are approaching the English border. Calm and collected I had been swimming for two days within the parameters of the Stockdale Paradox, entirely focused to get home, but equally making peace with the speed and situation I currently found myself in.

On the horizon was Berwick-upon-Tweed. A town of huge geographical significance for Great Britain, for over 400 years it's been at the centre of a 'border war' between Scotland and England and is now considered the most Scottish town in England. But for me, it was significant for an entirely different reason, since once I swam parallel to this small coastal town, we would have officially:

- Completed the first swim around Scotland.
- Entered back into English waters.
- Be 370 miles from Margate (and therefore the finish line).

I cannot stress how good that felt. Swimming, but consciously only breathing to my right to sight off the boat, I was covered in goosebumps as I watched the team gather on deck to watch Matt ceremoniously (and emotionally) take down the blue and white flag of Scotland from the mast and begin replacing it with the red and white flag of England.

The clock struck 2.30 p.m. and I took my final strokes in Scottish waters.

'Five, four, three, two, one … WE'RE BACK IN ENGLAND!'

The celebrations erupted on board *Hecate*. Every member of the family (crew) was in attendance that day as Taz, Harriet, Jemima and Peony danced around Suzanne who had found a fresh air horn and was attempting to get some tune or melody from it.

Filled with a blend of patriotism for England, newfound love of Scotland and a sense that every arm stroke was now taking me home, I felt like a homing pigeon on adrenaline. There was an instant temptation to take off like a shot and begin a sprint finish to Margate ... but 370 miles is a long sprint finish. Instead I chose to Control the Controllable that was my mind (the 'Inner Citadel'). Matt and I exchanged a look that had become our own silent, stoic form of celebration. It was essentially the Stockdale Paradox in celebration form, because we were both very aware we still had the entire length of a country to swim.

Moments later I was face down in the water (politely) ignoring the celebrations that continued on the boat. Instead, I swam with the words of famous English poet William Blake and his poem 'Jerusalem' playing on repeat in my head. I remember, back when I was a schoolboy over 20 years ago, it would be sung as a hymn in church during the St George's Day assembly. My favourite verse goes like this:

> I will not cease from Mental Fight,
> Nor shall my Sword sleep in my hand,
> Till we have built Jerusalem,
> In England's green and pleasant Land.

At this very moment, this was the perfect song choice for me. It served a dual purpose of reminding me of home while also providing a slow and rhythmic melody to which I could time my stroke. William Blake's 'Jerusalem' was, for me, the Stockdale Paradox in music form.

I even began to (semi) enjoy the swim again. Looking across the water with every stroke, I watched on as the serene, rural and entirely untouched coastline was decorated with ancient and abandoned castles that date back to Viking times. One by one I had the privilege of seeing them, as I floated past Dunstanburgh, Berwick and Bamburgh castles. This continued for one week (and over 100 miles) until we were forced to stop again. It seemed Storm Ali (which brought a halt to our swim in Dunbar) wasn't quite done yet and was staging one last 'fight' before leaving the British coastline for good.

But this time it was different. Still painfully aware of the situation with my dad, I was able to take stock and Control the Controllables, as we happily entered the harbour of Hartlepool to refuel, restock and recover before the sea decided the 'swimming pool' was open once again.

LESSON 15

- The ancient stoics believed we might become physically vulnerable and are often at the mercy of external events that are outside of our control (**the Uncontrollables**), but that our inner domain (**the Controllables**) cannot be conquered without our consent.
- Our emotions can be categorised as 'controllables'. Learn how to **Control the Controllables** – understand that you have power over your mind – and you can find the strength to tackle even the most difficult of tasks.
- As a coping strategy the '**Stockdale Paradox'** teaches us that we should never confuse faith that we will prevail in the end – which we can never afford to lose – with the discipline to confront the most brutal facts of our current reality, whatever they might be.

LESSON 16 | RESILIENCE CANNOT BE RUSHED, BUT QUITTING CAN

LOCATION: Hartlepool
DISTANCE COVERED: 1,505 miles
DAYS AT SEA: 122

Hartlepool

It's 8.30 p.m. on 1 October and I find myself immediately liking Hartlepool.

The hospitality we received as we arrived into the harbour was unlike anything we'd experienced around the entire British coast so far. Perhaps it's due to the fact that Hartlepool is home to the National Museum of the Royal Navy and HMS *Trincomalee*, Europe's oldest warship (still afloat) that was built shortly after the end of the Napoleonic Wars (1803–15). Proudly preserving its history, members of the museum would dress up as eighteenth-century sailors and fire cannons as part of educational re-enactments for local schools.

But the best thing about Hartlepool (aside from the cannons) were the cakes. We had been docked less than half an hour before the harbour master himself arrived bearing gifts of baked goods and chocolates. Whether he knew it or not, his act of kindness was immensely appreciated since (again according to Maslow's Hierarchy of Needs) it helped fulfil one of my most basic physiological needs ... food.

By 9.15 p.m. I had made a nest for myself in the corner of the galley next to the kettle (for extra heat) and wrapped myself in blankets and pillows. Like a bear, I had collected as many cakes and calories as I could find and was storing them among my layers of blankets, eating them one by one as I prepared to go into hibernation.

Eventually, I began drifting into a cake-induced slumber. Watching as my eyes got heavier and heavier, Suzanne quietly came into the galley and wrapped me in another blanket as she knew full well I needed to attend to another one of my basic physiological needs ... sleep.

That night I slept for more than five hours and it was bliss. This might not sound like much, but for me it was the most I'd slept since leaving Margate over 120 days ago.

As the clock struck 7.30 the next morning, I was woken up by voices outside the boat. Climbing out of the nest of blankets I'd created for myself, I unpeeled the pillows from my face and went outside on deck to see who was there. As I did I was welcomed by cheers, hugs and more cake. Again, I LOVE Hartlepool. This was far better than waking up with blood-soaked bedsheets fused to your neck like I had done for the entire south coast.

'Congratulations, only 285 miles to go!' someone shouted from the group.

'What's a jelly struggle cuddle to the face like?' another added as everyone burst out laughing.

There were maybe 10 people in total, but to me it might as well have been 10,000. For four months the only company I'd had were my own thoughts (for 12 hours a day) and the same six-person crew. Of course, we'd have the odd visitor, but this was the most people I'd spoken to since leaving Margate and each was so incredibly supportive.

A little overwhelmed, I responded to questions as best I could since I was very aware I was not well-practised in the art of socialising anymore, and also very conscious I had crumbs in my beard. Basically, I felt like a mildly famous, unwashed, niche sporting celebrity who'd fallen out of a biscuit tin.

I spoke for hours to the group and it turns out they were all members of the local triathlon and swimming communities, so they all had an innate understanding of the physicality of our swim. Wanting to know more about my average speed, stroke rate and pace for a mile, I paused to consider my response.

'In reality, there is no average,' I said. 'Every swim was different and impacted by waves and weather.'

'Okay, fine ... what about your top speed?' a member of the triathlon club asked, eager for answers.

'Sixteen miles per hour (14 knots) at John o' Groats,' I said laughing.

He looked confused until I explained about the powerful tides of the Pentland Firth. I then explained how swimming around Great Britain takes the principles of swimming and moves it outside of the conventional realm. It's essentially more closely related to sports like sailing, surfing and ocean rowing than it is to swimming.

I then added, while you can use athletic principles (like pacing strategies) you must think like an adventurer. You cannot be tempted by records, trophies and accolades and you cannot perform based on rules, regulations and metrics. Instead you must remain respectful (and adaptable) to Mother Nature whether you're at sea, on a mountain or crossing a jungle. This is why I so often say:

Resilience cannot be rushed, but quitting can.

They looked at me like they (semi) understood what I was saying. So, I invited everyone on the boat for cake for what would become an impromptu (and my first public) Stoic Sports Science Sea Seminar. A strange setting for a talk, I know, but I hadn't seen new people for over four months, so chatting to 10 others felt like I was performing on the main stage at Glastonbury.

IMPECCABLE PACING: THE BASICS

The brain (and body) craves consistency and sustainability. As a result, pacing was so important to every tide and every swim, every day. It's related to homeostasis and the psychobiological model of fatigue, but scientists believe the brain monitors cardiac integrity through myriad factors including heart rate.

They go on to say maintaining a consistent heart rate during race performance is critical in keeping the psychobiological model of fatigue in balance. A heart rate that is too high too early and for too long will signal to the brain the pace is unsustainable and we should shut down. This is why every swim would only start once I was happy to settle into a rhythmic style of swimming that consisted of a stroke rate you could set your watch to. I did this for two reasons:

1. Swimming for up to 12 hours a day meant there was very little time for rest, rehab or prehab. I would commence most swims with ligaments painfully contorted and wounds so raw that I would force myself to go slow initially, until the familiar numbing endorphins and cold water eased my pain and soothed my stroke.

2. Studies show that pacing strategies are considered crucial to success in events like ultra-marathon running, Ironman triathlons and long-distance swimming. How do we know this? Because, ever since the tortoise beat the hare in the classic fable, sports scientists have understood the importance of keeping the heart rate at sustainable levels.

Just what level, speed and intensity is 'sustainable' depends on the person and event. But it's generally accepted that sustainable efforts in ultra-endurance events (over six hours' duration) range between 50 to 75 per cent of your maximum heart rate. For most of us, this includes a heart-rate range of 110 to 160 beats per minute. Anything over this (especially early in a race) can quickly burn through vital sugar stores and (according to the psychobiological model of fatigue) provide 'scary' feedback to the brain about your current effort, saying it's not sustainable and you need to 'pull the hand-brake' or stop.

Of course, Roger Bannister's 4-minute mile remains one of the best examples of impeccable pacing as he assembled one of the world's greatest elite pace making squads. But today (working from the same blueprint) modern-day professors of pacing have emerged, and perhaps the best example comes in the form of the cycling's prestigious hour-record. A look back through history at some of the greatest hour-cycling specialists and it's clear to see the record requires scientific and strategic pacing with a level of accuracy the world of sport had barely seen before.

IMPECCABLE PACING: THE HOUR RECORD

The hour record is widely considered to be cycling's purest feat. Instead of requiring athletes to conquer a set distance, this event gives cyclists a set time of 60 minutes to pedal as many laps as they can around a velodrome. It's that simple. Also, whereas other competitive pursuits typically pit athletes against one another, the hour is a solo and lonely affair where your only competition is the clock.

It can trace its origins back to races on penny-farthing bikes that were popular during the 1870s and 1880s, but the first officially recognised record was set by Henri Desgrange at the Buffalo

Velodrome, Paris on 11 May 1893 with a distance of 35.325 km (21.950 miles), following the formation of the International Cycling Association (the first international governing body for cycling). Throughout history, various cyclists ranging from unknown amateurs to well-known professionals have held the record, adding to its prestige and allure. But today there is one unified record in which the current international governing body (the International Cycling Union) allow the use of endurance track bikes.

As a result, on 18 September 2014 the German cyclist Jens Voigt became the first rider to break the record under the new unified rules and set a new mark of 51.110 km to beat the previous best set by the Czech Republic's Ondrej Sosenka way back in 2005 by a colossal 1,415 m.

This ushered in a new era for cycling's hour specialists. Only six weeks after Voigt, Austria's Matthias Brandle wrote his name into the history books. Raising the proverbial bar even further on 30 October 2014, the Austrian clocked a distance of 51.852 km and beat Voigt by 742 m. With each attempt, it seemed we were collectively learning to master the hour and perfect our pacing.

So, when Australian Jack Bobridge declared he was stepping up to the plate the cycling world all stopped and took note. Many experts were convinced he would take the hour record with ease. He was a track legend and the world record holder in the individual pursuit when he covered 4 km (16 laps) in 4 min 10.534 s (which gives you an average time per lap of 15.6 s). In Australia's excellent team pursuit squad at London 2012, which won the Olympic silver medal, Bobridge would have been well used to covering a 250 m lap in 14.5 s or occasionally less.

So why, on 31 January 2015 at Melbourne's DISC velodrome, did he come up 552 m short in his hour record attempt? Managing a distance of 51.3 km, it made no sense. In short, he didn't pace properly. Experts of the hour record repeatedly state the trick is perfect pace management and banging out laps of 17.3 to 17.4 s with

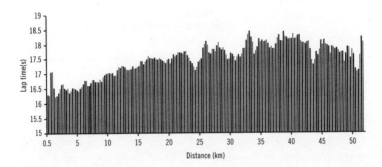

clockwork consistency and (if the body and mind is able) a slight acceleration right at the end to bring the record home.

But take a look at his lap times.

Looking like the Manhattan skyline this was never going to work.

Whether it was because of the cheers of the home crowd or the sheer adrenaline coursing through his body, his first two laps were clocked at 16.3 s which was far too fast considering he could occasionally dip under 14 s at the height of a world-class team pursuit.

Realising the mistake, he then over-compensated and delivered two laps at 17.1 s. Based on the blueprint laid out by Brandle and Voigt this was still too fast, but at least he was showing signs of patience and pacing. What should have happened at this point was a further reduction in speed to 17.4 s, but instead Bobridge hit the accelerator again and reeled off sub-17 s laps all the way to the 10 km mark.

The pace was incredible, but wouldn't (or couldn't) last. Indeed, only at the 16 km mark did he slow to the required to mid-17 s, but by then it was too late. His legs would have been bathed in fatigue at this point and his lungs would have been screaming to stop. Technically way up on world-record schedule, his goose was already cooked. What the crowd the witnessed was a pure display of heroism. But science teaches us this is useless unless paired with impeccable pacing. Afterwards, Bobridge described it as, 'The closest you can come to death without dying.'

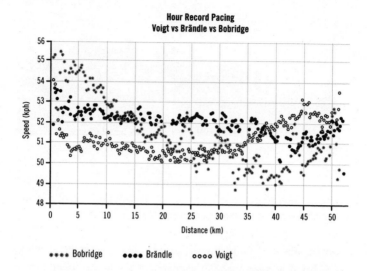

Hour Record Pacing
Voigt vs Brändle vs Bobridge

●●●● Bobridge   ●●●● Brändle   ○○○○ Voigt

At this point, I always think it's worth noting that Bobridge was one of the world's greatest cyclists. His physiology verged on super-human, with a lung capacity and power output in his legs that would rival a horse. Therefore, if a poor pacing strategy could trigger such a physiological collapse in him, think what it could do to a lesser trained athlete.

As his doomed record attempt continued, lap times started heading to 18 s and beyond, interspersed by wonderfully brave attempts to recover the situation with a quicker lap which only accentuated the problem. Ultimately, it was an absolute heroic achievement to reach 51.3 km, but Bobridge had written a blueprint on how *not* to break the hour record.

Taking notes, a fellow Aussie took up the challenge, determined not to repeat the mistakes of Bobridge. Rohan Dennis was a former world pursuit champion and team pursuit Olympic silver medallist from the London Games and had no doubt researched the above graph.

Then, a month later on 8 February 2015, and with the distinct advantage of having witnessed those who went before him, Dennis set a new benchmark of 52.491 km, beating Brandle's record by an astonishing 639 m.

Since then the hour record has fallen three more times: Britain's Alex Dowsett on 2 May 2015 with a distance of 52.937 km, followed by Sir Bradley Wiggins on 7 June 2015 with a distance of 54.526 km, and most recently the Belgian Victor Campenaerts, who on 16 April 2019 clocked a distance of 55.089 km.

But during every attempt, the key determinant of success was pacing.

THE PERFECT PACE STRATEGY

Setting the perfect pace is complex. This is because the precise mechanisms of fatigue are still debated, but what we do know is that as time passes and intensity increases (from aerobic to anaerobic) any theoretical steady state or maintainable pace is lost as oxygen use increases, heart rate elevates, fuel is burnt, chemicals build up which contribute to exhaustion, water is lost, heat accumulates, muscles fatigue and the molecular energy of the muscles (adenosine triphosphate) runs low.

Then consider how exercise stressors trigger signallers to tell the brain (as per the teachings of the psychobiological model of fatigue) and it's easy to understand how we stop or slow down. Experts believe the perfect pacing strategy is just below your anaerobic threshold. This is the point when your body must switch from its aerobic energy system to its anaerobic energy system. Represented on the graph, in theory it's where your use of the aerobic and anaerobic energy system is 50:50, but it's important to note:

- In reality, energy systems never work in isolation and are all working at different percentages at different times depending on the intensity and duration of that activity.

	AEROBIC	ANAEROBIC	
Weightlifting	0%	100%	100m sprint, golf and tennis swings, American football
Diving, gymnastics, 200m sprint	10	90	
Ice hockey			Basketball, baseball, volleyball, 400m sprint
Fencing, 100m swim	20	80	
Tennis, hockey	30	70	Lacrosse
	40	60	Soccer
800m run			
Boxing	50	50	200m swim, skating
2000m row	60	40	
1 mile run, 400m swim	70	30	1500m run
2 mile run	80	20	800m swim
3 mile run, skating 10km	90	10	
Marathon	100%	0%	Cross-country running, jogging

- Studies show the fitter you are (more efficient your cardiorespiratory system), the longer you can fuel your body with the aerobic system before the anaerobic system needs to take over.

How do you know which energy system you're predominantly using (aerobic or anaerobic)? As we discovered earlier, one of the easiest ways is to see if you can run and talk comfortably at the same time.

- If you speak in complete sentences, you're probably running at an aerobic pace, which is sustainable for a long time. This is the speed you 'cruise' at.
- If you cannot speak in complete sentences, you're probably running at an anaerobic pace, which is not sustainable for a long time. This is the speed you 'kill' at.

Not only is this sweet spot difficult to judge, but the hour record is raced from a standing start that threatens to immediately over-tax the anaerobic systems which can fatigue and deplete quickly. The dilemma for cyclists is: go out too slow and valuable speed is lost, but go too fast and you are plunged into an oxygen deficit that takes dozens of laps to repay.

Understand this and you will understand why Jack Bobridge's hopes of breaking cycling's hour record were impossible on 31 January 2015 with the pacing strategy he adopted. It's also why the modern-day sports science genius (and coach to Paula Radcliffe) Andrew Jones states, despite the confusion among the scientific community, 'Fatigue in endurance events has traditionally been linked to a reduction in muscle cell pH (acidity in the muscles) assumed to be reflected, albeit indirectly, by an accumulation of blood lactate.[112] Therefore, the ability to delay and/or tolerate an increase in blood lactate has been considered to be crucial to performance.'[113]

In summary, the exact science and terms are not important. The most important thing for an athlete or adventurer to understand is impeccable pacing to avoid a biochemical imbalance in the body that impacts muscles fatigue, muscle integrity and the psychobiological model of fatigue. It doesn't matter if you're a cycling fan or not, the lessons of cycling's hour record are clear for anyone. If you do not abide by the rules of physiology and pacing, your body and brain will fail you (since you simply cannot fight against your own physiology and psychology).

DON'T RUSH RESILIENCE

LOCATION: Hartlepool
DISTANCE COVERED: 1,505 miles
DAYS AT SEA: 124

It's 6.50 p.m. on 3 October and we are (sadly) leaving Hartlepool. The hospitality we were shown in Yorkshire made it a tough place to leave behind, but to be honest the welcome we received was only to be surpassed by the goodbye we got. That's because the harbour master had told us to make a brief stop by the watch tower, via the Royal Navy museum, before we left to resume our swim.

Not knowing what to expect, we made our way around the harbour and as the sun continued to rise, it revealed the dramatic silhouette of HMS *Trincomalee*. It looked stunning, but that was only half the show that morning. Standing next to it on the jetty were two men dressed as eighteenth-century sailors who then proceeded to roll out a giant cannon, light the fuse and ceremonially fire it (repeatedly) to mark our departure.

As the shots echoed throughout Hartlepool, cheers erupted from a small group of sailors who'd come to wave us goodbye and wish us luck. This was followed by the harbour master himself speaking over the PA system.

'To Ross and the crew of *Hecate* … wishing you fair winds and following seas.'

At this moment, I had to try hard to keep my emotions in check. This phrase is so often used among sailors before starting a journey and the very fact the harbour master would say that to me (accompanied by cheers from local seaman) almost felt like I'd been accepted in the sailing community.

Wanting to say something equally as meaningful back, I panicked.

'Thank you for the cakes and cannon.'

To this day I wish I'd found some better parting words, but regardless this was the best way to start the day (and any swim). I just had to ensure I managed my emotions and pacing strategy as I left the harbour walls. Since I knew we still had the entire length of the east coast of England to swim, and a promise to my dad to keep.

The next 20 miles of swimming, I have to say, were done with impeccable pacing. With no cargo ships to outswim or jellyfish to wrestle from my face, the coastline of Yorkshire offered miles of clear water where I could Control the Controllables (my pacing and mindset) and happily Accept the Uncontrollables (waves, weather and tides).

PACING AND THE IMMUNE SYSTEM

LOCATION: Whitby
DISTANCE COVERED: 1,525 miles
DAYS AT SEA: 124

It's 11.30 p.m. and we've arrived into Whitby in complete darkness.

Hartlepool was now 20 miles behind us and the cannons and cake already felt like a distant memory. But we had just arrived in one of Yorkshire's most famous seaside towns. Famous for its fish and chips and steam trains, Whitby is also home for thousands of seals, bottlenose dolphins and the occasional visiting minke whale.

But those things I have just listed are associated with Whitby during the day; at night it becomes famous for something else, something very different. For on the cliffs to the east, overlooking the North Sea, the ruins of the gothic Whitby Abbey served as inspiration for Abraham Stoker's horror story, *Dracula*. Published in 1897, it's a book that formed the foundations for an entire genre of literature and film, and inspired the world-famous Goth festival which takes place here at Halloween.

Climbing onto the boat, I joined Matt at the helm. After removing my goggles and unzipping my wetsuit, we then began the customary checking of wounds, scars and sea ulcers.

'Fantastic,' Matt exclaimed, smiling. 'Cuts, scars and chafing are bleeding, but still not infected.'

'I know, that's right ... and most of my tongue is still attached,' I replied, feeling quite proud of myself.

Now I acknowledge that to many this would seem odd, but after spending over 120 days at sea, both mine and Matt's perception as to what was 'healthy' was now completely warped.

Watching on, Jemima (Matt's oldest daughter) wasn't so sure. She had only joined the crew permanently a month before, so she wasn't far removed from society and was still quite civilised and normal in her understanding of a human being's basic health and welfare.

'I cannot understand this,' she said, baffled by our logic. 'If that happened back on land your first instinct would be to visit the hospital.

'But out here it seems your immediate thought is to add *more* duct tape and lubricant jelly,' she said while shaking her head in disbelief.

She had a point. Matt and I were aware this distorted view of medical DIY was far from conventional, but there were no rules or blueprints available when swimming these distances at sea, since no one had ever done it before. We thought if lube and tape had got us this far, why change a winning formula?

Jemima continued, 'What's remarkable is despite all the cuts, scars, bruising and bleeding, you've never missed a day's swimming, or even a single tide, because you're sick or ill. How's that?'

Sitting on the deck and applying disinfectant cream by moon-light (and torchlight) I then told the team how bulletproof my immune system was because of many complex factors, including my understanding of the importance of a nutrient-dense diet and the dangers of dietary deficiencies. But it was also because I had a basic understanding of the human immune system in general, as well as the impact an unsustainable swimming pace would have on it.

Beneath the stars that night I hosted another Stoic Sports Science Sea Seminar and explained the following. Firstly, it's very important to note science doesn't fully understand the intricacies of the immune system since, 'Exercise immunology has quite a short history relative to many branches of the exercise sciences, the modern era of careful epidemiological investigations and precise laboratory studies beginning in the mid 1980s.'[114] Secondly, of all these studies none were conducted during 157 days at sea.[115]

Basically, my situation was unique and as a result everything becomes a little more complicated. So I began researching from the more than two thousand peer-reviewed publications in exercise immunology that have been published since the formation of the International Society of Exercise and Immunology (ISEI) in 1989.

From these I formed a plan to care for my immune system that focused on pacing strategies and protein intake.

Why? Because the immune system is the body's defence against infection.

Through a series of steps called the immune response, the immune system attacks organisms and substances that invade body systems and cause disease. Most athletes will have experienced an 'immune crash'. It happens during periods of intense, heavy or high-volume training that have been too much for our bodies to handle. As a result, we're left beaten up and slowing down as our immune system waves the white flag.

Surrendering to any invading viruses or bacteria is known as 'exercise-induced immuno-depression' and it will prevent even the world's fittest athletes training to their potential as scientists claim, 'Heavily exercising endurance athletes experience extreme physiologic stress, which is associated with temporary immunodepression and higher risk of infection.'[116]

So, how was I not sick? The explanation lies in something called the J-shaped curve theory.[117] In the 1990s Dr David Nieman, a professor at Appalachian State University, formulated the J-shaped model to describe the relationship between exercise intensity and the risk of acquiring upper respiratory tract infections (URTI). Very common in athletes, this is a form of illness that's caused by an infection of the upper respiratory tract (nose, pharynx, sinuses or larynx). After analysing many athletes (from many sports) scientists found that moderate exercise has the ability to improve immune function compared to sedentary people sitting on the sofa doing nothing. But high-intensity exercise depresses the immune system[118] which means our resistance to various viral and bacterial diseases is weakened[119] and we're doomed to attend our next training session over trained, under motivated and 'burnt out.'[120]

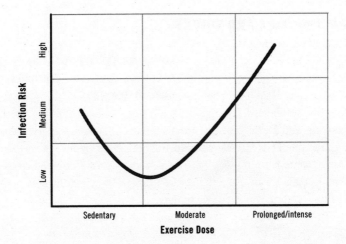

Represented on a graph the result looks like a 'J', hence the name.

All this means is a gentle 10-mile swim in calm waters complete with sunshine and dolphins might actually help boost the immune system. But sprinting through a busy shipping lane to avoid giant cargo ships has the potential to suppress the immune system.

It's significant that evidence to support this isn't yet conclusive.[121] It's also based on limited laboratory data[122] and (arguably) doesn't take into account the sheer complexity of the human immune system. But it does make intuitive sense. Besides, the fact I was miles away from land meant it was the only research I had to rely on.

So, while I swam – and waited for modern medicine to provide more studies and concrete science to help – I did my very best to pace myself and stay the correct side of the J-shaped curve theory, since modern medicine teaches us prevention is better than cure.

PACING: TIPS AND TRICKS

LOCATION: Robin Hood's Bay
DISTANCE COVERED: 1,530 miles
DAYS AT SEA: 125

It's 8.00 a.m. on 4 October and I am nearing Robin Hood's Bay in Yorkshire.

I'd been swimming for over 120 days through plastic, pollution and more obstacles than I could count, but today the sun was shining and the tides, waves and weather had decided to be kind to us (we really did have 'fair winds and following seas').

As a result, spirits were high on the boat and the old, picturesque fishing villages on the Heritage Coast of the North York Moors were very welcome sights as we passed them one by one ... with a pacing strategy you could set your watch to.

But that day I wasn't alone in the water. Three hours into that tide I was joined by a group of swimmers, just not of the human variety. Robin Hood's Bay is renowned for its wildlife and supports hundreds of species of fish, sea birds, dolphins and whales. But my favourite inhabitants, and training partners that day, were my old friends the grey seals (distant cousins of the ones I met on Lundy island). Always a privilege to share a swimming pool with them, at first they were sitting on the rocks, sheltered under the cliffs and watching as I swam past.

This is why I tried my best to be respectful and give them a wide birth. But moments later a few of the younger males decided to join me in the water to see what was going on. Diving off the rocks, they approached and began opening and closing their nostrils repeatedly to sniff me out. I've no idea how I smelt, but I hadn't showered in months so likely not great. Their huge eyes (and amphibious vision) then began looking me up and down as they tried to understand the origins of this strange new sea creature.

After a few more minutes, I felt I was (semi) accepted into the colony. They still weren't sure what I was, but knew I was very slow, completely safe and not a threat. As a result, the young male seals decided to keep me company as they effortlessly swam by my side while playing, ducking and diving along the way.

As the miles passed they watched my arms battle the water as they casually propelled themselves at the same speed. As I took 10 strokes to their two and 23 breaths to their one I looked so clumsy in comparison, but they seemed happy to babysit their new aquatically-deficient friend.

We did have one thing in common though: our mammalian dive response. Granted, theirs was much more advanced than mine, but we humans share a physiological mechanism that helps us control our breath, heart rate and blood flow, just like seals and other mammals such as otters, dolphins and muskrats. All you have to do to activate it is to stick your face in the water.

Once you do, a set of physiological reflexes are activated which enables the body to manage and tolerate a lower level of oxygen. The two main physiological changes in the body are:

- **Bradycardia**. This describes the slowing of the heart rate and studies show the human heart rate can slow down as much as 10 to 30 per cent, and up to 50 per cent or more in trained individuals.

- **Peripheral Vasoconstriction.** This describes a narrowing of blood vessels to reduce blood flow to the limbs ensuring that oxygen-sensitive organs like the heart and brain receive oxygen.

But even the breath-holding skills of the world's best human free-divers pale in comparison to my swimming counterparts that day.[123] One reason is because studies show seals can lower their body and brain temperature by up to 3°C. This in turn lowers their metabolism, oxygen consumption and heart rate to as low as 14 bpm,[124] shutting off blood supply to the limbs and directing oxygenated blood to the lungs, heart and brain.

Of course, my mammalian dive response wasn't that advanced, but this was the main lesson I took from my swimming coaches (the grey seals of Yorkshire) that day. From that day on every swim would start slowly, strategically and stoically as I entered the water and submerged my face to trigger the systematic slowing of my heart and shifting of my blood. Then (and only then) would I begin swimming with impeccable pacing that was only enhanced by my mastery and understanding of my mammalian dive response.

Yes, I know how strange this sounds, but I was now approaching the best part of half a year at sea and so was evolving into this strange sea creature. Not quite a man, not quite a seal, but something inbetween that would use every scientific tip and trick possible to get home and see his dad.

LESSON 16

- **Keeping the heart rate at a sustainable level is essential** for optimum performance in endurance events (**Impeccable Pacing**). If the heart rate is too high (or too low) this encourages the brain to send a signal to our bodies to shut down.
- A sustainable heart rate in ultra-endurance events (over six hours' duration) ranges from **50 to 75 per cent of your maximum heart rate**. For most of us, this is a heart-rate range of **110 to 160 beats per minute**.
- The **perfect pacing strategy** is just below your anaerobic threshold. This is the point when your body must switch from its **aerobic energy system** to its **anaerobic energy system**. But the fitter you are (and the more efficient your cardiorespiratory system), the longer you can fuel your body with the aerobic system before the anaerobic system needs to take over.
- In water, swimmers exhibit a **Mammalian Dive response** where physiological changes in their body result in a **slowing of the heart rate** and a **narrowing of blood vessels** to reduce blood flow to the limbs, ensuring that oxygen-sensitive organs like the heart and brain receive oxygen.

LESSON 17 | YOU'RE STRONGER WHEN SMILING

LOCATION: Grimsby
DISTANCE COVERED: 1,585 miles
DAYS AT SEA: 134

It's 10.30 a.m. on 12 October and I've gone temporarily blind.

For the past 12 hours I had been in the Humber estuary (the historic boundary between the counties of Yorkshire and Lincolnshire), but unlike the crystal-clear waters of the Yorkshire coast I had found myself swimming (and ingesting) a cocktail of brown, organic sediment that made breathing and sighting particularly tricky.

Later told the 'fertile water' gets its unique appearance from the eroding boulder clay cliffs along the Holderness Coast, for me it was like trying to move through gravy. Incredibly dense gravy too, since local coastguards told me up to 1.26 million tonnes of sediment may have been present in the water I currently found myself blindly travelling through. Basically, this made it a great home for birds and marine life, but a terrible swimming pool for me.

Also, although I usually breathe bilaterally (every three strokes), in the Humber estuary it was obvious the sea decides when you're allowed to breathe. This could be every three strokes, five strokes or even ten strokes, but you had to turn your head and take on oxygen between the random and brief breaks in the waves.

Despite being engulfed by gigantic brown waves, I stubbornly swam on for another hour, only to then be told by Mother Nature that the 'pool' was closed. For only the third time on the entire swim, our progress had been stopped by another storm. Storm Callum (the second storm of the season) was best described as Storm Ali's younger, angrier brother. Since, although Storm Ali stopped us in Dunbar with 105 mph winds, Storm Callum brought 85 mph winds that coincided with high spring tides which led to 10 ft waves overtopping sea walls in many coastal towns.

So that meant we had no choice but to retreat along with the other ships into the nearest harbour, which fortunately for us was the historic and heavily fortified docks of Grimsby. Quite possibly the best place to hide from a storm due to its high walls, solid structures and endless supply of award-winning fish and chips, sea trade out of Grimsby dates back to at least the medieval period, which means they were seasoned professionals when it came to inclement weather.

Of course, this wasn't my first storm either and the solitary confinement of Dunbar was still a fresh memory in my head. But this storm was different, and I didn't mind it for three reasons:

- Grimsby is in my home county of Lincolnshire.
- The people were incredibly welcoming.
- The next day was my birthday and friends and family were coming to visit.

That night, as the storm raged on outside my cabin, I had a blissful sleep. I was Controlling the Controllables and Accepting the Uncontrollables, all the while knowing that the next day (according to Maslow's hierarchy) my physiological, safety and social needs would be met when friends, family and crew gathered in the galley to eat, drink and wait for Storm Callum to pass.

STORMS, SMILES AND CELEBRATIONS: THE SCIENCE

It's 7.30 a.m. on 13 October 2018 and today I woke up 33 years old. Slowly crawling out of bed, I headed for the bathroom very aware that my skin seemed more weathered, scarred and salty than it was when I was 32. I was young, naive and much leaner back then, but since leaving Margate on 1 June, the seasons have changed and my tan, my six-pack and my youth have since faded ... lost somewhere in Scotland.

As I finished brushing my teeth, the door of my cabin opened.

It was Hester.

Now at this point I was very aware that I was basically a hairier, fatter and undomesticated version of the boyfriend she agreed to go out with years ago, but she didn't seem to mind. Attempting to give me a birthday hug, she couldn't quite get her arms around me due to my newly acquired girth and so we stood there in an awkward, chubby birthday embrace in the cosy 4 ft by 4 ft bathroom.

'Ooh ... you're so cuddly,' she said smiling.

To this day, I'm still not sure the word 'cuddly' was a compliment. After swimming for over 1,500 miles (around several countries) I was hoping for maybe 'heroic' or 'pioneering', but this is what I loved about Hester. It didn't matter what I did or how far I swam, I knew she would still be here whether I was fat, tall, small or skinny.

The same can be said for my family too. Climbing onto the deck, Mum and Scott had arrived equipped with presents and cake. All of which was immensely appreciated, but they knew the one thing I really wanted for my birthday couldn't be delivered that day. That's because Dad was too ill to travel, having started his immunotherapy treatment, so was resting at home under doctors' orders.

In the meantime Matt, Suzanne, Harriet and Taz had been awake since 6 a.m. decorating the boat in balloons and ribbons for my birthday breakfast. This was of course incredibly nice of all of them, but given the circumstances I would say it was also incredibly necessary too, and even now they probably have no idea just how much this actually meant to me.

You see, science shows that eating cake among family (old and newly adopted) has performance-enhancing benefits that go far beyond social needs and Maslow's hierarchy. In fact, experts now believe your mood, emotions and mental well-being can have a profound impact on your pace and resistance (and perception) to fatigue.

Looking at the swim reports it seems this was true. Although hard to accurately measure with tides, time, wind and waves, it seems there was some correlation between top speeds and distances covered when my mum, dad, brothers and girlfriend came on the boat.

One of the most memorable of these social swimming experiments happened back in the earlier days of the swim, in the seaside town of Portpatrick on the western shore of the Rhins of Galloway peninsula in Scotland. After wrestling with the tides around the Isle of Man (and setting a record of 100 miles in four days up the Irish sea) I'd arrived in Scottish waters successful, but sore. Sensing I'd be in bad shape (physically and mentally) my two brothers had a plan. Immediately packing their cars with cakes, flapjacks and chocolates they drove over 350 miles across England and Scotland to surprise me. Now, when I say 'surprise' I should mention I knew they were visiting the boat because they had spoken to Matt to find out which harbour we would stop in to refuel and restock. But the fact they arrived dressed as Popeye and Poseidon (complete with beard and toy trident) was something I wasn't expecting. I don't think the local fishermen of Portpatrick were either, as Craig and Scott were more than happy to stop and pose for pictures as they walked around the harbour.

Climbing onto the deck from my cabin I could barely speak since I was laughing so hard. I couldn't help but admire just how much they'd committed to this task.

'Where did you get the costumes from?' I asked.

'We thought this is what all sailors wear?' Scott said also laughing.

'Yes, we're just trying to blend in,' Craig said, now dancing on the boat with his wig and beard blowing in the wind.

Moments later Matt emerged from his cabin to see what was going on. Still severely sleep deprived from the Irish Sea, he had to rub his eyes to make sure he wasn't hallucinating .

'Oh ... you must be Ross's brothers.'

He then invited them aboard for breakfast, and for the next two days Popeye and Poseidon were the newest members of the crew, tasking themselves with making me smile during each swim.

And guess what? Shortly after Popeye and Poseidon had arrived I set a set a new speed record of 7.8 mph (6.8 knots) and covered 14.57 miles in just over four hours' swimming up the Mull of Kintyre (all despite a 100-mile warm-up through the Irish Sea).

So, what happened? Why was I stronger with a smile? According to a study published in the journal *Frontiers in Human Neuroscience* the answer lies in the psychobiological model of fatigue.[125] To test this theory, scientists from the UK's Institute for the Psychology of Elite Performance had athletes cycle to exhaustion as they were shown 'subliminal visual cues' of happy versus sad faces.

Subliminal visual cues are words and pictures that are unidentifiable to your conscious brain (since it doesn't have time to process and interpret) and instead happen so quickly (in a few milliseconds) that they're only absorbed at a subconscious level.

The results revealed that, 'Individuals cycled significantly longer when subliminally primed with happy faces.' They also added that the athletes rating of perceived exertion (RPE) during the time to exhaustion (TTE) test was also lower in the athletes 'primed with happy faces'.

They noted that 'these experiments are the first to show that subliminal visual cues relating to affect and action can alter perception of effort and endurance performance,' therefore more research is needed. But this is something the Royal Marines have been practising for years, so much so that it's actually part of their ethos, 'Cheerfulness in the face of adversity.'

This also supports the research in *Pain*, the official journal of the International Association for the Study of Pain, concerning maladaptive versus adaptive coping strategies for pain (which we covered earlier). But the final example of the science of a smile comes from one of the greatest explorers the world has ever known, Sir Ernest Shackleton.

STORMS, SMILES AND CELEBRATIONS: SHACKLETON

Shackleton was one of the world's toughest and most resilient adventurers. A British polar explorer who led three British expeditions to the Antarctic, he was one of the principal figures of the period known as the Heroic Age of Antarctic Exploration (1897–1922) when the frozen continent was first discovered and explored.

But it was Shackleton's 1914 expedition that cemented his place in history, when he set sail on his ship HMS *Endurance* to cross

Antarctica via the South Pole. The voyage began with food stores fully stocked consisting of an ample biscuit supply, the finest York hams, sheep tongues and 25 cases of whisky. But in early 1915, their ship became trapped in the ice and Shackleton's crew were forced to abandon it and seek safety on a floating iceberg. Watching his ship, food and the morale of his men sink to the bottom of the Weddell Sea, Shackleton now knew this was a very different type of expedition as written reports from the crew spoke of men blinded by hunger and sleepless nights plagued by fantasies of food.

But it's what happened next that defines the great man. Shackleton immediately began caring for his crew's physiological and safety needs (according to Maslow's hierarchy) as he began hunting for penguins and seals. It has been reported that he was partial to a little bit of elephant seal snout. Dinner one day even consisted of a sea leopard which attacked the boat and was seen as good fortune because its stomach was full of undigested fish that provided a delicious meal for the crew.

Once his men's physiological and safety needs were (partially) met, he then focused on sustaining morale by assessing their social needs. He did this by creating a unified team where everyone was equal. For example, he ignored the predominant class system of the time and had scientists scrubbing floors alongside seamen and university professors eating beside Yorkshire fishermen. While Shackleton was called the 'Boss' by his men, he did not differentiate himself from them, and in an attempt to help his crew get over the trauma of abandoning the *Endurance*, Shackleton literally served his men. Rising early in the morning, he made hot milk and hand-delivered it to every tent in the camp.

His mantra of unity and show of humanity was infectious. While his men were suffering from the most terrible deprivation, they often rose to his example and showed tremendous compassion for each other. When first officer Lionel Greenstreet spilled his much-needed milk on the ice, he seemed almost despondent over the loss.

So, one by one, the seven men who shared his tent silently poured some of their equally precious ration into his mug, refilling it.

Thankfully the story has a happy ending, when in 1916 Shackleton (with five men) went to find help and spent 16 days crossing 1,300 km of ocean to reach South Georgia and then trekked across the island to a whaling station. Securing help, he returned and rescued his remaining men in August 1916 and amazingly not one member of the expedition died.

Looking back over his career you can see Shackleton always understood the profound impact that morale could have on an adventure. On a failed expedition to the South Pole with Captain Scott in 1902, he famously surprised his tent-mates, hundreds of miles out from their base, by producing a Christmas pudding that had been 'hidden with his socks'. Historical records show the other men were suffering from signs of frostbite and scurvy at this stage, so would no doubt have been glad of the treat, in spite of Shackleton's not-entirely-hygienic choice of hiding place.

Basically, the entire life of Shackleton is inspiring and a masterclass in human resilience. Against all the odds, he managed the morale of his men and survived because he understood that central to any adventure is camaraderie and the science of a smile. It was also a story myself, Matt and the crew (including Popeye and Poseidon) continually tried to emulate throughout the remaining 200 miles of our swim.

LESSON 17

- Your mood, emotions and mental well-being can have a profound impact on your resistance (and perception) to fatigue.

- The Royal Marines practise a philosophy of **Cheerfulness in the face of adversity.** This is supported by research that shows that performance levels increase and perceived exhaustion levels are delayed when the brain is primed with **positive subliminal visual clues** ('happy' pictures or words absorbed by the brain only at the subconscious level).

- The great explorer **Ernest Shackleton**, in his expedition to cross Antarctica via the South Pole on his ship HMS *Endurance*, managed the morale of his men and survived because he understood that central to any adventure is **camaraderie** and **the science of a smile**.

LESSON 18 | YOU CAN SLEEP YOURSELF STRONGER

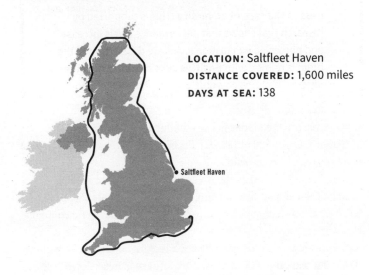

LOCATION: Saltfleet Haven
DISTANCE COVERED: 1,600 miles
DAYS AT SEA: 138

Saltfleet Haven

It's 5:30 a.m. on 16 October, and the threat of Storm Callum has passed. Cautiously leaving the safety and sanctuary of Grimsby dock two days before, we'd nervously made our way down the east coast as the storm had left behind an eerily calm sea that seemed to ripple and bubble away in the rising sun, threatening to erupt again at any time.

It was like swimming against a ticking time bomb. We were now midway through the British autumn and as winter approached we were all painfully aware that the frequency and intensity of storms around Britain was destined to increase. This meant our swim could (and would) change from being difficult to dangerous to outright impossible ... very quickly.

Anchored off the coast of Saltfleet Haven in Lincolnshire, Matt and I were both awake, unable to sleep, and sitting on deck. We were hesitant to make the 36-mile crossing from Lincolnshire to Norfolk across the Wash estuary for three reasons:

- It's BIG ... and stretches for over 100 square miles.
- It's ANGRY ... and part of the North Sea (a colder, harsher and angrier version of the Atlantic).
- It's DANGEROUS ... and home to a 35 km² (13.5 sq. mile) wind farm which we'd have to swim around.

Needless to say, if Storm Callum reappeared this would be tantamount to swimming suicide.

'How big are the blades in the windfarm?' I asked Matt.

'Hmm ... about 120 m [394 ft]. So, big enough to give you a haircut if we get too close,' he said.

'Oh, I see,' I replied as the severity of the situation sunk in.

Matt then sipped his morning tea and we both ate birthday cake left over from Grimsby that wasn't fresh, but wasn't stale enough to throw away yet.

'I know you're tired,' he continued looking at my sea-sore shoulders. 'But the only way to cross this estuary is head down ... for 36 miles ... with a relentless pace morning and night ... until we reach the harbour of Burnham Flats in Norfolk.'

I knew he was right, he usually was. For the past few months Matt had to continually change from being a sympathetic friend and sea mentor to a brutally realistic captain.

We knew giant rotating blades weren't the real enemy though. For today we were going into battle once more with the silent assassin that had been threatening to bring an end to this swim ... severe sleep deprivation. Plaguing myself and the entire crew as we relentlessly worked, sailed and swam with the tides that changed on a regular basis, we had been swimming day and night in six-hour intervals for over 130 days now and it was taking its toll physically and mentally.

We all knew this was a battle we would eventually lose, since sleep is inevitable and you can't fight it forever. We just hoped on this occasion we'd be able to fight long enough that we made it across to Norfolk.

Of course, everyone had their own coping strategies. Matt, for example, had resorted to chocolate-covered coffee beans which he rationed and medicated himself with during the night swims. I personally wasn't a fan since the taste was far too bitter for me. Instead, I relied on copious amounts of caffeine (in any and every form) while drawing on previous experiences from 48-hour training swims. The most brutal of these happened at the Royal Marines training centre down in Lympstone, in Devon.

Sitting on the deck that day waiting for the tide to turn, I told Matt the story as he crunched his supply of caffeine and I sipped mine.

MY 48-HOUR SLEEPLESS SWIM

It was 10 a.m. on 29 January 2018 at the Commando Training Centre in Devon. Tucked away in the southwest of England, this is the principal training centre for the Royal Marines. For over 75 years it has housed 3,000 officers and men in 74 huts on 54 acres of prime East Devon countryside and has a proud heritage of recruitment, training and selection for the British military.

Home to some of the fittest and most mentally resilient humans on the planet, it's a sacred place for many of Britain's bravest soldiers.

Then you had me. Although I have never served in the military, many of my friends from school and university have gone on to become decorated soldiers in the British armed forces. I was lucky enough that the Royal Marines decided to adopt me, this feral, nomadic athlete adventurer in need of somewhere to train.

Which is exactly what I was doing today. Heading to the swimming pool filled with blind optimism and child-like curiosity, I wanted to see how far I could swim non-stop in two days. Hearing of my plans, friends of mine (who happened to be physical training instructors) commandeered a swimming lane for 48 hours and as a team agreed to sleep by the side of the pool, and lifeguard and mentor me through sleep deprivation, hallucinations, gastrointestinal distress and chlorinated skin issues. Basically, they were great soldiers, but even better friends.

Arriving at the doors to the gymnasium and pool, it felt like walking into a museum. Every hallway was proudly decorated with trophies, framed pictures and athletic relics of some kind to inspire new recruits and remind them of their rich history and heritage that can be traced back to 28 October 1664 when the Royal Marines were formed.

Walking the halls, you couldn't help but feel inspired. It smelt historic, it felt elite and looked prestigious as performance and cutting-edge technology were fused with grandeur and tradition. The gym was the best example of this: barbells and machines crafted to a fine chrome finish which sat among wooden beams and ropes that felt so durable and 'industrially antique' as if they'd lasted years.

The swimming pool itself was the same. Blending sports science with a strange, old Edwardian splendour it had been custom-built to cater for everything from diving to swimming and even kayak drills. But for the next 48 hours this would be home for me, and the outside lane my kitchen as I carefully unpacked my food supplies.

The clock struck 11 a.m. and I was joined by my first two lifeguards. These were two friends who had helped me with every athletic adventure to date: Royal Marine Physical Training Instructor, Alex 'Benny' Benstead and Royal Marine Captain, Oliver Mason.

Benny's quite hard to describe, but imagine a Royal Marine power-lifting hybrid with the densest shoulder and moustache combination you've ever witnessed. Next there was Captain Oliver Mason, a six foot four, 120 kg rugby-playing ultra-marathon runner.

'Are you ready?' Benny asked.

'Yes,' I nodded nervously since the truth is I didn't know what 'ready' felt like when preparing to swim over 100 km with no sleep. I had done my research though and had printed out over a hundred journals and studies relevant to swimming and sleep deprivation.

Handing them to Benny, I pointed to the journal *Biological Psychiatry* and a particular study focusing on severe decrements in cognition (brain) function induced by sleep loss within the military.[126] Thumbing through the pages, Benny noted symptoms of mood disturbances,[127] biological stress[128] and impaired motor skills.

'Yup, that seems about right,' he said on closing the book. 'Best get cracking ... it will only get worse.'

I smiled through gritted teeth, since I knew he was right. But I was glad I was doing this training swim under solider supervision, since research published in the journal *Aviation, Space, and Environmental Medicine* found, 'Military operations, especially combat, expose individuals to multiple stressors, including sleep loss, food deprivation, and sustained physical activity.'[129]

Basically, those who've served in the military are very well practised in the adverse conditions described in Stoic Sports Science.

MY SLEEPLESS SWIM: THE START

Midday was upon us and it was time for the swim to begin. It was a slow and subdued start. No one cheered or clapped, it was almost anticlimactic because the physical training instructors in attendance knew exactly what was about to unfold over the next 48 hours. Among them was a good friend by the name of Sgt Matt Burley who only months before had set a record (in this very pool) by completing 34.46 miles underwater over 10 days (completing 166 lengths each day with only a 30 s rest period in between), raising thousands of pounds for charity as a result. Matt knew this pool better than anyone else and so equipped himself with a stopwatch to ensure I was adhering to the pre-agreed pacing strategy.

The first 32 hours went well as we clocked over 90 km. But it was after this point that the wheels began falling off the proverbial wagon. Why? Because scientists believe, 'Sleep is an important component of homeostasis, vital for our survival and sleep disorders are associated with significant behavioural and health consequences.'[130] So that explains why my body's inbuilt 'clock' – known as the body's circadian rhythm[131] – was well aware that the time was 8 p.m., the sun was going down and I should have been tucked up in bed. This is because your circadian rhythm is responsible for regulating the biological rhythms over a 24-hour period from the rise and fall of testosterone and cortisol levels to the synchronisation of sleep, wakefulness, mood, and cognitive performance.[132] So, when this malfunctions you're in trouble.

But it gets worse because a German physician called Jurgen Aschoff discovered our circadian rhythms are synchronised to the earth's 24-hour light cycle through external and environmental cues called zeitgebers.[133] For plants and animals, the daily pattern of light and darkness and the warmer and colder temperatures between day and night serve as zeitgebers, cues that keep organisms functioning on a regular schedule. For humans, societally imposed cycles, such as the schedule of the work or school day and regular mealtimes, can become zeitgebers as well.[134]

In order to keep your circadian rhythm (hormones and basic bodily functions) running like clockwork, your body relies on zeitgebers. But right now, I had no choice but to ignore them. Which you can only do for so long before your own mind starts to betray you.

'You okay?' Benny asked me during a brief biscuit break.

'Physically I'm fine, but mentally I'm struggling,' I replied.

Benny smiled sympathetically through pursed lips since he knew exactly what I was going through, having been there himself many times. He then delivered some much-needed home truths before I headed into my second night swim that weren't nice to hear, but were necessary to learn.

'This will become torture,' he said bluntly with no sugar coating.

He then told me sleep deprivation has been used as a form of torture for centuries. Yes, it might sound quite tame in comparison with other forms of torture, but in the hands of an expert interrogator it can be brutal and drastically reduce someone's resilience to physical pain and psychological enquiry.

Tracing its origins back to the fifteenth century, an Italian lawyer and doctor by the name of Hippolytus de Marsiliis was the first person to document sleep deprivation as a means of torture. He was best known for documenting the Chinese water torture method too, in which drops of water would consistently fall on a victim's forehead, causing them to go insane. But his work was later adopted by witch-hunters in Europe and North America who called this form of torture 'tortura insomniae' and used it to interrogate thousands of innocent women for alleged sorcery. American historian Andrew Dickson wrote, 'In this way, temporary delusion became chronic insanity, mild cases became violent, torture and death ensued.'[135]

It's worth noting that at this particular moment I was doing the exact opposite of swimming with a smile, and as a result the next four hours of training were brutal.

MY SLEEPLESS SWIM: THE BEGINNING OF THE END

With stories of Chinese water torture and witchcraft playing over in my head, I began to hallucinate in the early hours as I reached the

145 km mark in my swim. In fact, previous studies confirm, 'Perceptual distortions were most frequent in the late night-early morning hours (4.00 a.m.).'[136]

How bad was it? Well, I thought the lane markings were large fish and I bumped into the lane rope (twice) and thought it was another swimmer so apologised. Both times I said, 'Do help yourself to snacks at the end of my lane if you're hungry.'

It was at this point Benny knew something was wrong. He raced to the end of the pool containing the food, since he knew I would pop my head up eventually to feed and when I did he could assess my level of 'tortura insomniae'.

'How's things, buddy?'

'Oh, they're okay,' I replied since I genuinely thought I was.

'Well ... clearly not, since you just apologised to a lane rope and offered it biscuits.'

I looked around me. It was 8.00 a.m. in the morning and I was the only one in the pool. Realising I was slowly losing my mind, I decided to outsource common sense and asked Benny how I was.

'I don't think you'll die,' he said with a completely straight face. 'But I can't be 100 per cent sure yet.'

Proceeding to eat as many energy bars as my mouth and stomach could handle, I asked him why I was in this state.

'Well, we'll never know definitively whether or not a lack of sleep can be fatal to humans. But there are several studies on animals which demonstrate that staying awake indefinitely can indeed eventually kill.'

Indeed, there was plenty of evidence in the annals of time. In 1894, Russian scientist Marie de Manaceine started experimenting on puppies to test the effects of sleep deprivation. She wrote, 'I have found that by experimenting on 10 puppies that the complete deprivation of sleep for 4 to 5 days (96 to 120 hours) causes irreparable lesions in the organism's brain and in spite of every care these experiments could not be saved. Complete absence of sleep during this period is fatal to puppies.'[137]

An experiment in 1898 with dogs showed similar results. Italian scientists Lamberto Daddi and Giulio Tarozzi kept dogs awake by continuously walking them, only to find all the animals died after 9 to 17 days. The reasons for the deaths were not fully understood.[138]

In the 1980s, American sleep researcher Allan Rechtschaffen set up some controlled experiments using pairs of rats as his subjects. One of the rats was allowed to sleep but the other was forced to stay awake at all times. The control rats remained healthy but the rats subjected to total sleep deprivation all died after between 11 and 32 days. The exact cause of the fatalities was a mystery, the report (again) stating that 'No anatomical cause of death was identified.'[139]

'But there's good news,' Benny told me. 'You're not a dog or rat, and in humans it seems the more mentally stable and robust you are, the more resilient to sleep deprivation you may be.'

He then told me that from interviews and psychiatric tests involving 74 army volunteers at the Walter Reed Army Institute of Research (the largest biomedical research facility administered by the US Department of Defence), researchers found they could predict reasonably well which individual would find the experience most difficult and would report hallucinatory events.[140] He added (and while I don't agree with the ethics of this study) that researchers from McGill University found a similar connection between mental health and resilience to sleep deprivation when six chronic schizophrenic patients were kept awake for 100 hours. As sleep loss continued, these patients began to show acute symptoms that had not been seen for several years among them, such as auditory hallucinations (hearing voices in their head).[141]

I thought about all of the above while swimming through the night. I learned that the extent of a person's suffering under protracted sleep loss would seem to depend upon what we term 'mental health', and studies seem to highlight the point that symptoms occur sooner (and with greater intensity) in unstable individuals.[142]

As the sun came up, the end of my sleepless swim was in sight. As predicted by the psychobiological model of fatigue, my brain sensed the end was near and so lifted that psychobiological handbrake and allowed me to cruise to a finish after what was 48 hours and 175 km.

Emerging from the pool, my body was in pieces. I'd even developed early signs of trench foot, a painful condition caused by long immersion of the feet in cold water or mud. It's called 'trench foot' because soldiers seemed to develop the condition when engaged in trench warfare, when keeping the body (and feet) dry, warm and hygienic was often tricky.

But at the time I didn't care. I had finished.

I thanked everyone who (heroically) worked the lifeguard rota over those two days. Sleeping by the pool, their selfless act of sleep deprivation allowed me to learn some valuable lessons in resilience that you only gain from putting in the hard, dark miles ('getting wintered'). My most valuable lesson? On a notepad, I wrote:

Athletes are taught to perform at their *best*,
When they feel at their *best*.

Royal Marines are taught to perform at their *best*,
When they feel at their *worst*.

Through sore shoulders and seasickness on my Great British Swim I always thought back to this, and as I continued to make the 36-mile crossing from Lincolnshire to Norfolk, I had it playing on repeat in my head.

SWIM NOW AND SLEEP LATER

LOCATION: Lincolnshire
Windfarm
DISTANCE COVERED: 1,630 miles
DAYS AT SEA: 138

Lincolnshire
Windfarm

It's 11.30 a.m. on 16 October, and we are 20 hours into our Humber estuary crossing. As expected, my body's circadian rhythm was entirely confused. Although sleep deprivation had been a necessary evil of the past 130 days at sea and (to an extent) I was able to build up a certain tolerance to it ... the body and brain wasn't happy and the lack of rest and recovery had begun to manifest itself in the form of a dogged swim-stroke, snail-like pace and decision-making based on the mental capacity of an 11-year-old.

Basically, I was able to function but was never at my best. Nevertheless, inspired by the teachings of the Royal Marines, I was determined to at least try to perform at my *best* when I felt at my *worst* and continued swimming through the night. During this entire time I was sandwiched between Harriet in the smaller motorised rib and Matt at the helm of *Hecate*, to ensure that I stayed clear of the giant blades from the windfarm and so that they could check on my mental stability.

Both were easier said than done. For the first few miles I was breathing bilaterally and sighting off the lights from Matt and Harriet to maintain a steady course. But as we went further into the night, my basic sense of direction started to diminish and I swayed from side to side as the stars in the sky began to look very similar to the lights on the boats.

Deciding the best way to combat this would be to solely sight off the larger, brighter light on the bow of *Hecate*, this worked well for about a mile. That was until (with a sudden lapse of concentration) I mistook the boat light for the moon and then veered completely off course into the windfarm.

Harriet immediately gave chase in the small boat. 'ROSS ... STOP!' she shouted as I edged closer to the circulating blades.

Completely oblivious, I continued swimming since I was now deprived of both my senses and sleep at night. Deciding a different course of action was needed, Harriet quickly grabbed a banana and with pinpoint accuracy hit me on the back of the head with it.

As she did, I remember thinking *why am I hallucinating about bananas?*

Finally, as a last resort, she decided to run into me with the boat.

Now this isn't as bad as it sounds. Harriet was a very skilled driver and the rib was made from inflatable rubber so I basically just bounced off the side. At that point, on impact, I immediately knew I'd gone off course.

'Sorry,' I said half asleep.

Harriet smiled and felt bad she'd had to resort to hitting me with a boat, but I told her it was fine and better than getting a 'haircut' from the giant collection of windfarm blades. I gave her and Matt permission to bounce me like a pinball machine all the way across the estuary to Norfolk, which is exactly what they did ... all through the night until sunrise on 16 October when we arrived in Burnham Flats.

We crawled into the harbour, docked and took to our beds out of exhaustion. After 27 hours, we had made it from Lincolnshire to Norfolk and were now only 140 miles away from Margate, completing my swim and seeing my dad.

SLEEP NOW AND SWIM LATER

LOCATION: Burnham Flats
DISTANCE COVERED: 1,645 miles
DAYS AT SEA: 139

The time is 11.00am on 17 October and my alarm has sounded.

I had been sleeping ALL DAY. Waking in a delicate state, me and my immune system were no longer friends. I'm not surprised either, since studies show it's during sleep that your body is rejuvenated and replenished to keep you motivated, focused and functioning.

But during the past 27 hours, I hadn't done any of that and I had neglected my most basic biological 'house maintenance.'[143] And what about the effect of my lack of sleep on my performance levels? Studies conducted at Stanford University on basketball players analysed the impact sleeping ten hours a night had on player's performance after five to seven weeks. Previously, the players had only been sleeping six to nine hours and what the sleep scientists found was their performance dramatically improved.[144] 'Shooting accuracy improved, with free throw percentage increasing by 9 per cent and three-point field goal percentage increasing by 9.2 per cent ... Subjects also reported improved overall ratings of physical and mental well-being during practices and games.' What they concluded was, 'Improvements in specific measures of basketball performance after sleep extension indicate that optimal sleep is likely beneficial in reaching peak athletic performance.'

So where does this nocturnal magic come from? According to research published in *Frontiers in Systems Neuroscience*, it's closely related to our previously mentioned neurotransmitters.[145] Neurotransmitters are the chemicals that work to transmit signals from a neuron to a target cell across a synapse within the body. Pretty much every function within the body is controlled (or impacted) by neurotransmitters, from emotional states to mental performance and our perception to fatigue and pain. They are the brain's little chemical messengers and if they're not working correctly due to lack of sleep you can't expect to be very effective come match day.

Today mine refused to fire, motivation was low and I struggled to even lift my head from my pillow never mind contemplate a swim.

The importance of sleep is supported by scientists from the University of Toronto who monitored the sleep patterns of six runners following a 92 km ultra-marathon.[146] Results showed sleep time for each runner 'increased drastically' compared to 'normal sleep patterns' on each of the four nights after the marathon, illustrating the body's desperate need for quality sleep to recover. Using an electroencephalogram (EEG) in which electrodes measure brain electrical activity, they specifically found long periods of 'deep sleep' were induced on the first two nights. This led researchers to conclude this objective and quantitative increase in total sleep time, and particularly 'deep sleep', supports the theory that it's incredibly important for optimal recovery in athletes.

Another reason sleep is so critical to recovery is because it's during this time one of our most revitalising hormones peaks. Known as human growth hormone, it's a peptide hormone that stimulates cell reproduction, cell regeneration, growth and recovery. Which is why for all the energy bars and recovery shakes in the world, if you suspect you are overtraining and under-recovered, one of the best things you can do is head to bed.

Yet this was a luxury I (and the crew) wouldn't always have. I knew there would be times when I would be tired,[147] exhausted,[148] not optimally recovering[149] and my decision-making would be flawed and impaired.[150] Also, while there are few specific studies on this yet, I knew sleep deprivation would increase my (perceived) reasons to quit and reduce my (perceived) reasons to continue as exercise stressors and signallers were misinterpreted and/or exaggerated.

But equipped with my Royal Marine training philosophy and Stoic Sports Science, I knew I had the tools to battle my way through this.

LESSON 18

- To keep your **circadian rhythm** (hormones and basic bodily functions) running like clockwork, your body relies on **zeitgebers** (external and environmental clues such as mealtimes and natural light and darkness). Ignore these at your peril.
- Studies show that the more mentally stable and robust you are, the more resilient to **sleep deprivation** you may be.
- Nearly every function within the body is controlled (or impacted) by **neurotransmitters** (chemicals that work to transmit signals to target cells): from emotional states to mental performance and our perception to fatigue and pain. If the brain's 'little chemical messengers' are not working correctly due to lack of sleep, our performance levels will suffer.
- When you sleep, your **human growth hormone** stimulates cell reproduction, cell regeneration, growth and recovery. Feeling overtrained or exhausted? Then **head for bed!**

LESSON 19 | HEROICS IN HUNGER

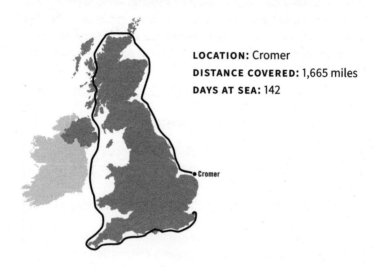

LOCATION: Cromer
DISTANCE COVERED: 1,665 miles
DAYS AT SEA: 142

Cromer

It's 3.00 p.m. on 20 October off the coast of Cromer, Norfolk. A coastal town with a long-standing connection to the ocean that was evident in its very architecture, we were anchored next to the famous pier that dominates the seafront. Standing 151 m (495 ft) long and serving as an enduring example of Victorian construction, incredibly it has withstood storms, tidal surges and even an attempt to blow it up during World War II.

But the townspeople's affiliation with the sea doesn't stop there. Each and every one of the stained-glass windows of the Cromer Parish Church has been designed to commemorate their beloved lifeboat crew, the most decorated in the history of the Royal National Lifeboat Institution (RNLI). Also, their local museum was named after Henry Blogg, who served for 53 years on Cromer's lifeboats and, alongside his crew, saved 873 lives from the North Sea.

This is essentially why I loved Cromer, a town populated with proud seafaring folk. They sensed with around 100 miles left to swim that this was the homestretch for us and so came out in force to support me and the team. I was even made an honorary member of the North Norfolk Crawlers swimming club, several of whom swam off the pier to hand-deliver a swim cap for me to wear during my time on the Norfolk coast.

But it was a single event that happened at precisely 4.10 p.m. during that day's afternoon swim that truly showed the unique spirit of the people of Cromer. I was two hours into that tide (swim) and settling into a steady stroke rate. Now no longer sleep deprived, my sense of direction was dramatically improved so I didn't need to be sandwiched between Matt and Harriet to keep me on course. But for one brief moment I thought I was still hallucinating ...

Completely confused, out the corner of my eye I thought I was imagining a man, in a boat waving sausages at me. A mile passed and the hallucination wasn't going away so I decided it was best to stop and check in with Matt.

'Can I ask you something?' I said swimming to the side of the boat.

Matt peered over the deck. 'What's wrong?' he asked concerned.

'Am I hallucinating or is there a man over there driving a boat and waving a bag of sausages at me?'

Everyone on the boat started to laugh. It turns out this wasn't a hallucination. He was a local butcher who'd called Matt so he could coordinate delivering a package of his award-winning sausages. All because he'd heard we weren't able to store fresh meat on the boat due to limited storage space in the fridge.

Swimming over to his boat (now knowing he wasn't a figment of my imagination) I couldn't thank him enough. For it wasn't just a bag of sausages he was giving me: it was fulfilling my basic, primitive physiological needs of food (according to Maslow's Hierarchy of Needs) and boosting morale like Shackleton's sock full of pudding.

This is why eating for me during the swim typically came in two forms:

- I would take my time, savouring the taste and texture of food since my brain continued to live in a world of sea-based sensory deprivation where sound, sight and smell were impaired.
- I would eat like an untamed, overweight whale, barely registering flavour but solely concerned with the precious calories and nutrients the food was providing.

Obviously, both types of 'dinner time' were needed at different times. For instance, it would never be wise to host a wine-tasting course in the Gulf of Corryvreckan with the Hag Goddess. But taking a brief moment (mid swim) to enjoy a sausage sandwich under the stars in Norfolk was something I will never forget.

Sailors, surfers, fishermen and swimmers all around the coast knew this too. They knew the very best form of support they could offer was food. From the incredible potato cakes of Solva harbour to the giant Cornish pasties of Newquay and award-winning fish and chips in Grimsby, often people didn't realise just how much it helped since storage and supplies on the boat were so limited.

I began to call them 'heroics in hunger', and do you know who are experts in this? The people of Scotland. Thanks to the kindness of strangers and the comfort of their food, they got me through some of my darkest moments of the swim as news of my dad's health continued to occupy my thoughts.

But there was one act of kindness that I will never forget. Her name was Iona and she was an open-water swimmer in Scotland. Maybe 40 years old (but hard to tell since she had those incredible Celtic Amazonian genetics) she had been following our progress around the Highlands and knew how cold the water was and how angry the storms were and so wanted to do something to help.

So, she decided to track our route and plot the exact point we would pass her house. Then, with military precision, she timed it so as we passed, her freshly baked, homemade fruit loaf was just out of the oven. Immediately putting on her goggles and swimsuit, she then mounted the fruit loaf (still piping hot) onto her head and ran down to the coast to intercept us.

To this day I have never seen anything like it (possibly on a par with my sausage wielding Spartan of Norfolk). Iona effortlessly swam breaststroke with one arm as she used the other one to balance the fruit loaf on her head. It's also no exaggeration when I say it was still warm and steaming by the time she delivered it to me.

But this is just one of many stories and every present, parcel and pastry meant so much. This is why I would so often say that 'resilience is best served with food' because both mental and physical fortitude *must* be fuelled. It's a basic human need and can make or break any adventure.

Back in Norfolk, and for the remainder of that tide (swim) I swiftly made my way around the northeast coast and thought about the great adventurers of the Heroic Age of Antarctic Exploration such as Roald Amundsen and Robert Falcon Scott.[151]

Their adventures can only be described as pure heroics in hunger.

HEROICS IN HUNGER AND ADVENTURE

In the early twentieth century, hunger played an important role in exploration's last great prize and the race to be the first person to reach the South Pole.

A number of explorers set out to claim it for their own, but in 1911 it was Britain's Robert Falcon Scott and Norway's Roald

Amundsen who went head to head to reach the most remote spot on earth. Scott had attempted to reach the South Pole once before in 1902 but his party were forced to turn back due to ill health and sub-zero conditions. It was always Scott's intention to return and, with the support of the British Admiralty and the government, he secured a grant of £20,000 for his latest attempt.

Scott recruited men from his original expedition and from Ernest Shackleton's ship HMS *Nimrod* which had recently returned from the Antarctic. His crew included naval seamen, scientists and paying members. His ship *Terra Nova* sailed from Cardiff on 15 June 1910.

Further north, Amundsen was a respected Norwegian explorer who was determined to beat the Brits to the South Pole. He kept his plans to head south very secret and set out with his crew on the *Fram*, appearing to head north round South America to the Arctic, but all the time intending to head south to Antarctica first and then continue north.

Fram reached the Ross Ice Shelf on 14 January 1911, Amundsen having chosen to land at the Bay of Whales. This gained the Norwegians a 60-mile advantage over Scott, who had landed at McMurdo Sound.

On 18 October 1911, after the Antarctic winter, Amundsen's team set out on its drive toward the Pole. Captain Scott began his trek three weeks later. At around 3 p.m. on 14 December 1911, Amundsen raised the flag of Norway at the South Pole. He had reached it a full 33 days before Captain Scott arrived. Amundsen and his crew returned to their base camp on 25 January 1912, 99 days and roughly 1,400 nautical miles after their departure.

Scott left his base camp with his team on 1 November 1911. He finally reached the South Pole on 17 January 1912, disappointed to learn that Amundsen had beaten him to it. The tortuous return journey was faced with stoicism and dignity. Weak from exhaustion, hunger and extreme cold, his last diary entry is dated 29 March 1912. He died in his tent alongside two of his men.

What was the deciding factor? Food.

For it was on the return from the South Pole that Amundsen and his team ate their dogs. One by one as their load got lighter and less kit was needed or used for the expedition, fewer dogs were required to pull the load and those dogs were looked upon as a commodity – breakfast, lunch and dinner – rather than man's best friend. Smart, but rather macabre.

In contrast, Scott's polar expedition was pulled by ponies (not dogs) which didn't work very well, either pulling the sledges or serving as a snack. Perhaps if Scott had brought along 'food' that could survive (the ponies are reported to have perished when falling through the ice) and walk on its own four legs in Antarctica, he may have won the prize of the Pole.

Amundsen's name also turns up in the north. Ten years before he conquered the South Pole, he humiliated the Brits by taking a very small boat along the Northwest Passage and becoming the first man to successfully navigate between the Atlantic and Pacific oceans.

One of the British men that Amundsen beat was Sir John Franklin, another polar hero, who died in his Northwest Passage attempt. Franklin, with his large, technologically advanced vessels HMS *Erebus* and HMS *Terror*, had packed what he believed to be his guarantor to the expedition's success: canned food. It was a revolutionary packaging of fresh grub which would keep his men fed for years, or so he thought, except that unfortunately the solder used to weld the cans was made of lead, which eventually caused lead poisoning and made most of his men go a bit mad before dying. Amundsen, on the other hand, hung out with the indigenous Inuits and learned how they hunted and survived in the Canadian wilderness.

Amundsen basically understood the heroics of hunger.

So how did I manage my own nutrition? Well, that is something the media now wanted to know. So, with less than 120 miles to go, I invited a journalist from the BBC onto the boat for breakfast, a cup of tea and a chat.

EAT ANYTHING AND EVERYTHING

LOCATION: Horsey
DISTANCE COVERED: 1,685 miles
DAYS AT SEA: 143

It's 7.10 a.m. on 21 October. Today was a great day! We were anchored off the northeast coast of Norfolk near a small village called Horsey, a place famous for its population of grey seals that were currently arriving ashore to give birth to this season's pups. Needless to say, after 130 days at sea (and sharing a 'pool' with them around Lundy and Robin Hood's Bay) I was feeling a little broody myself.

Looking through the porthole of my cabin for a better view, it was an honour to witness the tiny newborn seals with their distinctive white coats laying on the sandy beaches waiting for a milk delivery from their mums. It was a sight I would never forget.

But, putting the miracle of birth to one side, there's another reason today was a great day. Our time to swim, to have our breakfast and to progress with the tides had all aligned at quite a civilised hour of the day. This made a nice change from ripping blood-soaked bedsheets from my neck at 2.00 a.m. across the Irish Sea. Times like today when the stars aligned were rare, but when they happened everyone on the crew savoured them.

This is why Taz and Harriet had been up since 6.00 a.m. in the galley slicing and toasting several loaves of bread and preparing a giant cauldron of porridge that was bubbling away on the stove. The smell was incredible since Harriet always added cinnamon and spices to the oats. When she did this, no alarm clock was ever needed as I jumped out of bed to see whether she was adding peanut butter or cashew butter to the mix (or both).

What was also nice about this morning was there hadn't been such an immediate rush. So I had more time to make myself look semi-presentable before the BBC reporter was scheduled to arrive. Looking around the cabin I was struggling to find clean clothes, so in a moment of panic I decided to wear:

- My finest woollen hat, which a very kind Scottish lady had knitted for me in Dunbar (complete with bobble on top).
- A t-shirt that only had a few crumbs and creases in it.
- No trousers, only my trunks. Since all my trousers had holes or stains on them, so my logic was that wearing no trousers was better than wearing dirty trousers.

With my media outfit sorted, I then headed to the galley. At 7.30 a.m. breakfast was served and we were joined by the journalist. He was tall, smartly dressed, had immaculately combed hair and didn't have a single crumb or crease in his shirt or tie. He was in his mid-forties and based on first impressions I liked him, since he was very polite and hadn't battered an eyelid as I sat beside him without any trousers on.

No sooner had he arrived than the topic of conversation shifted to the giant cauldron of porridge and tower of toast that Harriet and Taz were creating.

'Will he [Ross] eat all that in a day?' he asked the crew, shocked at the sheer quantity.

'Oh no,' Taz replied. 'He'll eat all that in a morning ... this is basically breakfast and brunch.'

Shaking his head in disbelief, the journalist then took out his recording equipment, notepad and pen and began the interview.

'What foods do you eat?' he asked.

I smiled, since it wasn't as simple as that. When deciding what foods to eat I didn't want to strictly follow a specific diet plan, since we humans were never meant to eat through rules, regulations and checklists – they're simply too restrictive and we're biologically wired to seek variety. In fact, according to research in the *American Journal of Clinical Nutrition*, 'There would have been no single universal diet consumed by all extinct hominin species. Rather, diets would have varied by geographic locale, climate, and specific ecologic niche.'[152]

'Okay, but will you stick to a low-fat or high-carb way of eating?' the journalist continued.

I smiled and shook my head again. All nutrients are interdependent within the body. What this means is fats, proteins, carbohydrates, vitamins and minerals will all impact each other in more ways than we will probably ever know; all operating in a complex system of interrelationships where inevitably Monday's choice of breakfast will impact Friday night's choice of dinner. Everything is forever changing.

The problem is too often science fails to acknowledge this. Food is studied in complete isolation and nutritionists compartmentalise nutrients that are never compartmentalised in nature. We are unfortunately failing to take into account the complexity of the human body and all its different variables.

But for me things change every week, day, tide and swim. For me, when miles out to sea, the best way to approach my nutrition was to:

- Set a framework based on tried and tested guidelines.
- 'Fluidly' adapt and change within this framework, with each day, swim and tide depending on what my stomach could digest.

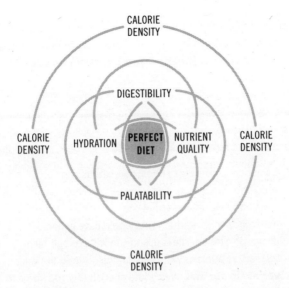

You must understand that at sea there wasn't time to strictly count calories, study sugar or work out the macronutrient composition of my breakfast. Equally, I was swimming for up to 12 hours a day which meant the very idea of pre-workout and post-workout didn't exist.

Put in a diagram it looks like this, as every meal, snack or shake was governed by these five basic principles:

- Calorie Density
- Nutrient Quality
- Palatability
- Digestibility
- Hydration

So that is how you fuel fortitude.

Now, worth noting is digestibility and hydration were topics I had learned long before Norfolk, as the shipping lanes of Dover and tidal streams of Portland Bill were my teachers on those particular themes. But the man from the BBC was keen to hear more about calorie density and just how many cauldrons of porridge oats I was eating every day.

LESSON 19

- Do not eat according to rules, regulations and checklists, since according to research: 'There would have been no single universal diet consumed by all extinct hominin species. Rather, diets would have varied by geographic locale, climate, and specific ecologic niche.'
- Instead, as humans we are biologically wired to seek **variety in our diet**. We should cherish this and strive to **balance our nutritional intake** rather than focus on one type of 'beneficial' nutrient.
- **All nutrients are interdependent** within the body, meaning fats, proteins, carbohydrates, vitamins and minerals will all impact each other in more ways than we will probably ever know, all operating in a complex system of interrelationships.
- The perfect 'diet' for a high-performance challenge is governed by five basic principles: **calorie density, nutrient quality, digestibility, palatability** and **hydration**.

LESSON 20 | RESILIENCE IS BEST SERVED WITH FOOD

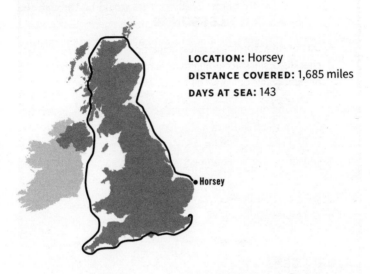

LOCATION: Horsey
DISTANCE COVERED: 1,685 miles
DAYS AT SEA: 143

• Horsey

It's 8.00 a.m. and we are one tower of toast and two bowls of porridge into our interview. As the vat of steaming oats continues to bubble away on the stove and more bread is freshly buttered, the entire galley has been turned into a sauna. I of course didn't mind since I still had no trousers on and this was one of the rare times I was actually hot. Our journalist friend, however, had removed his tie as droplets of condensation gathered on the roof and the portholes steamed up.

But, like a consummate professional, he continued with his questions.

'So how many calories do you eat per day?' he asked.

'Enough to fuel my swim, aid recovery and increase body fat for buoyancy and insulation,' I said.

He wrote that down in his notepad. 'But can you give me a figure?' he asked probing for an exact number.

'At a guess, I would say 10,000 to 15,000 per day.'

I then explained how, inspired by Robert Falcon Scott and Roald Amundsen, I knew my calorie requirements would be through the roof. Also, some days I'd be expending so much energy that I would desperately need to get my calories from anywhere and everywhere in order to continue.

This was of course easier in some places than others. For instance, trying to peel and force-feed myself a banana in 7-ft waves was tricky during my time on the south coast of England, especially when served in the middle of a shipping lane. But when family and friends visited the boat, hitting 15,000 calories was far easier, since they would often arrive equipped with my favourite snack in the form of a freshly baked, granary meatball baguette wrapped in a 10-inch stuffed crust pizza.

Yes, it's as good as it sounds.

CALORIE DENSITY

For years sports science has known that calorie intake forms a crucial role in successful performance for ultra-endurance athletes.

Take adventure racing for example. A sport where competitors compete over 10 days in various disciplines ranging from mountain biking, running, kayaking, climbing and mountaineering over a rugged, often remote and wilderness terrain. Scientists wanted to establish evidence-based nutritional recommendations for competitors and found, 'Energy expenditures of 365–750 kcal/hour have been reported with total energy expenditures of 18,000–80,000 kcal required to complete adventure races,' in addition to which, 'Large negative energy balances during competitions have been reported.'[153]

To put it simply, competitors were not able to eat enough. This is supported by a study which monitored the calorie intake of adventure racers during a 67-hour simulated laboratory experiment where athletes covered a total distance of 477.3 km. Food intake was recorded throughout the experiment and they found that even within the safe and controlled environment of the sports laboratory, 'Athletes' total energy expenditure was greater than their total energy intake (24,516 vs. 14,738 kcal).'[154]

That's a calorie deficit of over 9,000 calories.

This is why for all the advancements made in technology and sports supplements, scientists concluded, 'Athletes competing in ultra-endurance sports should manage nutritional issues, especially with regards to energy,' adding, 'Such a negative energy balance is a major health and performance concern'[155] and, 'Maintenance of nutritional and hydration status remains critical for successful participation in ultra-endurance exercise.'[156]

So, for my swim, we *estimated* I needed 10,000 to 15,000 calories per day. This is a rough guess, of course – no calorie counting equation could account for waves, tides, water temperature, salt water buoyancy and many more factors. But I knew on a very basic and primitive level that if I wasn't able to meet my calorie requirements, studies showed I wouldn't be able to swim at the same intensity,[157] recovery between tides would be greatly impacted[158] and even my immune system would begin to break down.[159]

Another reason for these colossal amounts of calories was body fat.

'How much do you need to put on?' the journalist asked.

'Well, I was 88 kg when I left Margate and now 140 days later I'm just over 100 kg,' I said. 'But this weight gain has been mainly dictated by nature and winter being round the corner.'

Clearing the steam from the porthole window, I then pointed to the beach of Horsey and the tiny seal pups that now inhabited it.

'My diet also takes inspiration from them,' I said.

Over a third bowl of porridge I then told him that a mother seal's milk is 60 per cent fat and has the consistency of condensed milk. This ensures the pup can gain weight quickly to survive the winter, often tripling their birth weight in just three weeks, gaining 2 kg per day to go from 15 kg to 45 kg during its time on the beach.

Obviously, 2 kg per day is a lot (even for me) but I was aware that, like the seal pups, I needed to store fat to become better prepared to take on the colder winter swims that lay ahead and have additional fat stores to tap into if needed. But without a plentiful supply of high-fat seal milk (and limited storage space on the boat), I instead relied on a giant supply of nut butters. High in fat (containing 9 calories per gram) I would add peanut butter, cashew butter and almond butter to anything and everything.

By 8.15 a.m. I was doing just that ... mixing almond butter with pieces of 80 per cent dark chocolate into my porridge as soon as it came out of the pot so it would melt. I then enriched it with whey protein, fruit, berries and anything else I could find lying around the galley cupboards.

'Do the berries make it taste nice?' the journalist asked.

'It's not just nice, it's necessary,' I replied.

Once I knew I was eating with enough calorie density, I next had to focus on nutrient density. This is why with my estimate of 10,000 to 15,000 calories per day, I began by consulting research from the *International Journal of Sports Nutrition* which analysed the nutrient intake of ultra-runners throughout a 1,005 km race completed over nine days. Since there was no diet for a 1,780 mile sea swim, I thought its recommendations were the closest to making logical sense for my challenge.

The researchers found, 'Daily energy intake with 62% from carbohydrate, 27% from fat and 11% from protein' was best and, 'If the guidelines for prolonged exercise are followed, then athletes can successfully complete ultra-endurance events.'[160]

'Does that mean you can eat anything?' the reporter asked .

'Uh ... not exactly,' I said smiling, although wishing that was the case.

Despite swimming for up to 12 hours a day and burning calories like a furnace, I had to adhere to the research published in the journal *Obesity Surgery*, 'It is a common belief that clinical vitamin or mineral deficiencies are rare in Western countries because of the unlimited diversity of food supply. However, many people consume food that is either unhealthy or of poor nutritional value that lacks proteins, vitamins, minerals, and fibre. The prevalence of vitamin deficiencies in the morbidly obese population is higher and more significant than previously believed.'[161]

Athletes' diets (and the nutrition of some people) are basically high in calories, but low in nutrients. In a survival situation, any calories are good calories. But studies show when possible you should always choose nutrient-dense foods. 'Ultra-endurance exercise training places large energy demands on athletes and causes a high turnover of vitamins through sweat losses, metabolism, and the musculoskeletal repair process. Ultra-endurance athletes may not consume sufficient quantities or quality of food in their diet to meet these needs. Consequently, they may use oral vitamin and mineral supplements to maintain their health and performance.'[162]

This is an idea echoed by others. 'Additionally, micronutrient needs may be altered for these athletes while dietary intake is generally over the Recommended Daily Allowance because of high caloric intake.'[163]

For that reason, the goal of every meal was always to eat calorie-dense and nutrient-dense foods during the hours I was awake and conscious (in the water or on the boat). Which, during a 24-hour period (when the tide changes every 6 hours to move in our favour so we can swim), could look like this:

THE GREAT BRITISH SWIM DIET

2:00am	2:30am	8:30am	9:00am	10:00am
EAT	SWIM		EAT	SLEEP
'Fat Fuelling Porridge' • 150g oats • 30g blueberries • 1 chopped banana • 2 tablespoons peanut butter • 50g dark chocolate • 30g scoop chocolate whey protein • 1 tablespoon flaxseed • 1 cup almond milk	'Swim Snacks' Eating easily-digestible carbohydrates every 30 minutes in the water (mid-swim) in the form of: Bananas Smoothies Sports drinks Fruit loaf Noodles Toast Granola bars Banana bread		Post-Swim/ Pre-Sleep Meal Starter: Wholewheat tortillas with shredded chicken and avocado slices Main: Ginger, garlic and olive oil chicken with brown rice and asparagus Dessert: Homemade fruit loaf and custard	

TOTAL CALORIE/NUTRIENT BREAKDOWN:

Now protein and carbohydrates contain 4 calories per gram and fat provides 9 calories per gram. Based on this, here's how 15,000 calories per day looked in grams with a 62 per cent carbohydrate, 27 per cent fat and 11 per cent protein food ratio.

- Protein = $(15,000 \times 0.11) \div 4 = 412.5$ g
- Fats = $(15,000 \times 0.27) \div 9 = 450$ g
- Carbohydrates = $(15,000 \times 0.62) \div 4 = 2,325$ g

2:00pm	2:30pm	8:30pm	9:00am	9:30am
EAT	SWIM		EAT	SLEEP
'Fat Fuelling Porridge' AND Hulk Splash Smoothie • 1 small apple • 1 kiwi fruit • 2 carrots • 80g kale • 15g raw ginger • 3 tablespoons lemon juice • 100ml apple juice • 100mg green tea powder	'Swim Snacks'		Post-Swim/Pre-Sleep Meal Starter: Tuna burrito with avocado and spinach Main: Whole chicken with coconut rice and stir-fried greens Dessert: Homemade dark chocolate and peanut butter brownie	

THE PROTEIN PILLOW

LOCATION: Great Yarmouth
DISTANCE COVERED: 1,695 miles
DAYS AT SEA: 143

Great
Yarmouth

It's 11.00 p.m. on 21 October and 14 hours since breakfast. The moon was rising, the journalist had long since left and we'd reluctantly, and abruptly, been forced to leave the baby seals of Horsey after Matt received news over the radio that harsh, northerly winds were arriving from a storm brewing in the North Sea. Completely exposed with no harbour on the north coast of Norfolk, we had to get to the safety of Great Yarmouth harbour further south as fast as possible.

As a result, we swam a very fast 15 miles that day racing against strengthening winds and choppy seas. On finally reaching the shelter of Great Yarmouth, I collapsed onto the boat near the entrance to the port. I was battered. After 140 days at sea, we worked out I had been swimming over 1,500 hours (or 90,000 minutes). This meant everything from my ligaments and tendons to my salt-infused skin and immune system was crying out for rest and recovery. The problem is these were things I couldn't give my body.

With the first signs of winter weather heading our way, this meant (at best) our progress to the finish would be slowed, but (at worst) it could stop it all together if the Thames Port Authority thought it was unsafe for us to swim the final 80 miles across the Thames Estuary in bad weather and heavy traffic.

At this point during the swim, we were basically trying to control and slow the inevitable catabolic breakdown of the body by any means necessary (again trying our best to limit limitations). One technique we had developed was eating and sleeping with supreme efficiency to ensure we maximised the time for both.

How did we do that? Taz would leave an entire cooked chicken on my pillow.

Yes, it's as odd as it sounds, but after months at sea together the crew could instantly tell when I was too tired to eat in the galley. They knew that I'd remove my wetsuit, dry myself and often fall into bed (which of course wasn't an optimal nutritional strategy for recovery). So by placing the chicken on my pillow, it meant I couldn't fall asleep without taking a bite. I would find myself sitting upright in my bed, propped up with pillows, and eating like a short, salty, hairy Viking (without trousers) with food in and around my face.

It wasn't always a chicken (since buying fresh meat was hard with limited storage on the boat). It could be a bowl of tuna, an omelette or a protein shake, but the theory was the same ... ensure I met my daily protein requirements for the day (to aid the repair, regrowth and recovery of my body) before passing out from fatigue.

I guess it must have worked, because over 140 days (and 1,600 miles) I still hadn't had a 'sick day'. That's not to say I hadn't been seasick of course (memories of Dover still haunt my stomach). But I didn't take one day off from a suppressed immune system and swam every tide that wasn't interrupted by a storm thanks to my 'pillow of protein'. In fact, studies show, 'The poor nutritional status of some athletes may predispose them to immunosuppression' and, 'Dietary deficiencies of protein have long been associated with immune dysfunction.'[164]

So how does protein help?

First, understand your immune system is a network of biological structures and processes that exist within our bodies to protect us against disease and foreign bacteria. These biological structures range from special cells and proteins to tissues and organs and each works in harmony with the other to keep us fit and healthy.

It's this masterpiece that's designed to work like clockwork. But then research from the Memorial University of Newfoundland in Canada found, 'Nutrition is a critical determinant of immune responses and malnutrition is the most common cause of immunodeficiency worldwide. Protein malnutrition is associated with a significant impairment of immunity.'[165] So, once my calorie requirements were met, eating a plentiful supply of protein to support my immune system was very much next on my dietary to-do list while at sea.

But what's still debated is how much protein we need in our diets. This of course varies from person to person, but we can make an educated guess and start with research from the often-quoted sports nutrition bible *The Complete Guide to Sports Nutrition*. It states that the International Olympic Committee Consensus on Sports Nutrition recommends strength and speed athletes consume 1.7 g of protein per kg of bodyweight, per day. This is considered the optimal amount to help the muscles repair and re-grow.

What if you're not a strength, speed or power athlete? Maybe you're an ultra-marathon runner or adventure racer or a short, salty Viking swimming around Great Britain. Well, research published in the *Journal of Applied Physiology* found endurance athletes need just as much protein as strength athletes. 'We conclude endurance athletes require daily protein intakes greater than either bodybuilders or sedentary individuals to meet the needs of protein catabolism during exercise.'[166]

Put simply, endurance athletes need protein to prevent their body breaking down. Which is why I swam like a swimmer and ate like a strongman.

THE POTENT FAT-CARBS FUEL

LOCATION: Orford Ness
DISTANCE COVERED: 1,730 miles
DAYS AT SEA: 147

Orford Ness

It's 8:23 p.m. on 25 October and we've arrived in Orford Ness. The finish line is now so close you can quite literally sense it in the sea as the sandy banks and strong tidal currents of the southeast coast give the water a distinct colour, taste and texture that I've not experienced in over 140 days. It's hard to describe, but savouring the swim that day it felt familiar and tasted like coming home.

But there was a problem. Separating me from my finish line was the 50-mile stretch of water that is the Thames estuary and right now the port authority tells us it's plagued with winter winds and heavy traffic, which means we must wait for our weather window to cross.

So, here we were in Orford Ness, patiently and strategically waiting to launch our sprint finish. It felt like there was no better place to plot our final swim. Orford Ness is a place forever cemented in Britain's military history and has helped (secretly) shape this country in more ways than many people know. First playing a pivotal role in the naval wars against French and Dutch forces between the seventeenth and nineteenth centuries, it later served as the country's covert, experimental military site during World Wars I and II where specialist structures were built for experiments and testing.

311

Later, at the height of the Cold War, the Atomic Weapons Research Establishment (AWRE) used these fortified buildings to further our understanding of atomic warfare, which continued through the 1960s until the buildings were abandoned. Today the ominous half-buried concrete structures (built to contain the most lethal weapons ever created) scattered across its bleak landscape serve as fading signposts to our recent history.

Anchored among this hallowed ground, we were plotting a final 'swimming siege' of the sea. Our weapon of choice? Something I call, 'fat-carbs'. This is the reason why every gigantic pot of food that Harriet and Taz cooked over the stove was laced with pure peanut butter, coconut oil, almond butter or cashew butter. Serving as a dual-fuel approach to every swim, it provided a plentiful supply of the body's two energy-yielding macronutrients (fats and carbs) that both have different properties and serve different purposes when considering a swimming siege 50 miles across the Thames Estuary.

Sitting in the galley that night I waited for my weather window, ate bowls of fat-enriched porridge washed down with a Hulk Splash smoothie and wrote the following in my diary to document the tools in my nutritional weaponry.

NOTES ON NUTRITION

Carbohydrates mainly come in the form of sugar and starch. As a nutrient, we often refer to them as our body's primary fuel source. This is because we're designed to store carbohydrates in the liver, brain and muscles where we can break down the sugar and starch into glucose, which we then use as energy to fuel our bodies and feed our cells.

We've had this basic understanding of carbohydrates for over 100 years, ever since 1887 when scientists noted that glucose uptake of the masseter muscle of a horse increased when it began chewing its food.[167] But today our comprehension of carbohydrates has evolved greatly.[168]

Studies at Loughborough University set out to quantify the difference carbohydrate intake made to a runner's performance. To test this, they took 18 runners, divided them into 2 groups and had them complete a 30-km time trial. Both groups consumed the same number of calories, however the diet of one group was predominantly made up of carbohydrates. The other group's diet was lower in carbohydrates and supplemented with fat and a protein powder supplement. Following the experiment scientists observed, 'The men in the carbohydrate group ran the 30 km faster after carbohydrate loading.' This led to the conclusion – and widely held belief – that 'dietary carbohydrate loading improves endurance performance during prolonged running.'[169]

This was supported by the Scandinavian Physiological Society, 'These results suggest that muscle glycogen (carbohydrate) availability can affect performance during both short-term and more prolonged high-intensity intermittent exercise,'[170] which led the Australian Institute of Sport to state, 'The recommendations of sports nutritionists are based on plentiful evidence that increased carbohydrate availability enhances endurance and performance during single exercise sessions.'[171]

So how much do we need? To put some exact figures on all this theory, research published in the *Journal of Sports Medicine* recommended, 'Carbohydrate intake ranges from 5 grams to 7 grams per kilogram of bodyweight per day for general training needs and 7 grams to 10 grams per kilogram of bodyweight per day for the increased needs of endurance athletes.'[172]

But the problem is we simply can't eat enough carbohydrates and store enough muscle glycogen to fuel long endurance events. This is why research conducted at Harvard Medical School said, 'Considering the total carbohydrate-based energy reserve from muscle glycogen, liver glycogen, and plasma glucose, it becomes clear that normal carbohydrate stores alone would be insufficient to fuel a marathon.'[173]

The solution? Add fat.

This is because studies found, 'The number of gruelling events that challenge the limits of human endurance is increasing. Such events are also challenging the limits of current dietary recommendations.' Which is why although carbohydrate-loading has been a widely used, performance-enhancing approach to nutrition for years, 'there are some situations for which alternative dietary options (adding fat) are beneficial.'[174]

This is because studies have found that working muscles consume a mixture of metabolic substrates, and the relative contributions of fat and carbohydrate to this mixture depend on exercise intensity and the size of available glycogen reservoirs. It's concluded, 'Carbohydrates account for a greater proportion at higher intensities, while

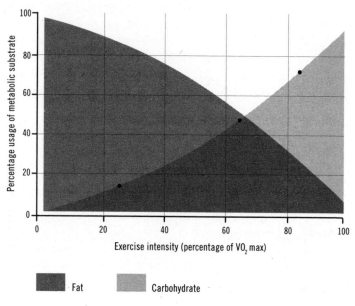

fat accounts for a greater proportion as available glycogen is depleted.'[175]

This chart shows the relative use of fat and carbohydrate as metabolic fuels depending on exercise intensity. Fractional usage of carbohydrate and fat are shown as functions of relative exercise intensity.

In summary, when faced with the task of sporadically sprinting across the Thames estuary to avoid ships, I was glad my body was fuelled by a plentiful supply of both fats and carbohydrates to cope with the differing intensities (cruise and kill).

LESSON 20

- The Great British Swim diet involved eating between **10,000 to 15,000 calories per day** and a **dual-fuel** approach of plentiful supplies of carbohydrates and fats.
- Sports science says, 'Endurance athletes require daily protein intakes greater than either bodybuilders or sedentary individuals to meet the needs of protein catabolism during exercise.'
- Sports nutritionists recommend **athletes consume 1.7 g of protein per kg of bodyweight, per day** to help the muscles repair and regrow.
- **Carbohydrates are the body's primary source of fuel.** A study found that, '… increased carbohydrate availability enhances endurance and performance during single exercise sessions.'
- Although carbohydrate-loading has been a widely-used, performance-enhancing approach to nutrition for years, according to sports scientists 'there are some situations for which alternative dietary options (adding fat) are beneficial.'

LESSON 21 | STOMACH OF STEEL

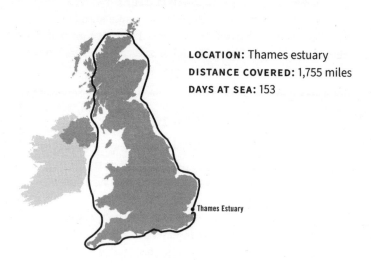

LOCATION: Thames estuary
DISTANCE COVERED: 1,755 miles
DAYS AT SEA: 153

Thames Estuary

It's 11.45 p.m. on 1 November and we've begun our swimming siege of the sea.

Our logic was we'd attack the Thames estuary at night and substitute any advantage that daylight offered (such as warmth and visibility) for fewer ships and fewer traffic hazards. For many this plan might have sounded dangerous, but for me, Matt and the entire crew ... it was just a Thursday.

After 154 days at sea we were no longer just a crew or a family, we were a finely tuned nautical operation capable of swimming through haunted whirlpools, armies of jellyfish, storms, sharks and seals ... day and night.

How? One weapon we had in our arsenal was bananas. Yes, the unsung hero of the swim so far. It was the final member of our team and the glue that kept us together. The reason for bananas becoming my preferred fuel source when in the water was they didn't have that synthetic, artificial taste typical of most sports gels.

As time went on, my taste buds developed a love for the soft, neutral and soothing texture of a banana and as such I was deeply indebted to every single one that had fuelled the swim so far.

But do you know the best thing about them? They are easy to throw (like a boomerang) and as a team we'd developed a unique way of administering sea snacks that minimised serving time. This meant precious time was no longer lost with me swimming to the boat to feed (particularly important when midway across a shipping lane).

So Matt kept a giant bunch of bananas by the steering wheel of the boat. Every time I was ready for a snack, he would effortlessly pick and throw a banana in my direction, almost like a pitcher with a baseball in slow motion. Worth noting is we were five months into the swim, so he was by now a world-leading expert in banana throwing. This was no exaggeration either; he could hit my hand from within a 30 m radius of *Hecate* and his record was a 41 m throw in a storm off the Scottish coast, that to this day remains one of the greatest banana-based physical feats I've ever seen.

Matt too was strangely proud of his newly acquired skill and had kept a 'banana tally' on the ceiling of the ship's helm. The different coloured pens Matt had used made it look strangely like the inside of the Sistine Chapel, and told a story as vivid as Michelangelo's painting – you could see when we were averaging one banana per mile through the Irish Sea, but cut back to a quarter banana per mile when swimming at 14 knots (16 mph) in the Pentland Firth.

Now in the Thames estuary we were cruising at half a banana per mile and had well and truly sharpened our sea skills. Matt didn't even need the daylight hours to find the target and could hit me with pinpoint accuracy using only the moon and its reflection on the water.

Then at 5.32 a.m. it happened ... The last banana was launched and the final tally was recorded. It was number 649.

A little mouldy and bruised, badly discoloured and with a questionable texture, that little yellow object had cemented its place in history.

'How does it taste?' shouted Matt.

'Like victory,' I replied, since 649 bananas eaten around the coastline of Great Britain remains a record I am particularly (and weirdly) proud of. So was Matt, as he delicately added the final tally to his own sistine chapel before standing back to admire his work. It wasn't just a roof with banana markings, it was a homage to our heroics in hunger.

~

It is 6.15 a.m. on 2 November and WE ARE 25 MILES FROM MARGATE!

We are so close that when the morning mist temporarily lifts you can vaguely see the outline of the unmistakable chalk, sandstone and clay cliffs of Kent that sit among the salt marshes, sand and shingle bays.

But we must temporarily stop swimming because the powerful tides of the Thames are now moving against us, which means these final 10 miles cannot be taken lightly. Feared by yachtsmen the world over, the fast-tidal currents churn up the sandbanks and create a brown ocean of water that's been featured in literature by some of history's most famous writers.

Describing the foreboding nature and 'sea solitude' of the place we currently call home, T S Eliot famously said the river was 'a strong brown god – sullen, untamed and intractable,' whereas Charles Dickens wrote 'the very shadow of the immensity of London seemed to lie oppressively upon the river.'

In 1,770 miles, we had learned to pick our fights carefully. Stopping for storms, hiding around headlands and winning against whirlpools, we knew that swimming against the tide in the Thames would end badly for us as we'd probably be swept out into the North Sea towards Belgium (at best) and the Netherlands (at worst).

So we decided the best course of action was ... breakfast. Assembling in the galley, Suzanne told us the journalist who visited us in Horsey days before had published his article. Within it he detailed how we were on the verge of making history and (very kindly) used terms like 'granite-like strength' and 'a resolve made of oak', but I must confess this wasn't true.

I wasn't a hero, I was just hungry. The entire swim had basically been an eating competition with a little bit of swimming thrown in. Since to swim 1,780 miles around Great Britain you didn't need 'iron will' ...

You needed a stomach of steel.

NOT A HERO ... JUST HUNGRY

It is 8.10 p.m. on 3 November and it's our last supper. WE ARE EIGHT MILES FROM MARGATE!

We've been camped in the Thames estuary for 24 hours waiting for the tides, the port authority, shipping lanes, family, friends and media to align and agree on a time we should arrive into Margate. As a result, it's given me an opportunity to reflect on the last 156 days and 1,772 miles, which has proved helpful before I rejoin society and integrate to life back on land.

Emotions are running high, but rations are running low on the boat. But it's no problem, as Suzanne could make a meal out of virtually anything. Also, the reality was I'd been swimming through shipping lanes and seawater for so long now that my taste buds no longer functioned or cared what I was ingesting.

I had developed a stomach of steel and it had become a valuable swimming superpower. As odd as it sounds, all endurance athletes should spend time training their stomachs by taking inspiration from the world of competitive eating.

This is based on research from the School of Sport, Exercise and Health Sciences at Loughborough University that found, 'The gastrointestinal tract plays a critical role in delivering carbohydrate and fluid during prolonged exercise and can therefore be a major determinant of performance,' but according to the study many athletes underestimate the importance and to date there's not been much research on the topic.[176]

Our stomach scientists then say, 'The intestinal tract is highly adaptable and it has been suggested that targeted training of the intestinal tract may improve the delivery of nutrients during exercise while at the same time alleviating some (or all) of the symptoms of gastrointestinal distress.'[177] They then go on to recommend 'training the gut' and state, 'Anecdotal evidence also shows that the stomach can adapt to ingesting large volumes of fluid, solids, or combinations. For example, serious contestants in eating competitions are known to "train" their stomach to hold larger volumes of food with less discomfort and – through regular training – are able to eat volumes of food within a small window of time that are unthinkable for the average and untrained person.'

Memorably, in 2018 American Joey Chestnut (yes, that's his real name) set a new world record in Nathan's Hot Dog Eating Contest, which takes places every year on 4 July at Coney Island in New York City. Chestnut, a titan of the competitive eating world, ate 74 hot dogs and buns – up from 72 the previous year – in ten minutes, beating his own record.

How did he do it? Well, competitive eaters use a variety of methods from drinking fluids and eating watermelons to expand the stomach to eating the competition foods and progressively increasing the volumes they eat and decreasing the time they eat it in.

A 2007 University of Pennsylvania study found this changes their physiology.[178] A normal human stomach is about the size of a small American football. At its biggest, it stretches about 15 per cent but competitive eaters can expand their stomachs two to three times their normal size. Nobody knows why exactly (again there's not been much research on the topic) but it demonstrates the adaptability of the stomach.

Conducting this 'stomach training' has two main effects:

- The stomach can expand and contain more food.
- The feeling of a full stomach is better tolerated and is not perceived as being so full.

Both aspects could be relevant to an exercise situation.

Our stomach science concludes with researchers saying, 'Future studies should focus on a number of areas, including the most effective methods to induce gut adaptations ... but it is clear that "nutritional training" can improve gastric emptying and absorption and likely reduce the chances and/or severity of gastrointestinal distress problems, thereby improving endurance performance.'

So the boat's galley wasn't just our kitchen, it was my stomach's gym.

LESSON 21

- All endurance athletes should spend time **training their stomachs**.
- According to research, 'The gastrointestinal tract plays a critical role in delivering carbohydrate and fluid during prolonged exercise and can therefore be a major determinant of performance.'
- A **normal human stomach** is about the size of a **small American football**. At its biggest, it stretches about 15 per cent but competitive eaters can expand their stomachs to two to three times their normal size.

LESSON 22 | RESILIENCE IS SUFFERING STRATEGICALLY MANAGED

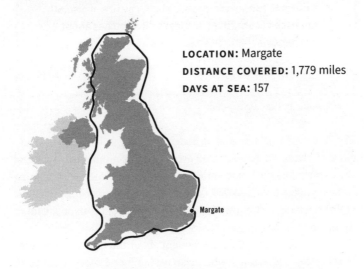

LOCATION: Margate
DISTANCE COVERED: 1,779 miles
DAYS AT SEA: 157

Margate

It is 7.50 a.m. on 4 November and WE ARE ONE MILE AWAY!

After 157 days, 1,779 miles and 649 bananas, the end is in sight. Also, having swum in harsh, cold and dark conditions across the Thames estuary the clouds dramatically cleared that morning and we were treated to an incredible sunrise, like a final gift from the ocean and Mother Nature.

I turned to Captain Matt and hugged him.

No words needed to be said. For over five months he had been a friend, coach and mentor, he had watched over me during every tide, mile and swim and had guided me home to ensure I could fulfil a promise I made to my family after hearing news of my dad.

Entering the water, I was already fighting back tears. I knew that once I'd completed my final swim, took my first steps on land since the start of summer and kissed the sand at Margate beach, three things would happen:

- The first swim in history around Great Britain would be complete.
- A paradigm shift in what we thought the human body and mind were capable of would occur.

But more important than all of this ...

- I would get to hug my dad.

The time was 8.05 a.m. and although the sea was kind, I was struggling to swim. I'd encountered every condition imaginable around the British coastline, but nothing could prepare me for swimming while trying to hold back 157 days of suppressed emotions, since the entire time I hadn't allowed myself to celebrate, think or dream of finishing.

To be honest, I hadn't even thought about the finish or what sort of reception I would get when I arrived. When I started out from Margate back in June, there had been maybe a hundred or so people on the beach comprised of local media, the mayor Julie and her husband Ray, family and friends. Now, five months on, I had invited 400 swimmers to join me for the final stretch into Margate, without genuinely believing that many would be crazy enough to swim a mile out to sea, at the start of winter, to meet a man they'd never met before.

I was wrong ... very wrong.

I didn't see them at first. But I heard them. Lining up in a human flotilla as the sound of their cheers reverberated across (and through) the water. Open-water swimmers of all shapes, sizes and ages. The entire formation was orchestrated by the Royal Marines who'd arrived in military kayaks, courtesy of Captain Oliver Mason who was there at the very start during training and now was here at the very end.

As our paths crossed and we met in the middle of the sea, I found it hard to actually put into words my feelings. I'd barely seen anyone other than the crew for half a year and now 400 swimmers had come to greet me.

You cannot describe it, only feel it. Tears followed by huge smiles and goosebumps all over as the emotions play with your physiology. I instigated a giant group-hug, there were hands and feet everywhere and I had to put my goggles on to hold back the tears, especially when the pilots from the acrobatic aircraft displays over the Moray Firth paid us another surprise visit, their smoke drawing a huge love heart in the sky to commemorate the finish.

As we arrived into the harbour the reception we received was incredible. But soon unbridled excitement was replaced with uncontrollable nerves as it dawned on me that thousands of people were on the beach (most with cameras) and I was about to emerge from the sea and attempt to walk after months of not using my legs on land.

I swam as far as I could in my watery comfort zone until eventually it was so shallow that I grazed the pebbles and sand on the seabed with my hand first. Realising it would look odd crawling onto the beach, I decided to tentatively touch down with my feet. Feeling stable enough (at first) I paused for a brief few seconds and then started to slowly walk, but with the cheers from the crowd amid the lights on the beach this walk turned into a somewhat ambitious sprint.

Almost falling three times, I managed to remain vertical long enough to arrive on the beach, but the immediate moments after were a complete blur. Having spent so long left alone with my own thoughts in the world of sensory deprivation that is the sea, the flashing lights from the assembled media throng were an assault on the senses and overwhelming, but in a pleasing way.

I was eventually handed a microphone and said a few words for the camera (to this day I'm not sure exactly what came out of my mouth) but amid the thousands in attendance on the beach that day, I just wanted to know where one person was ... my dad.

Delivering the biggest (and most overdue) hug in our family's history as he finally emerged from the crowd, I almost had to put my goggles back on to help hide the tears, but somehow I managed to fight them back by not speaking too much and despite the large lump developing in my throat.

But that was completely fine with my dad. He'd never been one to talk about his emotions anyway and that day he didn't have to. The very fact he was here spoke a thousand words, since he'd previously told doctors when starting his immunotherapy cancer treatment that no matter what happened, he was determined to watch his son finish his swim around Great Britain. So, under the agreement, he would be heavily medicated on painkillers and had to take a (precautionary) wheelchair in case he was too weak to walk ... and here he was with his arms wrapped around me.

I then hugged my mum, brothers and girlfriend, until Dad (again selflessly) told me to thank everyone who'd travelled so far to be here for the finish.

So, as a dutiful son, that's what I did. Making my way around the crowds, there were thousands of people who'd arrived from all around the UK (and world). One group arrived with giant, inflatable bananas holding banners with the words 'Rhino Neck' written in bold letters. Local school children had also made the journey with jellyfish made out of paper plates and bits of string, and fellow swimmers came equipped with far more than my usual 15,000 daily calories in the form of every cake, chocolate and cookie imaginable.

Eventually (as my lips turned blue from the cold and my belly became full from the cookies) I was 'shepherded' into the media centre by security where a warm shower and pizza were waiting for me in a dressing room. Not knowing whether to eat or shower first, I decided to do both. Holding the largest slice of BBQ pizza in one hand so I could shampoo my hair with the other, I spent the next hour getting reacquainted with *warmth* and *hygiene*, two long-lost friends I hadn't seen in over five months at sea.

Hours passed and I stood there, shell-shocked and showering, trying to make sense of the last 1,780 miles. But the truth is I couldn't. After a whole bottle of shampoo (and an entire pizza) I had no definitive answer on the legacy and final lessons of the Great British Swim. Which is why for the months that followed I began to deconstruct and reverse-engineer every nautical mile until I finished this book and came to the following conclusion ... a whole year later.

LESSON 22

Some statistics from the Great British Swim:

- o 157 days at sea
- o 1,780 miles (equivalent of swimming the Channel 85 times, or 57,679 lengths of an Olympic-sized swimming pool)
- o 0 sick days
- o 2.3 million strokes
- o 649 bananas eaten
- o Over 1 million calories consumed
- o Over 100 jellyfish stings
- o 2 minke whales
- o 1 basking shark
- o Over 1,000 seals
- o 5 rolls of gaffer tape used to fix broken skin
- o 3 kg of Vaseline for chafing
- o Worst conditions: 18 September 2018 with 105 mph winds during Storm Ali.

What lesson can we learn from this? **That anything is possible!**

EPILOGUE

It's 4 November 2019 in Cheshire, England.

Today, I am driving to one of my favourite places to swim. A lakeside watersports centre set within the countryside called Manley Mere, it's nestled among 10 acres of fields that come in every shade of green imaginable. Packed in the boot of my car are goggles, trunks and sports drinks. My two brothers (Scott and Craig) have also decided to join me for today's training. But for me, today was no ordinary swim session. No, today was extra special for two reasons:

- It is the anniversary of my Margate arrival.
- It was here that I finished the final chapter of this book.

A lot had changed since I arrived back on land and I could only truly reflect on what happened 365 days later once the whirlwind media tour had finished.

Matt and Suzanne returned to their farm in Devon to find the garden was now impressively overgrown and so spent the rest of the year taming it. Then, after a winter's work, they returned to sea and were last spotted sailing *Hecate* to Nazaré in Portugal in search of 50 ft waves to surf, with my 'sea siblings' (Taz, Peony, Jemima and Harriet) onboard.

As for my mum, she's happy my feet are back on dry land and is pleased she no longer has to protect me from Scottish storms. Not surprisingly she hasn't stepped foot on a boat since I stopped floating around Great Britain, but she sees me regularly. You see, her kitchen remains one of my favourite and most frequently visited places in 2019, as I make up for a year of missed home cooking.

Typically found foraging in the fridge, I'm rarely alone either as my dad joins me in hunting for cheesecake. Now a year on, he still remains the most stoically strong human that I know. Still having his immunotherapy treatment, he continues to fight AND beat cancer. I say 'beat' because he's returned to tennis coaching and this year received the Lifetime Achievement Award from the Lincolnshire Lawn Tennis Association, and a few months later celebrated his 40-year wedding anniversary with my mum.

Hester was also happy I was home. Now showered, shaven and (semi) integrated back into society, I'd foregone my feral ways and had also begun using a toilet again. She also hadn't stepped foot on a boat since Margate and had made me promise not to swim to, around or between any countries for at least a year. This is because after seven years together she knows me so well and can see what I'm thinking whenever we visit the coast.

And me?

Well, Margate was now a fond and distant memory, and stories of jellyfish wounds, sea ulcers and lacerations to my tongue have become immortalised within the media. But despite journalists (very kindly) writing articles about my perceived 'heroics', everything I had achieved I owed to the systematic application of Stoic Sports Science and The Art of Resilience.

Essentially, resilience is not some superhuman gift that is possessed by the brave and bold. It's innate within all of us, but is realised through stress and stimuli. This is exactly why according to naval medical research this idea of 'toughness' describes a range of psychological and physiological processes that enhance performance under stress.[179] It's also why 'resilience' is defined as the ability to successfully tolerate and recover from traumatic or stressful events and includes a range of physical, behavioural, social and psychological factors.[180]

Both of these have been extensively described throughout the pages of this book.

Which is why, (please) understand the main lesson from the swim (and the legacy of this book) is that I was NOT courageous. Courage is defined as strength in the face of pain or grief. I would argue that I had Stoic Sports Science in the face of pain or grief, founded on the collective teachings of some of the greatest minds and most resilient humans that have ever existed.

I was not fearless ...

I had undergone the Habituation of Stress (and understood Feral Fear Theory).

I was not bulletproof ...

I had built Resilience from tried and tested principles of sports science and strength.

I was not impervious to pain ...

I understood the Psychobiological Model of Fatigue.

I was not gifted with superhuman stamina ...

I understood the importance of Impeccable Pacing.

I was not emotionally invincible ...

I understood the Science of a Smile and how to Control Controllables.

I was not heroic ...

I was just hungry and understood I had to train for a Stomach of Steel.

In summary, my final hope is this. If you're reading this book you are now equipped with the tools you need to find your own Okugake. Fuelled by an intrinsic form of motivation for self-discovery through self-discipline and armed with Stoic Sports Science, you too now understand The Art of Resilience, and like the pioneers and heroes mentioned in this book (from Captain Webb to Emil Zatopek), can embark on your own athletic adventure.

ENDNOTES

Chapter 1

1   Duckworth AL, Peterson C, Matthews MD and Kelly DR (2007). 'Grit: perseverance and passion for long-term goals.' *Journal of Personality and Social Psychology* **92**(6):1087–101.

Chapter 2

2   Talpey SW and Siesmaa EJ (2017). 'Sports injury prevention: The role of the strength and conditioning coach.' *Strength and Conditioning Journal* **39**(3):14–19.

3   Fleck SJ and Falkel JE (1986). 'Value of resistance training for the reduction of sports injuries.' *Journal of Sports Medicine* **3**(1):61–68.

4   ibid.

Chapter 3

5   Asmussen E (1979). 'Muscle fatigue.' *Medicine and Science in Sports* **11**(4): 313–21.

6   Austruy P (2016). 'Neuromuscular fatigue in contact sports: Theories and reality of a high-performance environment.' *Journal of Sports Medicine & Doping Studies* **6**(4).

7   Knicker AJ, Renshaw I, Oldham AR and Cairns SP (2011). 'Interactive processes link the multiple symptoms of fatigue in sport competition.' *Journal of Sports Medicine* **41**(4):307–28.

8   Pennazio S (2009). 'Homeostasis: a history of biology.' *National Library of Medicine National Institutes of Health* **102**(2):253–71.

Lesson 1

9   Grøntved A, Brask T, Kambskard J and Hentzer E (1988). 'Ginger root against seasickness. A controlled trial on the open sea.' *Acta Oto-Laryngologica* **105**(1–2):45–9.

10   Deibert P, Berg A, Koenig D and Dickhuth HH (2005). 'The gastrointestinal system: the relationship between an athlete's health and sport performance: review article.' *International SportsMed Journal* 6(3):130–40.

Lesson 2

11   Wrzesniewski A, Schwartz B, Cong X, Kane M, Omar A and Kolditz T (2014). 'Multiple types of motives don't multiply the motivation of West Point cadets.' *Proceedings of the National Academy of Sciences of the United States of America* 111(30):10990–995.

Lesson 3

12   Ramesh G, Nagarajappa R, Madhusudan AS, Sandesh N, Batra M, Sharma A and Patel SA (2012). 'Estimation of salivary and tongue coating pH on chewing household herbal leaves: A randomized controlled trial.' *Ancient Science of Life* 32(2): 69–75.

13   Nielsen R, Akey JM, Jakobsson M, Pritchard JK, Tishkoff S and Willerslev E (2017). 'Tracing the peopling of the world through genomics.' *Nature* 541:302–10.

14   Collins M (2009). 'Genetics and Sports.' *Medicine and Sports Science* 54:102–9.

15   Scott RA and Pitsiladis YP (2006). 'Genetics and the success of East African distance runners.' *International SportMed Journal* 7(3):172–86.

16   Randall LW and Pitsiladis YP (2012). 'Kenyan and Ethiopian distance runners: What makes them so good?' *International Journal of Sports Physiology and Performance* 7(2):92–102.

17   Osterberg KL, Horswill CA and Baker LB (2009). 'Pregame urine specific gravity and fluid intake by National Basketball Association players during competition.' *Journal of Athletic Training* 44(1):53–7.

18   Casa DJ, Armstrong LE, Hillman SK and Montain SJ (2000). 'National Athletic Trainers' Association Position Statement: Fluid replacement for athletes.' *Journal of Athletic Training* 35(2):212–24.

19   Judelson DA, Maresh CM, Farrell MJ, Yamamoto LM, Armstrong LE, Kraemer WJ, Volek JS, Spiering BA, Casa DJ and Anderson JM (2007). 'Effect of hydration state on strength, power, and resistance exercise performance.' *Medicine and Science in Sports & Exercise* 39:1817–24.

Lesson 4

20   Koutedakis Y (2000). '"Burnout in Dance": the physiological viewpoint.' *Journal of Dance Medicine & Science* 4(4):122–7.

21   Lehmann MJ, Lormes W, Opitz-Gress A, Steinacker JM, Netzer N, Foster C and Gastmann U (1997). 'Training and overtraining: an overview and experimental results in endurance sports.' *Journal of Sports Medicine and Physical Fitness* **37**(1):7–17.

22   Parker S, Brukner P and Rosier M (1996). 'Chronic fatigue syndrome and the athlete.' *Sports Medicine, Training and Rehabilitation* **6**(4):269–78.

23   Kreher JB (2016). 'Diagnosis and prevention of overtraining syndrome: an opinion on education strategies.' *Journal of Sports Medicine* **7**:115–22.

24   Halson SL and Jeukendrup AE (2004). 'Does overtraining exist? An analysis of overreaching and overtraining research.' *Sports Medicine* **34**(14):967–81.

25   Gouarné C, Groussard C, Gratas-Delamarche A, Delamarche P and Duclos M (2005). 'Overnight urinary cortisol and cortisone add new insights into adaptation to training.' *Medicine and Science in Sports & Exercise* **37**(7): 1157–67.

26   Pichot V, Roche F and Gaspoz JM (2000). 'Relation between heart rate variability and training load in middle-distance runners.' *Medicine and Science in Sports & Exercise* **32**(10):1729–36.

Lesson 5

27   García-Pallarés J and Izquierdo M (2011). 'Strategies to optimize concurrent training of strength and aerobic fitness for rowing and canoeing.' *Sports Medicine* **41**(4):329–43.

28   Curtis T (1991). 'Strength training modalities: The perfect workout?' *National Strength and Conditioning Association Journal* **13**(6):83–5.

29   Midgley AW, McNaughton LR and Jones AM (2007). 'Training to enhance the physiological determinants of long-distance running performance: can valid recommendations be given to runners and coaches based on current scientific knowledge?' *Journal of Sports Medicine* **37**(10):857–80.

30   Kambouris M (2011). 'Predictive genomics profiling in athletics and sports performance.' *British Journal of Sports Medicine* **45**(2).

31   Wathen D and Baechle T (2008). *Periodization Essentials of Strength Training and Conditioning, 3rd Edition*. Human Kinetics/NSCA.

32   Magra M and Maffulli N (2008). 'Genetic aspects of tendinopathy.' *Journal of Science and Medicine in Sport* **11**(3):243–7.

33   Atkinson G and Reilly T (1996). 'Circadian variation in sports performance.' *Journal of Sports Medicine* **21**(4):292–312.

34   Deschenes MR, Kraemer WJ, Bush JA, Doughty TA, Kim D, Mullen KM and Ramsey K (1998). 'Biorhythmic influences on functional capacity of human

muscle and physiological responses.' *Medicine and Science in Sports & Exercise* **30**(9):1399–1407.

35   Deschenes MR, Bronson LL, Cadorette MP, Powers JE and Weinlein JC (2002). 'Aged men display blunted biorhythmic variation of muscle performance and physiological responses.' *Journal of Applied Physiology* **92**:2319–25.

36   Kanaley JA, Weltman JY, Pieper KS, Weltman A and Hartman ML (2001). 'Cortisol and growth hormone responses to exercise at different times of day.' *Journal of Clinical Endocrinology and Metabolism* **86**:2881–9.

37   Merrow M, Spoelstra K and Roenneberg T (2005). 'The circadian cycle: daily rhythms from behaviour to genes.' *EMBO Reports* **6**:930–5.

38   Tucker R and Collins M (2012). 'What makes champions? A review of the relative contribution of genes and training to sporting success.' *British Journal of Sports Medicine* **46**(8):555–61.

Lesson 7

39   Borghols EA, Dresen MH and Hollander AP (1978). 'Influence of heavy weight carrying on the cardiorespiratory system during exercise.' *European Journal of Applied Physiology and Occupational Physiology* **38**(3): 161–9.

40   Li TZ and Zhan JM (2015). 'Hydrodynamic body shape analysis and their impact on swimming performance.' *Acta of Bioengineering and Biomechanics* **17**(4):3–11.

41   Cohen RCZ, Cleary PW and Mason B (2010). 'Improving Understanding of Human Swimming Using Smoothed Particle Hydrodynamics.' *Proceedings of 2010 Singapore IFMBE, 6th World Congress of Biomechanics* **31**:174–7.

42   Kucia-Cztszczon K, Dybinkska E, Ambrozy T and Chwala W (2013). 'Factors determining swimming efficiency observed in less skilled swimmers.' *Acta of Bioengineering and Biomechanics* **15**:115–24.

43   Sacilotto GB, Ball N and Mason BR (2014). 'A biomechanical review of the techniques used to estimate or measure resistive forces in swimming.' *Journal of Applied Biomechanics* **30**(1):119–27.

44   Wanivenhaus F, Fox AJS, Chaudhury S and Rodeo SA (2012). 'Epidemiology of injuries and prevention strategies in competitive swimmers.' *Journal of Sports Health* **4**(3):246–51.

45   Talpey SW and Siesmaa EJ (2017). 'Sports injury prevention: The role of the strength and conditioning coach.' *Strength and Conditioning Journal* **39**(3):14–19.

46   Lauersen JB, Bertelsen DM and Andersen LB (2014). 'The effectiveness of exercise interventions to prevent sports injuries: a systematic review and meta-analysis of randomised controlled trials.' *British Journal of Sports Medicine* **48**(11):871–7.

47   Lauersen JB, Andersen TE and Andersen LB (2018). 'Strength training as superior, dose-dependent and safe prevention of acute and overuse sports injuries: a systematic review, qualitative analysis and meta-analysis.' *British Journal of Sports Medicine* **52**(24):1557–63.

48   Askling C, Karlsson J and Thorstensson A (2003). 'Hamstring injury occurrence in elite soccer players after preseason strength training with eccentric overload.' *Scandinavian Journal of Medicine and Science in Sports* **13**(4):244–50.

49   Hejna WF, Rosenberg A, Buturusis DJ and Krieger A (1982). 'The Prevention of Sports Injuries in High School Students Through Strength Training.' *National Strength Coaches Association Journal* (Feb).

50   Skelton DA and Beyer N (2003). 'Exercise and injury prevention in older people.' *Scandinavian Journal of Medicine and Science in Sports* **13**(1):77–85.

51   Pedemonte J (1986). 'Foundations of training periodization Part I: historical outline.' *Strength & Conditioning Journal* **8**(3): 62–6.

52   Issurin V (2010). 'New horizons for the methodology and physiology of training periodization.' *Sports Medicine* **40**(3):189–206.

53   Faigenbaum AD and Myer GD (2010). 'Resistance training among young athletes: safety, efficacy and injury prevention effects.' *British Journal of Sports Medicine* **44**(1):56–63.

54   Brooks JH, Fuller CW, Kemp SP and Reddin DB (2006). 'Incidence, risk, and prevention of hamstring muscle injuries in professional rugby union.' *American Journal of Sports Medicine* **34**(8):1297–1306.

55   Chumanov ES, Schache AG, Heiderscheit BC, et al. (2012). 'Hamstrings are most susceptible to injury during the late swing phase of sprinting.' *British Journal of Sports Medicine* **46**(2):90.

56   Heidt RS, Sweeterman LM, Carlonas RL, Traub JA and Tekulve FX (2000). 'Avoidance of soccer injuries with preseason conditioning.' *American Journal of Sports Medicine* **28**(5):659–62.

57   Byram IR, Bushnell BD, Dugger K, Charron K, Harrell FE and Noonan TJ (2010). 'Preseason shoulder strength measurements in professional baseball pitchers: Identifying players at risk for injury.' *American Journal of Sports Medicine* **38**(7):1375–82.

58   Windt J, Gabbett TJ, Ferris D and Khan KM (2017). 'Training load–injury paradox: is greater preseason participation associated with lower in-season

injury risk in elite rugby league players?' *British Journal of Sports Medicine* **51**(8):645–50.

Lesson 8

59   Aagaard P and Andersen JL (2010). 'Effects of strength training on endurance capacity in top-level endurance athletes.' *Scandinavian Journal of Medicine & Science in Sports* **20**(2):39–47.

60   Rønnestad BR, Hansen EA and Raastad T (2010). 'Effect of heavy strength training on thigh muscle cross-sectional area, performance determinants, and performance in well-trained cyclists.' *European Journal of Applied Physiology,* **108**(5):965–75.

61   Vikmoen O, Ellefsen S, Trøen Ø, Hollan I, Hanestadhaugen M, Raastad T and Rønnestad BR (2016). 'Strength training improves cycling performance, fractional utilization of VO2max & cycling economy in female cyclists.' *Scandinavian Journal of Medicine & Science in Sports* **26**(4):384–96.

62   Kucia-Cztszczon K, Dybinkska E, Ambrozy T and Chwala W (2013). 'Factors determining swimming efficiency observed in less skilled swimmers.' *Acta of Bioengineering and Biomechanics* **15**(4):115–24.

63   Vikmoen O, Ellefsen S, Trøen Ø, Hollan I, Hanestadhaugen M, Raastad T and Rønnestad BR (2016). 'Strength training improves cycling performance, fractional utilization of VO2max and cycling economy in female cyclists.' *Scandinavian Journal of Medicine & Science in Sports* **26**(4):384–96.

64   Lundberg TR, Fernandez-Gonzalo R, Gustafsson T and Tesch PA (2012). 'Aerobic exercise does not compromise muscle hypertrophy response to short-term resistance training.' *Journal of Applied Physiology* **114**(1):81–9.

65   Lundberg TR, Fernandez-Gonzalo R, Tesch PA, Rullman E and Gustafsson T (2016). 'Aerobic exercise augments muscle transcriptome profile of resistance exercise.' *American Journal of Physiology* **310**(11):1279–87.

66   Aagaard P and Andersen JL (2010). 'Effects of strength training on endurance capacity in top-level endurance athletes.' *Scandinavian Journal of Medicine & Science in Sports* **20**(2):39–47.

67   Wathen D and Baechle T (2008). *'Periodization' Essentials of Strength Training and Conditioning, 3rd Edition.* Human Kinetics/NSCA.

68   Zehr EP and Sale DG (1994). 'Ballistic movement: Muscle activation and neuromuscular adaptation.' *Canadian Journal of Applied Physiology* **19**(4):363–78.

69   Mangine GT, Ratamess NA, Hoffman JR; Faigenbaum AD, Jie K and Chilakos A (2008). 'The effects of combined ballistic and heavy resistance training on

maximal lower and upper-body strength in recreationally trained men.' *Journal of Strength and Conditioning Research* **22**(1):132–9.

70   Lauersen JB, Bertelsen DM and Andersen LB (2014). 'The effectiveness of exercise interventions to prevent sports injuries: a systematic review and meta-analysis of randomised controlled trials.' *British Journal of Sports Medicine* **48**(11):871–7.

71   Behm DG, Leonard AM, Young WB, Bonsey WA and MacKinnon SN (2005). 'Trunk muscle electromyographic activity with unstable and unilateral exercises.' *Journal of Strength and Conditioning Research* **19**(1):193–201.

72   Jenkins NDM (2012). 'Implement training for concentric-based muscle actions.' *Strength and Conditioning Journal* **34**(2):1–7.

Lesson 9

73   See www.pressandjournal.co.uk/fp/news/highlands/1471746/light-plane-crash -off-kintyre-likely-caused-by-poor-visibility/.

74   Scott A, Heinlein PT and Cosgarea AJ (2010). 'Biomechanical considerations in the competitive swimmer's shoulder.' *Sports Health* **2**(6):519–25.

75   Deschodt VJ, Arsac LM and Rouard AH (1999). 'Relative contribution of arms and legs in humans to propulsion in 25-m sprint front-crawl swimming.' *European Journal of Applied Physiology* **80**(3):192–9.

76   Counsilman JE (1968). *The Science of Swimming.* Prentice-Hall, Englewood Cliffs, NJ.

77   Hay JG (1993). *The Biomechanics of Sports Techniques 4th edition.* Prentice Hall, Englewood Cliffs, NJ.

78   Rushall BS (2013). 'Current swimming techniques: The physics of movement and observations of champions.' *Swimming Science Bulletin* **44**.

79   Czabanski B and Koszcyc T (1979). 'Relationship of stroke asymmetry and speed of breaststroke swimming.' *Swimming III* Terauds J and Bedingfield EW, eds. University Park Press, Baltimore, 148–52.

80   Laursen PB and Jenkins DG (2002). 'The scientific basis for high-intensity interval training: Optimising training programmes and maximising performance in highly trained endurance athletes.' *Sports Medicine* **32**(1): 53–73.

81   Tabata I, Nishimura K, Kouzaki M, Hirai Y, Ogita F, Miyachi M and Yamamoto K (1996). 'Effects of moderate-intensity endurance and high-intensity intermittent training on anaerobic capacity and VO2max.' *Medicine and Science in Sport & Exercise* **28**(10):1327–30.

82   O'Leary T, Collett J, Howells K and Morris M (2017). 'High but not moderate-intensity endurance training increases pain tolerance: a randomised trial.' *European Journal of Applied Physiology* **117**(11):2201–10.

Lesson 10

83   Weir JP, Beck TW, Cramer JT and Housh TJ (2006). 'Is fatigue all in your head? A critical review of the central governor model.' *British Journal of Sports Medicine* **40**(7):573–86.

84   Lambert EV, St Clair Gibson A and Noakes TD (2005). 'Complex systems model of fatigue: integrative homoeostatic control of peripheral physiological systems during exercise in humans.' *British Journal of Sports Medicine* **39**(1):52–62.

Lesson 11

85   Johnson MH, Stewart J, Humphries SA and Chamove AS (2012). 'Marathon runners' reaction to potassium iontophoretic experimental pain: pain tolerance, pain threshold, coping and self-efficacy.' *European Journal of Pain* **16**(5):767–74.

86   Freund W, Weber F, Billich C, Birklein F, Breimhorst M and Schuetz UH (2013). 'Ultra-marathon runners are different: investigations into pain tolerance and personality traits of participants of the TransEurope FootRace 2009.' *Pain Practice: the Official Journal of the World Institute of Pain* **13**(7):524–32.

87   Alschuler KN, Kratz AL, Lipman GS, Krabak BJ, Pomeranz D, Burns P, Bautz J, Nordeen C, Irwin C and Jensen MP (2019). 'How variability in pain and pain coping relate to pain interference during multistage ultramarathons.' *Journal of the International Association for the Study of Pain* **160**(1):257–62.

88   Tan G et al. (2008). 'Comparison of adaptive and maladaptive coping/appraisal as they relate to adjustment to chronic pain.' *Journal of Pain* **9**(4):57.

89   Zelman DC, Howland EW, Nichols SN and Cleeland CS (1991). 'The effects of induced mood on laboratory pain.' *Journal of Pain* **46**(1):105–11.

90   Büssing A, Ostermann T, Neugebauer EA and Heusser P (2010). 'Adaptive coping strategies in patients with chronic pain conditions and their interpretation of disease.' *BMC Public Health* **10**(1):507.

91   Weisenberg M, Tepper I and Schwarzwald J (1995). 'Humor as a cognitive technique for increasing pain tolerance.' *Journal of Pain* **63**(2):207–12.

92   Ayahuasca: made from a plant called the Banisteriopsis caapi, it's taken as part of a healing shaman ritual and is known for invoking positive spiritual revelations in people regarding their purpose in life.

93   Büssing A, Ostermann T, Neugebauer EA and Heusser P (2010). 'Adaptive coping strategies in patients with chronic pain conditions and their interpretation of disease.' *BMC Public Health* **20**(10):507.

94   Büssing A, Ostermann T, Neugebauer EA and Heusser P (2010). 'Adaptive coping strategies in patients with chronic pain conditions and their interpretation of disease.' *BMC Public Health* **10**(1):1.

95   Weir JP, Beck TW, Cramer JT, and Housh TJ (2006). 'Is fatigue all in your head? A critical review of the central governor model.' *British Journal of Sports Medicine* **40**(7):573–86.

96   Butler RK and Finn DP (2009). 'Stress-induced analgesia.' *Progress in Neurobiology* **88**(3):184–202.

97   Amit Z and Galina ZH (1986). 'Stress-induced analgesia: adaptive pain suppression.' *Physiological Review* **66**(4):1091–1120.

Lesson 12

98   Padgett DA and Glaser R (2003). 'How stress influences the immune response.' *Trends in Immunology* **24**(8):444–8.

99   Reiche EMV, Nunes SOV and Morimoto HK (2004). 'Stress, depression, the immune system, and cancer.' *The Lancet Oncology* **5**(10):617–25.

100 Vgontzas AN, Bixler EO, Lin HM, Prolo P, Mastorakos G, Vela-Bueno A, Kales A and Chrousos GP (2001). 'Chronic insomnia is associated with nyctohemeral activation of the hypothalamic-pituitary-adrenal axis: clinical implications.' *Journal of Clinical Endocrinology & Metabolism* **86**(8):3787–94.

101 Glaser R and Kiecolt-Glaser JK (2005). 'Stress-induced immune dysfunction: implications for health.' *Nature Reviews Immunology* **5**(3):243–51.

102 Thompson RF and Spencer WA (1996). 'Habituation: A model phenomenon for the study of neuronal substrates of behaviour.' *Psychological Review* **73**(1):16–43.

103 Van Paridon KN, Timmis MA, Nevison CM and Bristow M (2017). 'The anticipatory stress response to sport competition; a systematic review with meta-analysis of cortisol reactivity.' *BMJ Open Sport & Exercise Medicine* **3**(1):e000261.

104 Vera FM, Manzaneque JM, Carranque GA, Rodríguez-Peña FM, Sánchez-Montes S and Blanca MJ (2018). 'Endocrine modulation in long-term karate practitioners.' *Evidence-Based Complementary and Alternative Medicine* **2018**:1074801.

105 Salvador A (2005). 'Coping with competitive situations in humans.' *Neuroscience & Biobehavioral Reviews* **29**(1):195–205.

106 Meyer VJ, Lee Y, Böttger C, Leonbacher U, Allison AL and Shirtcliff EA (2015). 'Experience, cortisol reactivity, and the coordination of emotional responses to skydiving.' *Frontiers of Human Neuroscience* **25**(9):138.

107 Orlansky J (1989). 'The military value and cost-effectiveness of training.' NATO Defense Research Group Panel 7 on the Defense Applications of Operational Research. Research Study Group 15 on the Military Value and Cost-Effectiveness of Training. Institute for Defense Analyses, Alexandria, VA.

108 Gorman PF (1990). 'The military value of training.' Institute for Defense Analyses Paper P-2515.

109 Robson S and Manacapilli T (2014). *Enhancing Performance Under Stress: Stress Inoculation Training for Battlefield Airmen.* RAND Corporation, Santa Monica, CA.

110 Friedland N and Keinan G (1992). 'Training effective performance in stressful situations: Three approaches and implications for combat training.' *Military Psychology* **4**(3):157–74.

111 Beilock SL, Carr TH, MacMahon C and Starkes JL (2002). 'When paying attention becomes counterproductive: Impact of divided versus skill-focused attention on novice and experienced performance of sensorimotor skills.' *Journal of Experimental Psychology: Applied* **8**(1):6–16.

Lesson 16

112 Sjodin B and Svedenhag J (1985). 'Applied Physiology of Marathon Running.' *Sports Medicine* **2**(2):83–99.

113 Farrell PA, Wilmore JH, Coyle EF, Billing JE and Costill DL (1979). 'Plasma lactate accumulation and distance running performance.' *Medicine and Science in Sports & Exercise* **11**(4):338–44.

114 Walsh NP, Gleeson M, Shephard RJ, Gleeson M, Woods JA, Bishop NC, Fleshner M, Green C, Pedersen BK, Hoffman-Goetz L, Rogers CJ, Northoff H, Abbasi A and Simon P (2011). 'Position statement Part One: Immune function and exercise.' *Exercise Immunology Review* **17**:6–63.

115 Shephard RJ (2010). 'Development of the discipline of exercise immunology.' *Exercise Immunology Review* **16**:194–222.

116 Castell LM (2002). 'Exercise-induced immunodepression in endurance athletes and nutritional intervention with carbohydrate, protein and fat: What Is possible, what Is not?' *Nutrition* **18**(5):371–5.

117 Chamorro-Viña C, Fernandez-del-Valle M and Tacón AM (2013). 'Excessive Exercise and Immunity: The J-Shaped Curve.' *The Active Female* 357–72.

118 Shephard RJ (2010). 'The history of exercise immunology.' In: *The History of Exercise Physiology*. Tipton C, ed. Human Kinetics, Champaign, IL.

119 Shephard RJ (1997). *Physical Activity, Training and the Immune Response*. Cooper Publishing Group, Carmel, IN.

120 Brenner IK, Shek PN and Shephard RJ (1994). 'Infection in athletes.' *Sports Medicine* 17:86–107.

121 Oliver SJ, Laing SJ, Wilson S, Bilzon JL, Walters R and Walsh NP (2007). 'Salivary immunoglobulin A response at rest and after exercise following a 48 h period of fluid and/or energy restriction.' *British Journal of Nutrition* 97(6):1109–16.

122 Nieman DC, Nehlsen-Cannarella SL, Markoff PA, Balk-Lamberton AJ, Yang H, Chritton DB, Lee JW and Arabatzis K (1990). 'The effects of moderate exercise training on natural killer cells and acute upper respiratory tract infections.' *International Journal of Sports Medicine* 11(6):467–73.

123 Lindholm P and Lundgren CEG (2009). 'The physiology and pathophysiology of human breath-hold diving.' *Journal of Applied Physiology* 106(1):284–92.

124 Hindell MA and Lea MA (1998). 'Heart rate, swimming speed, and estimated oxygen consumption of a free-ranging southern elephant seal.' *Physiological Zoology* 71(1):74–84.

Lesson 17

125 Blanchfield A, Hardy J and Marcora S (2014). 'Non-conscious visual cues related to affect and action alter perception of effort and endurance performance.' *Frontiers in Human Neuroscience* 11(8):967.

Lesson 18

126 Lieberman HR, Bathalon GP, Falco CM, Kramer FM, Morgan CA and Niro P (2005). 'Severe decrements in cognition function and mood induced by sleep loss, heat, dehydration, and undernutrition during simulated combat.' *Journal of Biological Psychiatry* 57(4):422–9.

127 Scott JP, McNaughton LR and Polman RC (2006). 'Effects of sleep deprivation and exercise on cognitive, motor performance and mood.' *Physiology & Behaviour* 87(2):396–408.

128 Tobaldiniab E, Costantinoa G, Solbiatia M, Cogliatic C, Karade T, Nobilif L and Montanoa N (2017). 'Sleep, sleep deprivation, autonomic nervous system and cardiovascular diseases.' *Neuroscience & Biobehavioral Reviews* 74(Part B) 321–32.

129 Lieberman HR, Niro P, Tharion WJ, Nindl BC, Castellani JW and Montain SJ (2006). 'Cognition during sustained operations: comparison of a laboratory simulation to field studies.' *Aviation, Space, and Environmental Medicine* 77(9):929–35.

130 Chrousos G, Vgontzas AN and Kritikou I (2016). 'HPA Axis and Sleep.' In: Feingold KR, Anawalt B, Boyce A, et al., eds. Endotext [Internet], South Dartmouth, MA.

131 Dijk DJ and Czeisler CA (1995). 'Contribution of the circadian pacemaker and the sleep homeostat to sleep propensity, sleep structure, electroencephalographic slow waves, and sleep spindle activity in humans.' *Journal of Neuroscience* 15(5):3526–38.

132 Reppert SM and Weaver DR (2002). 'Coordination of circadian timing in mammals.' *Nature* 418:935–41.

133 Arendt J and Broadway J (1987). 'Light and Melatonin as Zeitgebers in Man.' *Journal of Biological and Medical Rhythm Research* 4(2):161–85.

134 Wever RA (1980). 'Phase shifts of human circadian rhythms due to shifts of artificial Zeitgebers.' *Chronobiologica* 7(3):303–27.

135 West LJ, Janszen HH, Lester BK and Cornelisoon FS Jr (1962). 'The psychosis of sleep deprivation.' In: Sankar S, ed. 'Some biological aspects of schizophrenic behavior.' *Annals of the New York Academy of Science* 96(1): 66–70.

136 Babkoff H, Sing HC, Thorne DR, Genser SR and Hegge FW (1989). 'Perceptual distortions and hallucinations reported during the course of sleep deprivation.' *Perceptual and Motor Skills* 68(3):787–98.

137 Kovalzon VM (2009). 'Some notes on the biography of Maria Manasseina.' *Journal of the History of the Neurosciences* 18(3):312–19.

138 Bentivoglio M and Grassi-Zucconi G (1997). 'The pioneering experimental studies on sleep deprivation.' *Sleep* 20(7):570–6.

139 Everson CA, Bergmann BM and Rechtschaffen A (1989). 'Sleep deprivation in the rat: III. Total sleep deprivation.' *Sleep* 12(1):13–21.

140 Morris GO and Singer MT (1961). 'Sleep deprivation.' *Archives of General Psychiatry* 5:453–61.

141 Koranyi EK and Lehman HE (1960). 'Experimental sleep deprivation in schizophrenic patients.' *Archives of General Psychiatry* 2:534–44.

142 Luce GG (1973). 'Current research on sleep and dreams.' US Dept of Health, Education and Welfare, Public Health Service, National Institute of Mental Health.

143 Brand S, Beck J, Gerber M, Hatzinger M and Holsboer-Trachsler E (2010). 'Evidence of favorable sleep-EEG patterns in adolescent male vigorous football players compared to controls.' *World Journal of Biological Psychiatry* **11**(2-2):465–75.

144 Mah CD, Mah KE, Kezirian EJ and Dement WC (2011). 'The effects of sleep extension on the athletic performance of collegiate basketball players.' *Sleep* **34**(7):943–50.

145 Diekelmann S (2014). 'Sleep for cognitive enhancement.' *Frontiers in Systems Neuroscience* **8**(1):46.

146 Shapiro CM, Bortz R, Mitchell D, Bartel P and Jooste P (1981). 'Slow-wave sleep: a recovery period after exercise.' *Science* **214**(4526):1253–4.

147 Pilcher JJ and Huffcutt AI (1996). 'Effects of sleep deprivation on performance: a meta-analysis.' *Sleep* **19**(4):318–26.

148 Honn KA, Hinson JM, Whitney P and Van Dongen HPA (2019). 'Cognitive flexibility: A distinct element of performance impairment due to sleep deprivation.' *Accident Analysis & Prevention* **126**:191–7.

149 Alhola P and Polo-Kantola P (2007). 'Sleep deprivation: Impact on cognitive performance.' *Neuropsychiatric Disease and Treatment* **3**(5):553–67.

150 Van Dongen HPA, Maislin G, Mullington JM and Dinges DF (2003). 'The cumulative cost of additional wakefulness: Dose-response effects on neurobehavioral functions and sleep physiology from chronic sleep restriction and total sleep deprivation.' *Sleep* **26**(2):117–26.

Lesson 19

151 Widdowson E (1980). 'Adventures in nutrition over half a century.' *Proceedings of the Nutrition Society* **39**(3):293–306.

152 Cordain L, Eaton SB, Sebastian A, Mann N, Lindeberg S, Watkins BA, O'Keefe JH and Brand-Miller J (2005). 'Origins and evolution of the Western diet: health implications for the 21st century.' *American Journal of Clinical Nutrition* **81**(2):341–54.

Lesson 20

153 Ranchordas MK (2012). 'Nutrition for Adventure Racing.' *Sports Medicine* **42**(11):915–27.

154 Zimberg IZ, Crispim CA, Juzwiak CR and Antunes HKM (2008). 'Nutritional intake during a simulated adventure race.' *International Journal of Sport Nutrition and Exercise Metabolism* **18**(2).

155 Nikolaidis PT, Veniamakis E, Rosemann T and Knechtle B (2018). 'Nutrition in ultra-endurance: State of the art.' *Nutrients* **10**(12):doi10.3390/nu10121995.

156 Peters EM (2003). 'Nutritional aspects in ultra-endurance exercise.' *Current Opinion in Clinical Nutrition & Metabolic Care* **6**(4):427–34.

157 Rodriguez NR, Di Marco NM and Langley S (2009). 'American College of Sports Medicine position stand. Nutrition and athletic performance.' *Medicine and Science in Sport & Exercise* **41**(3):709–31.

158 Economos CD, Bortz SS and Nelson ME (1993). 'Nutritional practices of elite athletes. Practical recommendations.' *Sports Medicine* **16**(6):381–99.

159 Venkatraman JT and Pendergast DR (2002). 'Effect of dietary intake on immune function in athletes.' *Sports Medicine* **32**(5):323–37.

160 Eden BD and Abernethy PJ (1994). 'Nutritional intake during an ultraendurance running race.' *International Journal of Sport Nutrition and Exercise Metabolism* **4**(2):166–74.

161 Kaidar-Person O, Person B, Szomstein S and Rosenthal RJ (2008). 'Nutritional deficiencies in morbidly obese patients: a new form of malnutrition? Part A: vitamins.' *Obesity Surgery* **18**(7):870–6.

162 Knez WL and Peake JM (2010). 'The prevalence of vitamin supplementation in ultraendurance triathletes.' *International Journal of Sport Nutrition and Exercise Metabolism* **20**(6):507–14.

163 Applegate EA (1991). 'Nutritional considerations for ultra-endurance performance.' *International Journal of Sport Nutrition and Exercise Metabolism* **1**(2):118–26.

164 Gleeson M and Bishop NC (2000). 'Elite athlete immunology: importance of nutrition.' *International Journal of Sports Medicine* **21**(Suppl 1):S44–50.

165 Chandra RK (1997). 'Nutrition and the immune system: an introduction.' *American Journal of Clinical Nutrition* **66**(2):460S–463S.

166 Tarnopolsky MA, MacDougall JD and Atkinson SA (1988). 'Influence of protein intake and training status on nitrogen balance and lean body mass.' *Journal of Applied Physiology* **64**(1):187–93.

167 Chauveau MA and Kaufmann M. 'Experiences pour la determination du coefficient de l'activite nutritive et respiratoire des muscles en repos et en travail.' *Comptes Rendus Hebdomadaires Des Seances De L'Academie Des Sciences* **1887**(104):1126.

168 Ivy JL (1999). 'Role of carbohydrate in physical activity.' *Clinics in Sports Medicine* **18**(3):469–84.

169 Williams C, Brewer J and Walker M (1992). 'The effect of a high carbohydrate diet on running performance during a 30-km treadmill time trial.'

European Journal of Applied Physiology and Occupational Physiology **65**(1): 18–24.

170 Balsom PD, Gaitanos GC, Söderlund K and Ekblom B (1999). 'High-intensity exercise and muscle glycogen availability in humans.' *Acta Physiologica Scandinavica* **165**(4):337–45.

171 Burke LM, Cox GR, Culmmings NK and Desbrow B (2001). 'Guidelines for daily carbohydrate intake: do athletes achieve them?' *Sports Medicine* **31**(4):267–99.

172 ibid.

173 Rapoport BI (2010). 'Metabolic factors limiting performance in marathon runners.' *PLoS Computational Biology* **6**(10):e1000960.

174 Brown RC (2002). 'Nutrition for optimal performance during exercise: carbohydrate and fat.' *Current Sports Medicine Reports* **1**(4):222–9.

175 Romijn JA, Coyle EF, Sidossis LS, Gastaldelli A, Horowitz JF, Endert E and Wolfe RR (1993). 'Regulation of endogenous fat and carbohydrate metabolism in relation to exercise intensity and duration.' *American Journal of Physiology* **265**(3):E380–91.

Lesson 21

176 Jeukendrup AE (2017). 'Training the gut for athletes.' *Sports Medicine* **47**(Suppl 1):101–10.

177 Jeukendrup AE and McLaughlin J (2011). 'Carbohydrate ingestion during exercise: effects on performance, training adaptations and trainability of the gut.' *Nestle Nutrition Institute Workshop Series* **69**(1):1–17.

178 Levine MS, Spencer G, Alavi A and Metz DC (2007). 'Competitive speed eating: truth and consequences.' *American Journal of Roentgenology* **189**(3):681–6.

Epilogue

179 O'Donnell A, Morgan CA, Jovanov E, Andrasik F and Prevost MC (2002). *The Warfighter's Stress Response: Telemetric and Noninvasive Assessment.* Naval Aerospace Medical Research Lab, Pensacola, FL.

180 Meredith LS, Sherbourne CD, Gaillot SL, Hansell L, Ritschard HV, Parker AM and Wrenn, G (2011). *Promoting Psychological Resilience in the US Military.* RAND Corporation, Santa Monica, CA.

ACKNOWLEDGEMENTS

The Great British Swim (and therefore this book) was only made possible because of the incredible team of people who kept me afloat. This (of course) begins with Captain Matt Knight, whose heroics throughout the five months are impossible to put into words. In 157 days he never got a single tide, weather reading or passage plan wrong. What he did was simply incredible and will go down in sailing history. Next, we calculated that Suzanne must have bought, boiled, roasted and cooked well over 1 million calories for me alone; without her 'heroics in hunger' the swim simply wouldn't have been possible, as she remained the glue that held the swim and our ship together. Equally, I don't know what I would have done without my sea siblings, Taz, Harriet, Peony and Jemima, who each crossed 'hell and high water' (time and again) as they guided me through shipping lanes, storms and 10-ft waves. Put simply, in no way was this ever an individual sport and I will never be able to thank this family enough.

Next, to *my* family. There's no doubt that without the love and support of my mum, dad, brothers and (incredibly patient) girlfriend I wouldn't even have considered stepping foot on Margate beach. That is because many considered this adventure 'swimming suicide', but when I first told them the idea (over a Sunday roast dinner) they immediately began to plot and plan the best harbours, ports and headlands to visit and deliver rations to me in the form of cheesecake. For me, this epitomises how lucky I am, and I acknowledge that all I have achieved is really just a by-product of having them in my life.

But among all the heroes I've mentioned in this book, there is one you will not find, because he is impossibly modest, prefers to remain 'behind the scenes' and, during the entire time I was at sea, was back on land (never sleeping), handling the logistics of the entire project. His name is Richard Bowen, and despite 99.99 per cent of people claiming this entire adventure was a bad idea, he became head of media for the whole thing and single-handedly produced an online series that reached over 500 million people. A pioneer of modern digital media, he's an incredible director, but an even better friend and I'm forever indebted to him and his team (Craig, Tom, Ben, Euan and Harvey), who travelled all around Britain with their cameras to document the swim.

Finally, to the amazing publishing team at HarperCollins. Without them, this entire book would only exist as long, often incoherent scribbles in a sea-soaked notebook, but because Oliver Malcolm and Ed Faulkner shared my vision to create a book that would educate and empower millions, I was given the opportunity to write. Then, months later, with the help of the marketing, editing and design team (Orlando Mowbray, Tom Whiting, Sarah Hammond, Isabel Prodger and Simeon Greenaway), those scribbles became a finished manuscript and my dream of publishing my philosophies and theories on resilience became a reality.

INDEX

Page references in *italics* indicate images.